Praise for *Three Minutes for Mom*

"*Three Minutes for Mom* is the perfect companion for motherhood. The daily reflections will leave you feeling more empowered, connected, and confident."

—WHITNEY GOODMAN, LMFT,
creator of Sit with Whit and author of *Toxic Positivity*

"*Mom*, the most beautiful and impactful job we'll ever do. Yet the desire to do it right is as overwhelming as society's tendency to tell us what we're doing wrong. Finally, with *Three Minutes for Mom*, we have a compassionate and educational blueprint for how to do this job the best way we can—no judgment; all love."

—MICHELLE DEMPSEY-MULTACK, MS, CDS,
author and founder of *Moms Moving On*

"While moms continue to try to be superhumans, I love how this book gives them permission: to slow down, to think outside the day-to-day grind, and to experience the fruits of all their labor more often—and more immediately. While motherhood is so much about the future of our children, being able to live in the moment and appreciate the here and now is so crucial to the mental health of mothers—and the mental health of everyone in the family. The beauty of this book is in its simplicity and very supportive tone. I know *Three Minutes for Mom* will provide moms with exactly the kind of comfort and affirmation they need to live more in the moment—and to be present to enjoy it as it is."

—SIGGIE COHEN, PhD

"Erin thoughtfully addresses some of the most profound topics facing today's parents, providing practical techniques and insightful reframes that empower this generation without demanding excessive time or resources. Her approach enables families to focus on what truly matters, fostering a sense of confidence and purpose in parenting."

—NEHA RUCH,
founder of Mother Untitled and author of *The Power Pause:*
How to Plan a Career Break after Kids—and Come Back Stronger Than Ever

three minutes for mom

365 Days of Empowerment, Encouragement, and Growth for a More Connected Motherhood

ERIN MORRISON, MA, EdM, Creator of The Conscious Mom

ADAMS MEDIA

NEW YORK   AMSTERDAM/ANTWERP   LONDON   TORONTO   SYDNEY   NEW DELHI

Adams Media
An Imprint of Simon & Schuster, LLC
100 Technology Center Drive
Stoughton, Massachusetts 02072

First Adams Media hardcover edition April 2025

ADAMS MEDIA and colophon are registered trademarks of Simon & Schuster, LLC.

For information about special discounts for bulk purchases, please contact Simon & Schuster Special Sales at 1-866-506-1949 or business@simonandschuster.com.

The Simon & Schuster Speakers Bureau can bring authors to your live event. For more information or to book an event, contact the Simon & Schuster Speakers Bureau at 1-866-248-3049 or visit our website at www.simonspeakers.com.

Interior design by Erin Alexander

Manufactured in China

10 9 8 7 6 5 4 3 2 1

Library of Congress Cataloging-in-Publication Data has been applied for.

ISBN 978-1-5072-2325-3
ISBN 978-1-5072-2326-0 (ebook)

DEDICATION

To my greatest wisdom teachers, Jonah and Ellie.

CONTENTS

INTRODUCTION

To the Mother Holding This Book,

Mom. It's the name you respond to the quickest, the name you hear called out the most, and it's the name that's forever changed your life.

You knew there would be sleepless nights and never-ending days. You knew there would be the most precious moments watching your children grow into their own unique, individual selves. What you might not have known was how much becoming a mother would inspire you to better yourself, love yourself, and understand yourself more.

In the busiest days of motherhood, sometimes all you have is a few moments for yourself—and that's just where this book comes in. In *Three Minutes for Mom*, you'll find everything you need to make the most of that brief pause, that essential time to connect with yourself. With 365 entries covering every aspect of motherhood, you'll find exactly the comforting and realistic voice you need to inspire, encourage, and motivate you every single day. First, you'll find an inspirational yet relatable message, then you'll discover an exploration of how that message applies to your role as a mother, and finally you'll engage in a reflection on how you can bring the meaning of that message with you into your day in small and achievable ways. In just three minutes, you'll get the connection you need—whether that's a reminder to take care of yourself or a fresh new way to look at your relationship with your child.

This book was made for you to take a moment . . . not to slow you down, but to fill you up and to remind you how incredibly important, powerful, and capable you are. You can read the entries in order or flip through the pages until you find one that applies to your life on a particular day. Then take comfort in the advice, laugh at the craziness, and feel the compassion of knowing you are not alone in the journey of motherhood.

So instead of letting the challenges of motherhood overwhelm you, grab this book. Make three minutes of your day centered in strengthening, loving, and supporting you . . . every day.

With all my love, Erin

Day One:
Water What You've Got

Water what you've already planted and watch how much will bloom.

It's easy to be swayed by the parenting world warning you of all the mistakes you could be making as a mother. Here's what to do instead: Look around and notice how you've already created a beautiful environment for you and your child. Just like when you plant a garden, if most of your efforts are focused on tending to what you've planted, not only will you enjoy it more—you'll encourage more growth. So don't spend too much of your time focused on the weeds of motherhood—of course they'll pop up from time to time! But if you remember to water what you've already planted, you'll see so much bloom.

Today take a few minutes to draw your attention to the solid foundation you've created in your family and what grows there: Maybe it's fun and silliness, respect, and kindness, or maybe it's love, comfort, trust, and honesty.

Day Two:
It's Okay to Not Know

In motherhood, there's one thing you can be certain of:
You'll never be certain.

No matter how old your child is, not a day goes by where you aren't faced with a new challenge in motherhood; some days it may be the challenge of getting your child to sleep, and other days it's answering your child's existential life questions. It's impossible to have all the answers, and actually, you're not supposed to have all the answers. Here's what you *do* have: the ability to allow yourself to take a moment, an hour, or a day to find the answers you need. Your child will learn an incredible lesson from you admitting when you're unsure or when you require time to think about an answer. This shows your child what it's like to be human, to not have all the answers, and to be able to find those answers with time, patience, and support. Just as much as you're teaching your child how to be a human, you're learning, too—the more understanding and compassion you allow yourself in this process, the more room you'll create for growth.

If you find yourself in a challenging situation with your child today, remind yourself that you may not have the answer right away and allow yourself the time to find that answer.

Day Three:
Prepared, Not Perfect

You'll never be a perfect mother, but you will be a prepared mother.

Of course you'd love to be the perfect mother, but there's another type of mother that's even better because it's actually attainable: the prepared mother. You prepare yourself for the fact that you'll certainly mess up, that you'll make mistakes, and that you may not have the right words to say. As a prepared mother, you may not know it all, but you do know that you'll always do your best by being prepared with open-mindedness, compassion, and humility. Here's the best part about being a prepared mother: Your child watches you navigate through your mistakes and learns how to treat themselves when they mess up too.

Today when you run into a parenting moment that feels less than perfect, pause and ask yourself which prepared mother quality will help you best in this situation: open-mindedness, compassion, or humility?

Day Four:
It's Not Personal

Your child's behavior isn't personal to you; it's personal to them.

Of course it feels personal when your child says, "You're the worst mom ever!" You work so hard to be the exact opposite of that. But when it happens, take a moment to let the sting of those words fade enough to notice that your child's behavior isn't personal to you; it's personal to them. Because your child communicates their tough feelings through behavior, try to be on the lookout for the feeling that lies *beneath* their behavior. Not only will this help you understand your child more, but it will keep you less reactive and more responsive to what your child needs.

Rather than take your child's behavior personally, ask yourself what about their behavior tells you how they're feeling. The more you practice tapping into what's really going on with your child, the more you'll be able to rise above your own reactivity and tap into your own feelings as well.

Day Five:
Add a Little Magic

If you don't show your child that life can be magical, who will?

As a mom, you work so hard to keep your family on schedule, on time, and on top of it all. Yet sometimes the monotony of life can take the reins, leaving you feeling in a bit of a rut. Think of that rut as a reminder that you not only need but *deserve* to sprinkle a little more fun into your life. Of course not everything in life can be fun, but when you practice sprinkling fun into your days, you're teaching your child that they can always choose to find the fun in life. After all, if you don't show your child that life can be magical, who will? Adding the magic of fun into your family's day-to-day life is how your children learn that life is full of responsibilities, but that doesn't mean you have to be miserable doing them—fun can be found, sought after, and experienced anytime you choose.

Sprinkle a bit of fun into your day by asking your children to imitate you or another family member or make it a game of family charades; this not only shakes things up, but gives you a great perspective on how your children view their family.

Day Six:
The "Why" Behind Whining

When you get curious about what bothers you,
you move away from judgment and closer to compassion.

When you are bothered by your child's whining, first notice that it is absolutely an unpleasant experience to hear your child in a helpless state (honestly, there isn't a parent in the world who enjoys this!). Yet if you have a visceral reaction to your child's whining, it's important to look at what your relationship to vulnerability and helplessness has been. Have you been able to openly complain and be heard? Were you allowed to express your unhappiness? You may find that what bothers you the most about your child is a part of you that you struggle to accept, understand, or express. Getting curious about what irritates you will help you move away from judgment and closer to understanding and compassion.

When you're irked by your child's whining, ask yourself, "What judgment am I making about my child's complaint?" Do you believe they should be happy? Do you wish they wouldn't be honest about how they feel? With curiosity, rather than judgment, see what you find in your answers.

Day Seven:
You Don't Have to Say, "I'm Fine"

Everything doesn't have to always be fine; it can simply be undefined.

There's nothing wrong with saying you're "fine" except that most of the time, the word "fine" is used as a placeholder for how you're really feeling. Whether you aren't ready to share how you feel or just aren't sure of how you feel, practice saying just that: "I'm not sure how I feel" or "I'm not ready to talk about how I feel." Tiny acts of honesty with yourself are what cultivate a stronger sense of self-trust, which is the foundation for showing up as the mother you know you are: attuned, compassionate, and confident.

Today when you're uncertain about how you feel, allow yourself to say just that. The more honest you can be with yourself, the more confident you'll become in trusting yourself in the toughest moments of motherhood.

Day Eight:
"I Am" versus "I Feel"

*In the hardest moments of motherhood,
remember, you are not what you feel.*

Moms experience a lot of emotions and big feelings in a day. If you ever find yourself feeling trapped in your feelings, there's a small shift you can make to get out of that rut. Rather than say, "I am sad," say, "I am *feeling* sad." It's not just semantics; this tiny play on words creates a separation from who you *are* and what you are *feeling*. That space between you and your feeling is the real you, the one experiencing emotion. Not only does this allow you to feel the feeling and move on, it also allows you to see your child in this same way: a human experiencing a constant flow of temporary emotions.

*If you feel stuck today, ask yourself, "Am I sad or am I feeling sad?"
That separation will allow you to move through your feelings more
freely and remind you that you won't be cemented in your current
feeling forever.*

Day Nine:
Why You Feel Triggered

Your child often points to the areas in
your life where you need the most healing.

If your child poked you where you had a bruise on your arm, it would hurt—you'd jump back, shout, and maybe even swat their hand away. If your child poked your other arm, without a bruise, you would have a much milder reaction. This example shows why you feel triggered by your child: Your child is poking at something that is already there—an unhealed part of yourself that hurts when it's poked at. Rather than feel awful when you're triggered by your child, you can feel a sense of relief and control, knowing that this is something within you that you can heal.

Today when your child does something that triggers you, ask your-self where else you've felt triggered like that before. Is it a feeling of not being listened to, appreciated, or respected? Allow yourself to acknowledge that your reaction is less about your child and more about the wound inside you that needs healing.

Day Ten:
You're Doing It Right

You're doing way more right than you're doing wrong.

In a world that keeps moms on a treadmill of achievement, driving you to want more, do more, and be more, take a moment to notice how much you're already doing right. Free yourself of the expectations of what you *should* be doing, how you *should* be parenting, and really look at what's working for you and for your family. From packing a healthy lunch box to giving your child a hug and telling them you love them, every moment counts, no matter how big or how seemingly small. When you stop and look at your day, you'll find that there's way more you're doing right than you're doing wrong.

Today take a moment to note three things you've already done right. Jot them down on a notepad or simply make a quick mental list. Take a deep breath and remind yourself to let go of perfection—you've already got this just as you are.

Day Eleven:
When Your Child Is Mad at You

*A child who is unconditionally loved
will tell you when they're mad at you.*

When your child tells you, "I don't like you!" or " You're mean!" or "You're the worst mom ever!" sure it doesn't feel great, but here's why you can actually be proud at those moments: Your child feels so unconditionally loved that they feel safe to share their truth, even when it means that they don't like you at the moment. You have created an environment where your child feels like they can express themselves freely without the threat of your love being taken away from them. That is something to be unbelievably proud of and something to hold on to in moments like this. So rather than immediately punish your child for their harsh words, pause to let them know that you can tell how deeply hurt they are because of the words they've chosen. Acknowledging their hurt doesn't make you weak; rather it strengthens your connection to your child. Your child will be much more receptive to a replacement behavior after they've calmed down and felt heard.

The next time your child shares how unhappy they are with you, take a moment to soak in the deeper realization that your child knows you'll always love and accept them, even when they try their hardest to push you away. Once your child has calmed down, have a discussion by saying, "You were so upset earlier, can you think of another way you can let me know you're upset without using those hurtful words?" You can also offer two preferred phrases to use as a replacement phrase.

Day Twelve:
Genuinely Enjoying Your Life

Connection is what creates the happiest, most enjoyable lives.

As a mom, it's easy to get so caught up in the daily tasks and responsibilities of life that you forget about enjoying your days. Luckily, there are two things you can do every day to genuinely enjoy your life more. The first is to reach out to someone you care about to share how you are genuinely feeling. The second is to reach out to someone you care about and ask how *that person* is genuinely feeling. Positive, connected relationships with others is the path to creating healthier, happier lives. So start getting in the habit of creating small, genuine moments of connection throughout your day. Maybe it's a quick morning phone call after school drop-off or it's an afternoon check-in text message after lunch. Creating a routine of connection with the ones you love will become an anchor to enjoying your life just a little bit more.

Today take the time to text a loved one: Think about who you feel most comfortable with sharing how you're truly feeling each day and make a note to reach out to that person today. Not only will they feel loved for your genuine check-in, but you'll also feel a greater sense of connection to them and yourself.

Day Thirteen:
The Ebb and Flow of Feelings

Your feelings are like the waves of the ocean:
They ebb and flow; they come and go.

As a mother, you can experience a full range of emotions in a twenty-four-hour period, sometimes even in a one-hour period. Not only is this difficult to navigate, but often no one teaches you how to manage this ever-changing flow of feelings. So here's where to start: When you're frustrated, when you're angry, when you're hurt, or when you're feeling *any* unpleasant feeling, visualize the ocean. A simple visualization of the ocean can remind you of something very important: Feelings aren't forever. The waves of the ocean are just like your feelings: They ebb and flow; they come and go. Some of those waves will wipe you out and others will help you continue to float along, but every wave—and every feeling you experience—doesn't last forever. The waves are a reminder of the impermanence of what you may be feeling. Let the idea of them be the flotation device you need in the moments when your feelings (or your child's feelings) have inundated your day.

Today when you experience an unpleasant emotion, close your eyes to envision it as a huge wave that's crashed into the shore. Then at some point, later in the day, think back on that wave of emotion and notice that this thing that once crashed hard into your day has subsided: This after-the-fact noticing is what will allow you to weather the storms that are the emotions of motherhood.

Day Fourteen:
Healthy Mom Guilt

Healthy guilt guides you toward where you want to be.

Here's how to take your "mom guilt" and turn it into something good: First, there are two types of guilt: healthy guilt and unhealthy guilt. Functional, healthy guilt says, "I don't like what's going on here and I want to change it." Unhealthy guilt says, "No matter what choice you make, you'll still feel guilty." Regardless of which guilt you experience, the trick is to examine the whole situation before you let the guilt affect you. For example, if you feel guilty for not playing with your child after dinner and you realize it's because you truly haven't had enough connection time with them today, this is healthy guilt pointing you toward where you want to be. However, if you realize you have had a lot of connection time with your child today, then this is unhealthy guilt that is no longer serving you and you can be proud that you've identified it and redirected yourself to a more positive, connected relationship with guilt.

The next time you experience mom guilt, take a moment to ask yourself, "Is this guilt moving me closer to where I want to be?"

Day Fifteen:
Say Yes to Yourself

A no to someone else can be a yes to yourself.

Being a mom requires saying yes to endless amounts of practices, playdates, and parties. Sure, you understand the benefits of staying connected to your family, friends, and community, but when the yeses pile up, it leaves very little room for you. But the reality is, you need room for you. While spa days and meditation retreats are absolutely encouraged, the room we're talking about is room for you to *not* have to be constantly on the go and instead have space to just be. Does it seem impossible to say no to the status quo of always being on the go? If saying no feels hard for you (especially when there isn't an actual schedule conflict), allow yourself to see the other side of the no: A no to someone else is a yes to yourself.

The next time you feel like you want to say no to plans but worry it will let someone down, ask yourself if this will actually be a yes to yourself. It's okay to choose yourself; it's okay to choose time to just "be" with no reason other than you need it.

Day Sixteen:
The Three Steps to Repair

You can't repair what you won't acknowledge is there.

You're bound to make mistakes as a mother. After all, you're human. The good news is that you can repair your mistake with your child each time this happens, using a quick, simple formula: acknowledgment, accountability, and action. First, *acknowledge* what happened: "I just yelled at you." Second, take *accountability*: "I shouldn't have yelled at you; that was my fault and I'm sorry." Lastly, take *action* to do things differently, which can look like trying again or moving forward with a promise to do your best. Not only will using this technique help repair your parent-child relationship, but it will also teach your child how they can repair a situation when they make mistakes too.

The next time you need to repair a mistake you made with your child, try utilizing acknowledgment, accountability, and action. Give yourself time to adopt this new formula and be sure to use your own words so that your repair feels authentic to you and your child.

Day Seventeen:
Practicing Patience

You must embody the very virtues you want your children to possess.

You can help your child develop the skill of patience in three small steps. First, create small moments of recognition when your child is patient. For example, when your child is trying to get your attention, let them know you need a second and then make note of their patience: "Thanks for being so patient while I finished my task." Second, understand that patience is the ability to sit in uncomfortable emotions, waiting for something we want or waiting for something we don't like to end. Acknowledge the natural discomfort of learning to be patient, and with empathy, be in those uncomfortable moments with your child. Third, note your own relationship with patience. For example, when you're in traffic, notice how you teach your child to handle the discomfort of waiting. If needed, make tiny adjustments not only to help your child with patience but also to help yourself create a healthier, more enjoyable relationship with patience.

The next time you're in traffic, monitor your level of patience. If you'd like to feel less impatient, try saying out loud to your child, "Wow, it's tough for me to be patient right now. I wonder what we could do to have fun while we wait?"

Day Eighteen:
When Your Child Is Struggling

*Your child will struggle, but they have a secret weapon:
They have you by their side.*

As a mother, it can be eerily familiar to learn that your child struggles with school or friendships like you once did. While you are hardwired to pull from your own life experiences to make sense of the world around you, when it comes to your child, it can get tricky to not insert your past experience into their present experience. Here are three ways to support your child: First, even though you may have a similar experience, your child is a different person, with different parents, friends, and so on. Separate your experience from your child's experience. Second, listen to your child. Rather than assume what your child is going though, listen, ask, observe, and notice that your child isn't an exact replica of you. Lastly, your child has you as a mother. You alone are one of the most beautiful resources your child has to help them navigate their struggles.

When you hear about your child's struggles, after your heart drops into your stomach, pick it up to remember you've lived through something similar and can guide them with empathy, open-mindedness, and discernment. While you may not have the answers right away, you can be with your child as you navigate their struggles together.

Day Nineteen:
Find a New Path

Give yourself permission to "reroute" as many times as you need.

Imagine driving along a new route using your GPS to navigate. When you've made a wrong turn, the GPS doesn't give up or continue down the wrong path; it reroutes until you're back on course. The same can be said for when you've taken a wrong turn in parenting. You are allowed to reroute as many times as you need. You can always find a new path and try again. The best part is that not only does this give you grace, it also models accountability and self-compassion for your children. If you want your children to be confident in their ability to reroute when they make a mistake, those lessons have to start with you. Learn to make this skill a natural instinct in your everyday life.

Today allow yourself to reroute without judgment. Say it out loud when you encounter a difficult moment: "I didn't like how I handled that; let's try that again." Saying this out loud will help your child learn how to handle the same kinds of situations in their lives. The more you have patience for yourself, the more they will too.

Day Twenty:
Validate Your Feelings

*The more you validate your feelings, the less
your feelings will control you.*

Have you ever found yourself in a difficult parenting situation, only to minimize your feelings and downplay your experience? It's likely you've said things like "It's no big deal" or "Other people have it worse!" While you're not intentionally invalidating your feelings, over time it may become difficult to identify or trust what you feel. So the next time you find yourself downplaying a tricky situation, try acknowledging that you actually have a good reason to feel what you feel. Try saying things like "I understand why I am upset; this is tough" or "It makes sense that I'm exhausted; even though other mothers have sleepless nights, it doesn't make mine any less difficult." The more you validate your own feelings, the more you'll develop a stronger sense of self-trust—a strength that will continue to help you in your motherhood journey.

If you catch yourself in a tough moment today, take a few minutes to validate what you're feeling. Nope, this isn't self-pity; it's self-acknowledgment that simply states whatever you feel is valid and warranted. This is the path to a stronger connection to yourself.

Day Twenty-One:
Be a Good-Enough Mother

The good-enough mother grants permission for the good-enough child.

At the beginning of your child's life you are devoted to meeting every single one of their needs: You soothe them, feed them, and take care of each aspect of their life. As your child grows, you're probably noticing that it's becoming more difficult to meet *every* need: You can't always play with them or give them what they want, when they want it. The truth is, this is a natural part of development *and* because of that, there is no perfect mother—but there is a good-enough mother. As a good-enough mother, you'll be able to show up *most of the time* as an attuned, empathic, and available mother. And in those moments when you can't show up? Then you are normalizing what it's like to be human. As a good-enough mother, you're teaching your child to be a good-enough child. You are no longer striving for impossible perfection, but instead trusting that doing your best is always going to be enough.

Today notice how often you're a good-enough mother. It's likely there are countless ways you've been good enough. This isn't being overly optimistic; it's being appropriately realistic—you're a good-enough mother; you just have to train yourself to see it.

Day Twenty-Two:
Small Changes Matter

Small shifts each day are what create true, lasting change.

Showing up each day is *exactly* what lays a strong foundation for change. Sure, the world will want to convince you that radical, life-altering parenting methods like spending thousands of dollars on a program or throwing out every toy in your home are the only ways to see results. But for the everyday mother like you, who is ready for achievable, sustainable change, it's the tiny shifts each day that add up to create lasting change. Don't discount the small moments you show up or the little things you do, because it's in those moments that you're making an impact that adds up and absolutely matters.

Think about something you do every day for your child that truly makes a difference. Maybe it's a special way you wake them up, a note in their lunch, or a back rub at night. Every little thing you do matters.

Day Twenty-Three:
Good Moms Have Bad Moments

A good mom will have bad moments, but because she does much more right than she does wrong, she doesn't let them define her.

You will have bad moments, but that doesn't make you a bad mom. This is because "Good moms have bad moments," and here are three reasons why this phrase should live rent-free in your head: First, it allows you to take accountability for your actions, but doesn't let them define you. Second, it helps you utilize healthy guilt: The bad moment registers as a reminder to shift course because that moment isn't aligning with your usual approach. Lastly, your child is going to watch you make mistakes, take accountability for them, but then also forgive yourself and move on. Seeing you do this will instill the same self-confidence and self-caring in them.

It may sound cheesy, but practice saying, "Good moms have bad moments" three times to yourself right now. Set a calendar reminder in your phone at the end of the day with the phrase or send it to a friend when she's upset about her bad parenting moment. Keep this phrase at the front of your mind to remember: You're a good mom who has bad moments.

Day Twenty-Four:
When In Doubt, Listen

In the moments when you aren't sure what to say, listen.

In the moments when you're not sure how to respond to your child, you're not sure what to say, it's natural to blurt out the first thing that comes to mind to soothe, fix, or ameliorate the situation. But here's the thing: You don't have to react right away. Instead you can do something that's incredibly helpful: You can listen. As moms, we tend to assume we know exactly what our child is feeling or thinking, which can lead to disconnection and frustration. So give yourself permission to listen just a little bit more. Not only does listening de-escalate the situation, it also gives you more data to assess what's going on so that you can respond to your child in a more attuned and connected way.

Today when you have a moment to talk to your child, practice truly listening to what they're saying. It's common to want to interject or redirect, but just take a moment to listen without needing to respond and notice what it feels like to be fully present for their words.

Day Twenty-Five:
Making Mistakes

Making mistakes makes you honest, relatable,
and a role model for your child.

It's a good thing to make mistakes in front of your child. Why? Because your child will learn that making mistakes is a natural part of life. The next time you make a mistake, think of it as a way to teach your child *how* to make mistakes. First, don't deny your mistake; own up to it. Say, "Wow, I really messed up there." Second, don't beat yourself up; build yourself up by saying, "That was a mistake, it happens, and I definitely want to do better next time." Making mistakes doesn't weaken your parenting; it strengthens it. Your children learn to respect you for being honest and accountable—qualities you likely want your child to possess as well. The path to being a more conscious, connected mother starts with being human, so the next time you make a mistake, file it under the "I'm showing my child how to be human" category and be as kind to yourself as you want your child to be to themselves.

The next time you make a mistake in front of your child, use it as an opportunity to model accountability and self-compassion. Your child will be grateful that you've modeled what it's like to be human so that when they mess up, they can follow your lead.

Day Twenty-Six:
HALT: Hungry, Angry, Lonely, and Tired

*The more you can tune into yourself, the more
you can tune into your child.*

The next time your child has a meltdown and you can't for the life of you figure out what's going on with them, remember the acronym "HALT": "hungry, angry, lonely, tired." This is a checklist of the four states that are often responsible for people not being their best selves. Our children are rarely aware that they are hungry, angry, lonely, or tired, but we can certainly keep HALT in mind to better understand our child's current state and meet them where they're at. Using this checklist will help you feel more compassion and give you a road map to support your child in their tough moments. The bonus here is that you'll start using that checklist on yourself too. At any given moment a meltdown can occur, so keeping HALT in your back pocket will be a supportive tool for you.

While you may be attuned to when your child is hungry or tired, the feelings of anger and loneliness can be trickier. Try tapping into how much connection your child has had today: Could they be angry that they haven't gotten what they needed? Could they be lonely and needing some one-on-one time? If all else fails, ask yourself why you'd act how they're acting. You may gain great insight there as well.

Day Twenty-Seven:
Do What's Right for You

There's doing the right thing and then there's doing what's right for you.

When you think about the phrase "Do the right thing," what comes to mind? Does it make you think about doing right by all? Does doing the right thing also include doing what's right for you? Many women were taught as little girls to be kind, polite, and obedient in order to do what's right. While this is done with the best intentions, the message doesn't always include making sure it's right for *you*. As a mother, you might struggle with choosing what's right for you (or your child) when it isn't what's best for the majority. An example would be knowing your child is too tired to make a playdate, but because the "right thing to do" is to be polite and not cancel, you push your child past their limit. Or when your teen is burned out from a tough week at school and needs rest, but you insist they attend a family party because it's the "right thing to do." As you navigate motherhood today, ask yourself, "When I look back at this moment, whose best interest will I have prioritized, and is that my true priority?"

When you feel torn on how to respond to a situation, stop and ask yourself, "Is doing the right thing the same thing as doing what's right for me?"

Day Twenty-Eight:
Redefine Balance

Redefining balance is the key to finding balance.

Finding balance in motherhood can feel like finding a unicorn: It's only something you read about in fairy tales. Each day you're on a quest to find the mythical creature that is *balance*. But how exhausting and depleting it is to try and chase something that doesn't exist! So, what if instead of trying to achieve a perfect, daily balance, you expanded your definition of balance to include a week, a month, or a season? The truth is, your life will continue to ebb and flow, contract and expand, based on your own needs and the needs of your family. So there is no need to try to fit it all in each day. Instead expand your view of balance and allow yourself to see a bigger picture. Not only will this help you see how much you truly do achieve as a mother, you'll also be cultivating self-compassion and self-appreciation, which are feelings you absolutely deserve in your life.

Take a moment before you start your day and ask yourself, "What are my realistic expectations for balance today?" If there is one task that will consume most of your time, zoom out to see when a more usual balance will resume. Doing this will help you see the bigger picture and affirm that you are always doing your best!

Day Twenty-Nine:
Quality over Quantity

*Ten minutes of true connection is worth more
than ten hours of disconnected togetherness.*

As a mother, it can be easy to get caught up in measuring every little thing you do, including how much time you spend with your child. This is why it's important to remember that the quality of your time is worth more than the quantity of your time. You can't always be attuned, attentive, and engaged, and that's okay. It's quality over quantity: Rather than count the minutes you've played with your child, drop into that play for ten minutes and give it your all—get into character, watch how your child's incredible imagination works, and get curious about anything they share with you. Making the most of what you have will always bring you closer to connection. That's where you can draw from; the moments you give will create a breeding ground for more and more. Continue building yourself up for all you do and watch how it continues to grow.

Today focus on the quality of the time you spend with your child rather than the quantity. Perhaps it's your full attention chatting on the way to school, imaginative play they've been begging you to participate in, or a fully present bedtime story complete with all the silly voices—it's the moments you make count that matter.

Day Thirty:
You Get What You Get

"You get what you get and you absolutely can *get upset."*

You've likely heard the phrase "You get what you get and you don't get upset," and with good intentions it tries to teach us that we can't always get what we want. But let's update this phrase to support you and your child in accepting that you can't always get what you want, but you absolutely *can* be upset. Why? Because disappointment is a normal human emotion that you and your child will experience, and rather than not allow that feeling, you can welcome it without needing to shut the feeling down or avoid the feeling. For example, the next time your child gets a cupcake at a birthday and it's not the icing color they wanted, rather than tell them they can't get upset or swapping the cupcake out, you can say, "Ah, I wish you got a yellow cupcake, too; I know that's your favorite color. I'd be upset, too, but this is the one they handed you, so do you want to give it a try?" Getting comfortable with discomfort is a practice, so be gentle with yourself and your child as you give all feelings permission to flow freely in your family.

When your child gets upset, rather than alter the situation or change their feelings, try identifying with their disappointment. When you relate to your child's feeling of disappointment, it will reduce feelings of anger or embarrassment and instead breed compassion, understanding, and collaboration to help them through what they are experiencing.

Day Thirty-One:
Connection Before Correction

When in doubt, use connection before correction.

As a mother, you are constantly in correction mode with your child: "We use gentle hands," "Bottoms on the couch—jumping isn't safe," "You can be mad, but you can't be mean." However, if you are constantly correcting a behavior that doesn't quite make sense, try focusing on connection to get to the root of your child's behavior. Every human, your child included, is hardwired to crave connection: We want to feel important, loved, and needed and will alter our behavior to get the connection we need. When you meet the needs of your child's desire for connection, you clear away the behaviors your child has been using to seek attention. For example, if your child screams when you're on the phone—no matter how many times you've told them not to—try having the same focused conversation with your child that you're having on the phone. Whether it be a role-play, a silly conversation with your child pretending to be someone else, or an actual conversation with your child, giving them the one-on-one connection they need can allow the connection-seeking behavior to retire.

If you need to correct your child's behavior today, check in and get curious whether your child is seeking connection through their behavior. If you suspect connection is the motivator, use that moment as an experiment: Stop what you're doing and drop into connection mode to see what happens with your child's behavior.

Day Thirty-Two:
Receiving Apologies

It's not your job to make someone feel better about their mistakes.

Think about the last time someone unintentionally hurt you. How did you reply to their apology? You may have said, "No worries" or "It's okay" when, in fact, it didn't sit right with you. Forgiveness is beautiful because it allows us to move on, but to truly heal we have to be honest with our pain. Now, it's not always a big deal when someone offends you, but over time not honoring your feelings builds up to create a knot of resentment. So when you want to move on or avoid holding a grudge, the more you validate your own experience, the closer you'll get to feeling comfortable and confident being you. The next time someone apologizes, practice using a self-validating reply like "I appreciate your apology"; "I wasn't okay with that, so thanks for acknowledging you're sorry"; or a simple "Thank you." Not only will this strengthen your self-trust muscle, but it is also a beautiful way to model for your child how to honor their feelings *and* move forward with forgiveness.

It's time to replace "No worries" with a self-validating reply. Circle the one that feels best for you: "Thank you for apologizing"; "I appreciate that"; "Thanks for saying you're sorry, I needed to hear that"; and of course the simple "Thank you," which will absolutely be a safe, self-validating response.

Day Thirty-Three:
You Aren't a Self-Improvement Project

*You already have enough projects; don't
create more work for yourself.*

This book won't twist, bend, and shape you into the perfect mother. This book doesn't promise to magically transform you into a new and improved version of yourself. Why? Because you're not a self-improvement project and you already have everything you need. Yes, it's absolutely wonderful to change parts of yourself that no longer serve you, but there is something to be said about enjoying the good stuff you've already worked so hard to create. After all, if the focus of your life is to always seek change, improvement, and growth, you won't have time to soak in and savor all that's already within you and right in front of you.

Today enjoy the parts of yourself you've already invested time and energy into by asking, "What am I most proud of myself as a mother?" Whatever your answer, soak it in and allow yourself to feel good about it. Savoring will only help you create more of the good you already have, so give it a try.

Day Thirty-Four:
Practicing Self-Compassion

Understanding is the gateway to self-compassion.

What is your relationship with self-compassion? Are you and self-compassion best friends or are you not sure you've ever met? The truth is, you learn self-compassion from your caregivers, so if it wasn't modeled for you, it is likely you and self-compassion are strangers. Sometimes self-compassion can even leave you feeling uncomfortable because it's associated with self-pity. So let's take baby steps. First, start with simply understanding because understanding is the gateway to self-compassion. Understanding basically means "I understand why I feel the way I feel." Understanding is giving yourself a slight nod, a hint of approval that your feelings are warranted. Stay with that; let it simmer until it becomes comfortable and a normal practice. Over time, understanding will transform into self-compassion, allowing you to say, "I understand, allow, and feel love for myself." Eventually you'll show yourself compassion like you do for your child: with kindness, acceptance, and love.

The next time you mess up, forget something, or make a mistake, note how you speak to yourself. Would you address your child in that same manner? If not, how can you use understanding as a gateway to self-compassion?

Day Thirty-Five:
How to Be Mad

"You can be mad, but you can't be mean."

Anger is an important, inevitable, and powerful emotion. The key to anger, just like all the other emotions, is how to effectively express it. It's likely your child has expressed anger in ways you would consider mean, rude, or inappropriate. Why? Because your child must learn *how* to be mad. The first part in teaching your child how to effectively express anger is to separate feelings from behaviors. The phrase "You can be mad, but you can't be mean" can be used when your child's anger hasn't been expressed in a healthy way. This phrase helps your child (and you) remember that while all feelings are allowed, all behaviors are not. Now, when your child is in the throes of anger, it's unreasonable to expect them to adopt a new behavior. However, after that storm has passed, you can discuss effective ways they can express anger: walking, jumping, drawing, writing, talking, crying, punching a pillow. This can become a trial-and-error process where your child learns they're never in trouble for how they feel and they get to choose safe and healthy methods to feel their anger.

"You can be mad, but you can't be mean" is an anchor for you in the moments when your child's behavior feels out of control. This phrase will ground you in your truth, knowing that your child can absolutely feel what they feel and you will teach them how to express those feelings with safe, healthy behaviors.

Day Thirty-Six:
The Power of the Pause

When in doubt, pause.

Imagine your child just yelled at you, "You're the worst mom ever!" You feel your body tense up, your face flush, and you're ready to launch back with a reaction that matches your child's energy. This is where you can use the *power of the pause*. The pause creates a space between you and your child. The pause gives you a moment to regroup and invite your "adult" brain to come back online. The pause reminds you, "Wait, I have control here. I'm not taking the bait; instead I am going to reel in my child because I have control over my response." Now, what happens when you don't pause? You end up matching your child's dysregulated energy, opening up the door for a Ping-Pong match of hurt feelings and power struggles. The pause will become your best friend. Silence will allow you to not take it all so personally and to remember that there is a person who you love very much who is learning how to manage their very big feelings. The more you allow pauses in your day-to-day parenting, the more you'll have the reins, guiding your family to more productive, healthy conversations.

Your pause is true power. While it may seem passive to stay silent, you are anything but passive in that moment. Use your pause to remember it's you and your child against the situation at hand, not you against your child. Let the pause disarm your reaction and empower your response.

Day Thirty-Seven:
We're on the Same Team

It's not me against my child; it's my child and me against the challenge.

How many times has it felt like you and your child are on opposing teams? Feeling this way is not the parent-child relationship you want. Not only is this narrative false—of course you're on your child's team; you're their biggest cheerleader—it disconnects you from your child. To restore connection, here's a small phrase that makes a big shift: "It's not me against my child; it's my child and me against this challenge." Let's use the example of bedtime: The usual "My child won't go to bed; they won't listen to me" furthers the divide, creating a "you versus them" mentality—this is not creating a united front to solve the problem. Now, if you adjust your view to "My child and I are in this bedtime struggle together; how can I get us through?" it brings you back to a connected, more effective mindset, remembering you're not an opponent; you're on their team. Sometimes you're coaching them and other times you're cheering them on, but no matter what, you're in it together.

Practice reframing parent-child struggles by saying to yourself, "We're on the same team" or "My child and I are navigating a tough moment together." Your belief in this is the most powerful tool in getting through the tough moments of motherhood.

Day Thirty-Eight:
Depersonalizing Motherhood

Your child isn't rejecting you; they're rejecting the task at hand.

You're bound to face resistance from your child. After all, it's your child's job to test the limits and it's your job to set the limits. But no one tells you how difficult it can be to constantly hold those limits because that resistance can feel personal. This is why it's important to have this phrase slapped on your proverbial forehead: "My child isn't rejecting me; they're rejecting the task at hand." Sure, you might want to make it about you, but it isn't. Your child is only resisting you because you are the enforcer of the rules! Your child isn't trying to make bath time difficult; bath time feels difficult for them. Your child isn't mad at their curfew because of you; they're mad at the fun they imagine they're missing out on. Yes, they will be mad at you, they will reject you, they will resist you . . . but you must remember to depersonalize this part of motherhood. The more you depersonalize your child's resistance, the more you can feel empathy for your child and the more you can stay connected to your child.

Today be on high alert for your child's resistance so that you can "try on" this new approach to depersonalizing motherhood. Note any changes you feel in your emotions, reactions, and how you respond.

Day Thirty-Nine:
When Your Child Won't Talk to You

Not every child wants to talk about their feelings
while they're feeling them, and that's okay.

If your child shuts down when they're upset, wants nothing to do with you, or refuses to talk to you, here are three ways to parent through those moments: First, accept how your child feels right now. It's easy to worry that they'll always cope with their feelings by shutting down, but if you stay in the now and accept your child as they are, it's the most powerful form of love they can receive. Second, remember that your child does need you to help them navigate their tricky emotions, but it might not be at the time or in the form you're offering. Lastly, even though you have the best intentions, you can't force your child to talk to you. Instead give your child the space and tools to express themselves in the way that feels best for them. Your child might want to draw, write, text, or act out how they feel. Once you accept where your child is at and remember that they do need you, you can create the space for communication that's effective for them.

The next time your child pushes you away, remember that behaviors are a way to process feelings. Your child does need you; they're just learning how to cope with their feelings. If your child needs space, let your child know you love them and you'll keep checking in so they know you're there for them when they're ready.

Day Forty:
Shadow Puppet Behaviors

Your child's behavior is as big as their feelings.

Remember playing shadow puppets with a flashlight as a child? Can you envision how small your hand was and how big that shadow puppet would get? It felt so powerful to be able to make something so small be seen in a big way. This is a great visualization to use when your child is expressing their feelings through their behaviors. Your child has very big feelings, yet they only have so many ways to show you, or communicate, the magnitude of what they feel. That's where those big bursts of behaviors come in—the yelling, the stomping, the throwing—those big actions make a statement, just like a big shadow puppet. Knowing your child's big behaviors are actually communication will help you reevaluate how you handle the moment.

When your child engages in a big behavior, you need to keep them and others safe. Once that's done, let your child know, "Wow, you have such a big feeling right now, I can see how mad you are, how sad you are, and you know what, I believe you and I understand why you wanted to do XYZ."

Day Forty-One:
When Your Child Sees You Cry

*Normalizing your emotions allows your child
to not be afraid of their own emotions.*

If your child ever sees you sad and crying, because you're human and it happens, here are three ways to keep your interaction healthy. First, use appropriate honesty by saying, "Yes, sometimes when we're sad, we cry, and Mommy is sad right now." Appropriate honesty means you don't have to divulge the reasons or details of why you are sad. Second, let your child know that all feelings are temporary, including sadness: "Sometimes we feel happy; sometimes we feel sad. It's normal for our feelings to change." Third, if your child lovingly tries to console you, thank them for their kindness *and* reassure them that because you're an adult and they are your feelings, it's your responsibility to handle them. This makes sure your child knows that feelings are normal *and* that it's never their job to make sure you're okay.

You never plan on crying in front of your child, but like any other interaction in motherhood, your ability to accept what's in front of you with compassion will allow you to handle it in the best way possible. Tears are your body's way to self-soothe. Trust your body and allow yourself to have that moment that you know will eventually pass.

Day Forty-Two:
Successful Moms

As much as we teach our children, parenting teaches us too.

The success you've had in life prior to becoming a mother—in education or your career—is likely from being tenacious and having focus and control over your efforts. These skills have taken you far, yet as a mother you may feel wildly unsuccessful when you apply those same efforts to parenting. One of the hardest realizations mothers have is that the skills used to succeed in life before having kids are often not the skills needed to succeed in motherhood. Not only can it be infuriating, but it's also exhausting: How in the world could you have gone so far in your pre-kids life only to be stumped and frustrated by a tiny little human you love so much? Motherhood calls you to lean into the softer side of yourself, learning to accept and allow rather than force and control. A new version of success is born when you expand and adapt your hard-earned skills to motherhood.

It can feel counterintuitive to let go of control as a mother, so rather than envision the extreme of having no control, ask yourself, "What do I desperately attempt to control that hasn't been successful?" Give the areas that come to mind space to envision less control and more curiosity: Can you soften? Can you shift? Can you lean out enough to see what changes with less force?

Day Forty-Three:
Being Your Child's Sounding Board

When it comes to children, your unwavering
presence speaks louder than words.

As your child grows and has relationships with siblings, friends, classmates, and family, you become the sounding board when problems arise; you hear it all. It's natural to jump in, problem solve, and share all your wisdom. Yet, for most of us, as much as we want support, we also want to be listened to, validated, and understood. A beautiful practice to adopt not just in parenting, but in all relationships, is to ask what is needed of you: "Would you like me to just listen or would you also like my input?" This practice widens the space for your child to explore their feelings and come to a new understanding on their own. While it can be hard to witness your child feel unsure, your unwavering presence and listening communicates that they can get through their situation and if they do want your direct support, you're right there by their side.

Get in the practice of asking your child, spouse, friends, and family, "I hear you; do you want me to just listen or would you also like my opinion?" It may sting to hear that your input isn't wanted. But at this moment, it's not personal to you; it's personal to them. Know it's an honor that they've entrusted you with the very important task of witnessing their experience.

Day Forty-Four:
Plan to Not Make Plans

Making plans to not make plans is productivity for the soul.

If you find yourself constantly up to your neck in practices, playdates, and parties, you may feel the need to slow down, but still somehow end up filling every minute of your day with plans. While there is always an excess of options to stay busy, the deeper part of yourself knows that less will allow you to feel more: more energized, connected, and grounded. Look at your upcoming month and make a plan to not make plans. Make a calendar note that for a set number of hours or maybe even a whole day, the plan is to not make plans. Intentionally creating space in your family's schedule to simply just *be* is productivity for the soul. Your mind may rationalize or justify why plans are needed, but challenge yourself to simply be.

The next time you find yourself overbooked, overscheduled, and overplanned, open up your calendar and make a plan to not make plans. Pay attention to what comes up for you; what judgments or assumptions are you making about creating intentional rest for your family? Rather than judge, be curious and see what it feels like to take a breather and simply be.

Day Forty-Five:
You're Not Complaining

A mother sharing her struggle isn't complaining;
it's sharing and honoring her truth.

Getting honest with yourself is the key to feeling more comfortable in your own skin. You need to try less self-doubt and more self-compassion, knowing that you trust yourself, your feelings, and your experience. The path to getting honest with yourself can be paved by sharing your truths with someone else—a partner, a parent, a friend, and of course another mother. Remember, you are not complaining; you are being honest about your truth. If talking about your struggles in motherhood makes you feel uncomfortable in some kind of way—ungrateful, embarrassed, or inadequate—that's okay. Start small and let a loved one know that "I just want to be honest." It's the tiny steps you make toward validating, honoring, and acknowledging your truth that shows you that you are allowed to have the full range of human emotions and that you can navigate through them with the support of your loved ones.

A simple way to honor your truth in motherhood is by saying, "I'm upset about my child not listening to me and I understand why I feel this way." This is a small step to validation, and practicing this will compound into more self-trust, confidence, and comfort in your own skin.

Day Forty-Six: Overheard Compliments

*Catch your child being kind or doing good
and watch the shifts in your child unfold.*

Today you're about to make the best mistake. A mistake that's going to make your child feel great. You're going to "accidentally" let your child overhear a compliment about them. You can be on the phone chatting about how hard they tried on their math test, or you sing their praises to another loved one about how thoughtful they are when they hold the door open. Doing this gets you in the habit of tending to the good in your child. You know it is there, but too often you are distracted by the busyness of life that you forget to slow down and acknowledge the endless good your child does. How you see your child is how your child learns to see themselves, so compliment the good they do and watch the shifts in your child unfold. When your child receives positive confirmation about who they are—"I'm a kind person" or "I am curious and creative"—they will feel and behave in a way that is proud, confident, and competent.

Don't get too focused on what to compliment your child on—anything that comes to mind goes a long way. Need a starting point? Here are few areas to focus on: kindness, helpfulness, thoughtfulness, self-care, self-love, creativity, patience, gentleness, and simply being themselves.

Day Forty-Seven:
Try Not to Judge Your Child's Feelings

Behind every behavior that doesn't make sense
lies a feeling that absolutely makes sense.

When your child is having a tantrum or a meltdown, you might find yourself unintentionally judging your child's feelings. In your head you may be saying, "This is not a big deal," "You're overreacting," or "You shouldn't be feeling this way." Truth is, regardless of what you think, your child is feeling the way they are feeling. When you judge that your child's feelings are invalid, you create a separation between you and your child, which makes it harder for you to help them through the tough moment. In order to make your life easier *and* to help your child, you can approach the situation differently and ask, "What is the feeling beneath my child's tantrum?" Often the outburst is rooted in something like disappointment or powerlessness—feelings that you have no doubt felt in your own life at some point. Identifying the feeling makes your child's meltdown relatable and allows you to be less reactive, more understanding, and able to guide your child through the tough emotions you've also experienced.

It's easy to forget your child is equipped with all the same emotions as you, just without any instruction manual. You are that instruction manual. As hard as it is to weather what seems to be an unreasonable tantrum, remember to find the feeling beneath the behavior.

Day Forty-Eight:
Anger As a Tool for Growth

Your child is a mirror reflecting every part of yourself.

Do you feel like you are always yelling at your child? Are you tired of being an angry mom? Here's a different approach to use the next time you're angry with your child. Look at your child as if they are holding a mirror, reflecting back parts of yourself that you might not be happy with. One, it could be a part of yourself you don't want your child to embody like being inflexible, needing to be right, or struggling with being on time. Two, your child could be reflecting back parts of yourself you weren't ever allowed to experience: the ability to complain or openly share their feelings. Perhaps you were never allowed to express yourself, so you have no idea how to handle those feelings in your child. Three, it could also be that your child's lack of emotional control reflects back how out of control you feel. Noticing that your anger is a reflection of something inside you is huge. Start with compassion for yourself that you've carried this around for years before your child even entered the picture. Know that your openness to seeing things differently will take you where you need to go.

The next time you are angry with your child, before you react, stop and visualize the mom mirror. What about your child's current behavior is so infuriating for you? Take a moment to reframe your thinking and have some empathy for where your child is coming from.

Day Forty-Nine:
Empathy Through Disappointment

Your job isn't to make your child happy; it's to walk them through the experience of being human.

It is a daily occurrence for your child to not get their way, to not get what they want, and to feel disappointed. However, it's unlikely that your child calmly says, "Mommy, I am so disappointed I can't have more ice cream." It's more likely that your child shows disappointment by crying, complaining, or calling you "the worst mom ever." In the storm of all the emotion of disappointment, remember to see past your child's behavior and anchor to the feeling they are experiencing. Can you tap into what it feels like to not get what you want and not have any power to change that? It's not easy to handle disappointment and powerlessness all at once. When you feel compassion for your child in their experience, rather than agree with how they are behaving, it allows you to react as the parent you want to be. Your job isn't to always make your child happy; it's to walk them through the experience of being human.

The next time your child is raging over not getting what they want, remember the word "disarm." Your first goal is always to disarm yourself, and that can be done by relating to your child's feelings of disappointment and powerlessness, feeling that compassion, and moving through it with understanding.

Day Fifty:
Staying Calm

*You can be calm with your child to the
extent that you can be calm with yourself.*

Validating your child's feelings has many benefits; it allows your child to know what they feel is real, allowed, and accepted. The trouble you may run into is how *long* your child stays in their feelings. Sure, you can give them a few minutes to cry, yell, and rage, but after five minutes go by, you can start to feel your patience dwindle and your ability to stay calm diminish to nonexistent. No, you aren't a bad mother; you're a mother doing everything you can to be there for your child. Here's what's actually going on: You can only sit and be calm in the storm of your child's feelings to the extent that you sit in the storm of your own feelings. You can only validate your child's feelings to the extent that you can truly validate your own feelings. So while you have the best intentions with your child, know that this is an inside job where you can practice staying with and validating your own feelings.

The next time you struggle to stay calm during your child's big feelings, zoom out of that moment and think about how you handle these feelings on your own. Do you tend to push them away by getting busy, minimizing them, or pretending they don't bother you? What would it feel like to stay in those feelings without your usual cover-up? This curiosity is growth; give yourself time to see where it takes you.

Day Fifty-One:
Bare Minimum Parenting

Sometimes your best version is your bare minimum.
Why? Because you're human.

There are times in life when you simply cannot give it your all in motherhood. Whether you're physically sick, mentally exhausted, emotionally drained, or there's just too much going on within your family, know that you are allowed to downshift into *bare minimum parenting mode*. Bare minimum parenting mode means that you are giving yourself permission to do what is needed to get through the day so that you and your children are healthy and safe. All the extras—the home-cooked meals, the perfectly brushed hair, and the quality one-on-one time—all go out the window, not because you don't care about your family, but *because* you do care about your family. Knowing and acknowledging this allows you to conserve your energy to get through this challenging time. This means you give you and your family compassion and leave judgment at the door. Bare minimum parenting mode is not only allowed, but it's necessary to allow you to be the best version of yourself in the not-so-best moments of life.

It may feel silly, but officially declare when you are entering bare minimum parenting mode. Tell yourself and tell someone else. You can even spin it positively to your child, like making it a pizza night since you're not cooking dinner or having an impromptu movie night with blankets and pillows on the floor because you need that downtime to just be.

Day Fifty-Two:
Catch the Ball

When your child throws their emotions at you, don't throw those emotions back at them—instead, catch them.

Your child just said, "I hate you!" These words mean your child is having very big feelings and wants to make sure you know how they feel. It's like they are taking their feelings, rolling them into a ball, and throwing them at you. Your reaction may be to smack that ball right back with the same level of energy and anger by using threats or punishment to show them you're going to win this match. You have another choice, though, and that is to *catch the ball*. You don't want to play this game, especially since you know how it will end: a lose-lose with tears, regret, and a whole lot of repair that needs to be done. Instead catch the ball, put it down, and show your child that their feelings won't deter you from being their safe, sturdy place.

Imagine you and you and your child standing at opposite ends of a Ping-Pong table. Your child spikes the ball. Rather than hit it right back, you put your paddle down and catch the ball. This is what you'll do with your child's anger; don't keep their anger in play by reacting. Pause, remind yourself it's not personal, and respond knowing you can help your child through their feelings.

Day Fifty-Three:
Tell On Yourself

Confidence is built by knowing and trusting what you feel.

Telling on yourself is one of the quickest ways to take your bad mood down a notch. When you wake up cranky, when you feel your patience hanging by a thread, rather than clench your jaw, pretending to be okay, try "telling on yourself." Whether you say it to yourself or out loud to your family, acknowledging when you aren't feeling your best releases the pressure to pretend everything is fine. Moments like these, when you're honest with what you feel, are what continue to solidify your self-trust and confidence.

Once you get comfortable "telling on yourself," you can add in bits of humor about how you feel. You can make fun of yourself, act out how tired you are, or even ask your child to act out what you feel like. Doing this creates a path for you to move through your feelings and maybe turn your cranky mood into fun.

Day Fifty-Four:
Appropriate Honesty

*"You're not responsible for my feelings,
but you are responsible for your actions."*

"Are you mad, Mommy?" If you've ever gotten this question, you know it's not an easy one to answer, especially when you *do* feel angry with your child. Here is a two-step approach to handle this situation using *appropriate honesty*. Appropriate honesty means you can be truthful with your child about your feelings: "Yes, you're right, I am angry." Validating what your child sees not only creates trust in your parent-child relationship, it also teaches your child to trust themselves. Keeping what you share appropriate means you let your child know "I was frustrated that you didn't listen to me. You're not responsible for my feelings, but you are responsible for your actions." This will allow you to find a balance that's honest and healthy in managing your feelings in motherhood.

Your child is learning how to handle their emotions by watching you. Letting your child know that you have feelings that are affected by others—but you still take ownership of them—will allow your child to do the same.

Day Fifty-Five:
Calling In Sick to Motherhood

*Motherhood is the one job where you're irreplaceable,
which is exactly why rest is a necessity.*

You've probably heard people say, "Moms don't get sick," but guess what—you do, and you will, because you're human. And because motherhood is the one job where you're irreplaceable, you absolutely need ways to care for yourself when you're under the weather. You may not be able to take a few days off, but you can "call in sick" by shifting into *bare minimum parenting mode*. Bare minimum parenting mode is checking your usual high expectations and all the extras at the door. When you're not feeling well, you're only doing what is necessary to care for your family—get them dressed, fed, and cared for—without the guilt of it being inadequate. Whether it means baths are skipped, hair isn't brushed perfectly, or dinner is a frozen meal, fast food, or a simple PB&J, the goal is to meet your family's basic needs so you can get the rest and healing you deserve.

Create a sick day plan now by noting what three automatic go-to plans you'll have set next time you're under the weather. What will you serve for dinner that takes very little effort? What parts of grooming can you let go of? What activity can your children engage in to maximize your downtime?

Day Fifty-Six:
Realistic Repairs

*Most of parenting is just showing your child
how to do this thing called being human.*

Repairing is a healthy parent-child relationship practice, and it doesn't have to be a long, drawn out, overly remorseful process. Here's an example: Let's say you've repeatedly asked your child to get their shoes on; you lose your cool, yell, and then want to apologize. Your realistic repair sounds something like "I am frustrated from asking you to get your shoes on ten times. I'm sorry I yelled; that wasn't okay. Let's figure out a different way to get through this." A realistic repair shows your child how to be human: It's okay to make mistakes, take accountability, and move forward. If you find yourself trying to convince your child to forgive you, pause and remember, your goal isn't to make sure your child forgives you; it's to create a relationship where you model honesty, openness, and empathy that will naturally allow that forgiveness to blossom.

The next time a repair is warranted, take a moment to think about how you'd like to be apologized to and use that exact approach. It's likely you would want someone to own their mistake, apologize, and show that they care about your hurt feelings by changing their behavior.

Day Fifty-Seven:
Give Grace Instead of Nagging

When you change the way you approach your child,
the way your child approaches you changes.

Of course you don't want to be a nag. Yet you might be asking your child to do the same things over and over again. While there's no magic formula to get your child to do every little thing they're asked to do, there is a way to stop nagging. Try using the phrase "I think you forgot to . . . " or "Oh no, I don't think you remembered to . . . " This approach moves away from the feeling that your child is in the wrong and instead gives them grace and the opportunity to do what they've been told. When you give your child the benefit of the doubt, it gives them the space and confidence to make better choices.

Think about some other phrases or approaches that could give your
child the benefit of the doubt. Assuming they've forgotten is one way.
Another way might be assuming they're too tired to get the task done.
If your child agrees, you both can brainstorm a way to make it easier.
Get creative not just for your child, but for you, too—it never hurts to
add a little variety and fun to your day.

Day Fifty-Eight:
Disarm Yourself

If you want to change the relationship with your child,
you have to disarm.

If you've ever wanted to shift the dynamic with your child—but you haven't been sure how to do it—it's time you focus on disarming. Believe it or not, you walk around this world wearing invisible armor. This armor has been around way before you became a mother and it protects you from potential harm—yes, even from your child. Your armor is what anticipates a fight before it begins—not because you want an argument, but because your armor's job is to keep you safe. While it may prepare you for battle, your armor keeps you in a constant state of defensiveness, which keeps you disconnected from your child. Your child can feel this separation and responds accordingly. This cycle can end right now by committing to dropping your armor and disarming.

Here's your first step to disarm: Keep a mental note at the front of your mind that your goal in every interaction with your child is to disarm. Find a phrase to help you: "I am not here to fight," "I don't need my armor," or "My goal is to connect, not fight." This thought alone will shift your parent-child relationship.

Day Fifty-Nine:
It's Normal to Be Annoyed

You're absolutely allowed to get annoyed with your child.

Did you know it's absolutely normal to be frustrated with your child? When your child doesn't follow your directions or makes a mess out of the house you just cleaned, of course you're going to be annoyed at them. How could you not? You're human! If you've ever been under the assumption that somehow you can achieve eternal calm, please know that can't happen! The goal in motherhood isn't to avoid feeling normal, human emotions. The goal is to show your child how to feel normal, human emotions *and* how to use those feelings to respond. Get in the practice of saying to yourself, "Yep, it makes sense why I am frustrated." When you own, allow, and normalize your feelings, you can choose something different from yelling and screaming. This simple validation allows you to be right where you are and then make a choice to respond in a way that feels aligned to your parenting practice.

Today practice separating your frustration from how you respond by imagining catching your frustration in a jar like you would a firefly— you catch it in the jar, look at it long enough to know you don't want to keep it bottled up, and then let it go so you can respond.

Day Sixty:
Resetting Outside the Home

A child's behavior is often their most powerful form of communication.

If your child has ever had a tantrum or meltdown or has acted out of sorts at a social gathering, it probably left you feeling embarrassed about their behavior. The next time this happens, keep in mind that your child's behavior is always a form of communication. When it comes to events, parties, and large social gatherings, there's an abundance of moods, feelings, and personalities that are interacting with your child and it's likely that they may be feeling overwhelmed, overstimulated, and/or overtired. Before reprimanding your child, try taking them into a quieter space, lowering your voice, and getting down on their level and saying, "Wow, there's so much going on, I wanted to be just with you for a moment." Give your child that space for a pause, because not only could they use some time away from the crowd, but you might also benefit from a reset too.

The next time your child is acting out at a social event, try to practice giving your child the benefit of the doubt. When you lean in with empathic curiosity, you're much more likely to create a space where your child can share what's going on, which will allow you to support them through it.

Day Sixty-One:
Feeling versus Fact

What is feeling and what is fact?

You love your child, so naturally when they are sad, hurt, or upset, you're going to feel compassion and empathy and you might even experience their same feelings. But it can be tricky when you take on your child's feelings, because their new feelings merge with your old experiences. For example, your child comes home from school upset about not being included in a game of soccer. Being with your child in their sadness is validating and healthy. But let's say in your childhood, you had an ongoing difficult experience making friends, so now you're not just sad with your child, you're also bringing your own feelings and past experiences into the present day, imagining your child will end up with the same hurt and pain you had. This is where your feelings get mixed up with your child's facts. Here's a phrase to help you keep your experiences separate: "What is feeling and what is fact?" The feeling: Your child is sad; the fact: Your child wasn't included in a game of soccer. Everything else that's a worry or hasn't happened yet can be disregarded. This is what will help you focus on supporting your child through their tough moments.

Can you identify sensitive spots from your childhood years? Take note so that if your child has even one ounce of struggle in any of those areas—whether academic or social—you'll be prepared to separate what is yours and what is theirs.

Day Sixty-Two:
People-Pleasing Recovery

Am I doing this because of love,
or am I doing this because I fear losing love?

People-pleasing is such a sweet, sneaky way of feeling in control. This behavior gives you a false sense of control by keeping others happy so you can feel at ease. The thing is, in motherhood, being a people pleaser leads you to being overly busy, stressed, and resentful. So here's a way to shift away from people-pleasing behaviors: Start paying attention to the drive behind why you're doing what you're doing. If you feel the urge to say yes to someone, to take on a favor, or to run someone an errand, ask yourself these two questions: One, is this yes coming from a place of love? Meaning that you love this person and you have the capacity to do this task. Or two, is it coming from a place of fear of losing love? Meaning that if you don't do what this person asks, you won't receive their love anymore or you'll lose their approval even though you don't really have the time or energy for the task. Learning to differentiate between what's coming from love and what's coming from fear will allow you to sort out what you truly want to spend your valuable time doing.

Today when you're asked to do something for someone else, pause to ask yourself, "Am I doing this because of love, or am I doing this because I fear losing love?"

Day Sixty-Three:
Seeing the Good

*Don't be so focused on what you are doing wrong
that you forget to see all you're doing right.*

The next time you feel like you just aren't cutting it as a mom, try to remember vegetable garden parenting. Imagine you've grown an amazing garden of vegetables and even though you see how great those vegetables are growing, you're more focused on the weeds that keep popping up. This is what's happening to your view of your parenting skills: You're so focused on what you're doing wrong that you've forgotten all the beautiful things you've gotten right as a mom. Here are three things you can expect from the vegetable garden parenting approach: First, you'll realize that you've been doing way more right than you've done wrong. Second, seeing more of the good will give you the confidence to handle the not-so-good (when the weeds pop up). Lastly, your child will follow your lead; they'll naturally see and appreciate the good in themselves because that's what they know from watching you.

It's time to start vegetable garden parenting: Today grab an imaginary basket and walk through your motherhood timeline collecting the moments that have made you feel best.

Day Sixty-Four:
When Everyone Wants You

"There's two of you and only one of me."

When you have more than one child (or more than one person in your home that needs you: a spouse, parent, or even a pet), you know how often you're needed in two places at once. As a mother, you feel called to do it all, and when you can't, it's easy to get frustrated that you're always needed. When this happens, try to remember that it *is* impossible for you to do more than two things at once. Get in the habit of confirming this real truth: "There are two kids and only one mom." Say it out loud and say it frequently when you feel pulled in multiple directions at once. Your children will get familiar with this phrase and will soon realize that you will take care of their needs; they just have to be patient. Eventually they will even feel comforted by the phrase in moments when you aren't tending to their needs and wants.

Try saying the phrase in a playful, overly exaggerated way to help cut the tension and even get your children involved in how to "solve" it. Making tiny shifts like this can help you navigate the stressful moments of motherhood.

Day Sixty-Five:
Parenting Yourself

Parent yourself the way you'd parent your child.

One of the biggest misconceptions in motherhood is that the love you have for your child should be enough for you to always stay calm. As much as you love your child, remember that you've lived decades of life before becoming a mother, meaning you have decades of untended-to, unprocessed feelings swirling around inside you. The incredibly authentic and raw connection you have with your child can awaken those old feelings. It can feel confusing that the unconditional love you have for your child doesn't trump those old feelings. These moments are less about parenting your child and more about parenting yourself. Treat yourself with the same kindness and love that you would treat your child with. Give yourself permission to feel what you are feeling and don't beat yourself up for it. You are learning to love all the parts of yourself, just like you love all the parts of your child, even when those parts are filled with uncomfortable, unpleasant feelings.

The next time you are uncomfortable with the feelings that come up for you in motherhood, practice parenting yourself the same way you'd parent your child. Let yourself know that it's okay to feel how you feel, that those feelings will pass, and that over time, the more you allow yourself to experience them without judgment, the less power they'll have over you.

Day Sixty-Six:
Being the Safe Place Parent

A child who honestly shares how they
feel is a child who feels unconditionally safe.

When your child says, "I don't love you anymore!" or "I hate you!" it feels like a punch to the gut. Here's the thing: You know that it's normal to get angry at your parents—you can even think back to your childhood and feel incredibly mad at your own parents. Yet, at the core of every child, is the desire to be loved by their parents. So when your child says those hurtful words, know it's a sign that they feel safe enough and loved enough to express their hurt. As hard as it is to see, that's a win. Rather than shut down their feelings with your words, you can pause and remember that you know your child loves you—they're just hurting and want you to know it in the most aggressive way they know how to express it. You don't have to be a punching bag (you can take time away, change your setting), but you can hold space for them, and yourself, and know that your love for them won't ever fade no matter how harsh their words get.

Next time your child uses harsh words with you, try not to take them personally. Stop and remind yourself that those words are an expression of your child's hurt. Letting your child move through their feelings and addressing their choice of words later is how you can assure them that all their feelings are accepted, but that all their actions aren't.

Day Sixty-Seven:
Parent Performance Review

*Seeing yourself through your child's eyes
will shift how you show up as a parent.*

It's funny how motherhood experts suggest the best ways to be a mom and yet rarely suggest that you check in with how your child feels about you, their mom. Not that you're looking for an actual performance review, but taking a moment to see yourself through your child's eyes can be a helpful, a reassuring, and an awakening tool. The next time you and your child have a free moment together, ask your child, "Tell me your favorite things about Mommy" and "Tell me the things about Mommy you wish would change." Listen with discernment and compassion and know that whatever your child shares with you is their truth in that moment. Savor the good and soak in the love your child feels from you. Hold space for the not-so-good, too, remembering that you're a mom who loves her child—but also holds boundaries that make her child feel upset.

Have fun with this prompt. Allow your children to share their input about their other parent and their grandparents and teachers. You'll learn from their sharing and will encourage an open line of communication, which is a pivotal part of your parent-child relationship.

Day Sixty-Eight:
Family Chores and Belonging

A child thrives when they feel a sense of belonging.

Family chores and family jobs are helpful to keep your family functioning, but one of the most impactful effects that family roles have on children is often overlooked. While children require love and support to thrive, they also require belonging. To belong means to know you matter, you make a difference, and you're needed and wanted. Giving your child family tasks is a great way to build their sense of belonging. If you struggle with how to assign chores and responsibilities, start with tasks that your child can easily accomplish and that are visibly helpful to the family. Your child will see the impact they have on their family and strengthen their self-confidence and sense of belonging. Be sure to savor the moments you witness your child absorbing how important they truly are, not for what they do, but for who they are—a loved, important member of their family.

Start small when you add new responsibilities to your child's routine. Try coming up with three possibilities and allowing them to choose which one to start with. Balancing belonging with autonomy will show your child that you not only value their impact, you value their input too.

Day Sixty-Nine:
Growing and Knowing

The desire for growing is best supported by your deep inner knowing.

You're reading this book for two opposing reasons: to grow into an amazing mother and to know you're already that amazing mother. What a beautiful thing, growing: to want to better yourself, learn more about who you are, and be the best version of yourself. And what a beautiful thing, knowing: seeing how you embody all that you seek. This is the path to loving yourself into your natural evolution as a mother. Today take a moment to savor what it is you already know to be true about yourself and in what ways you'd like to continue on that path to growth.

When you have the desire to change something about yourself, make space to see what that desire is rooted in: Is it rooted in a place of love or rooted in a place of fear that you're not enough? If it's the latter, find a part of you that is rooted in a place of love and grow from that space—it will take you further down the path you desire.

Day Seventy:
The Power of Listening

You always have the option to pause and listen.

"What do I do when my child _____ [fill in the blank]?" There are end-less scenarios you face as a mother. As lovely as it would be to have a perfectly prepared plan for every encounter you face, you already know it's not possible. What *is* possible is something you already know how to do: *Listen*. It may be your instinct to jump into action, make assumptions, and take control—even when you're unsure yourself! Listening might be the last thing you want to do when you have to solve a problem that's right in front of you. But when you remember that listening is a parenting superpower, you'll create more time and space to assess what your child needs and reduce the need for repairs and apologies.

Throughout your day today, notice how often you are thinking while your child is speaking rather than actually listening. Don't be hard on yourself; it's common to be in your head anticipating your response. Instead use this as a reminder to gently return to listening and it's likely you'll find more comfort, calm, and confidence in responding to your child.

Day Seventy-One:
The Little Things Matter

*It turns out, the little things aren't so little at all—
they're actually the biggest things.*

You have so much to do as a mother, yet at the end of the day, you aren't even sure what you accomplished. That's why it's important to be reminded that *it all matters*. What you do matters. Every little thing you do for your child matters. Every little back rub, every time you make their lunch, every time you give them a hug, every time you care about the story they tell you: It matters; it matters big. The love, compassion, and values you instill in your child matter more than ever right now. What you give to your child is what your child in turn then shares with the world, so don't for one second discount the small acts of love that you share with your child.

Stop to think about one value you've instilled in your child that you feel incredibly proud of and look for it in your child and yourself throughout the day.

Day Seventy-Two:
Validate and Move Forward

When you allow your child to feel, you allow your child to heal.

You want your child to have confidence and a strong sense of self-trust, so you validate their feelings. It's pretty impressive that you've created such a healthy family tradition with your child. Something to keep in mind is that you can validate your child's feelings without keeping your child stuck in their feelings. Validating your child's feelings can be a short and sweet process where you acknowledge what you see, help them name the feeling, and then pave a path forward. Children must learn how to process their feelings and that includes how to move *past* their feelings rather than stay *stuck* in them. Offering your child a path forward can be done by being goofy, making up a song or dance, setting up an activity—anything that shows your child that you can have difficult feelings, but that you also have access to the enjoyable ones too.

Today think about how your child handles their tough feelings. Do they tend to stay stuck in them? If so, get creative with how you validate that what they're feeling is real while also offering them a way to move through that feeling.

Day Seventy-Three:
What You Want Most

*What you want most for your child is
often what you need most for yourself.*

Think about what you want most for your child. Not so much material things, more the core feelings and beliefs you want them to embody. Maybe it's feeling unconditionally loved, accepted, confident, or knowing they are enough. How beautiful that you want to give your child those things. Have you ever thought to see if those are the same things you want to feel inside yourself? If you've struggled to feel confident in yourself or never learned to love yourself, it's likely you've made it your mission to make sure confidence and self-love are things your child *does* feel. When you realize that what you want most for your child is often what you need most for yourself, you can get a clearer picture of which of those qualities your child already possesses and which are areas you want to support within yourself.

Today you're going to do a deep dive by reflecting on the qualities you want your child to embody and noting which you wish you had embodied as a child.

Day Seventy-Four:
Buffet Parenting

Take what you want and leave the rest.

As a mother building your own family, it's natural to look back at your own childhood. Maybe you've reflected and found things you loved that your parents did, and maybe you've realized there are certain things you certainly won't choose to carry on as you parent. You don't have to use an all-or-nothing approach when it comes to parenting. Just like you would at a buffet, you can pick and choose what works best for you and your family. Pile on what will nourish and help your family grow and certainly pass by what doesn't leave a good taste in your mouth. Each generation has the opportunity to carry on what feels right and get rid of what no longer serves them.

Reflection time: Jot down two parts of your childhood you'd like to pass on to your child as well as two new traditions or practices you'd like to add to your family's legacy.

Day Seventy-Five:
The Impact of Raindrops

Every drop of love you give your child matters.

There are days in motherhood when no matter how hard you've tried to be the best mom you can be, it doesn't feel like it's enough. Those moments can feel discouraging and make you believe that all you do to show up as a patient, present, and loving mother isn't making an impact. The truth is, you are one of the most impactful people in your child's life. Your impact is like a raindrop: One small droplet doesn't seem like much, but the ripples it creates and how it continues to expand show you the impact it has. This is the same as each drop of love, effort, and input you contribute to your child's life. The individual drops may be small, but as they collect, they create the most important force of love in your child's life.

Take time to think back to a "little thing" someone in your family did for you that ended up creating quite the big ripple effect in your life.

Day Seventy-Six:
Managing the Juggling Routine

Just because you can doesn't mean you should.

Motherhood is synonymous with multitasking; at any given moment you could be doing two things at once. While your ability to juggle it all is impressive, it doesn't necessarily mean you always have to be juggling. Here's the thing: *Just because you can do something doesn't mean you should do it.* Meaning just because you have an extra ten minutes to take a relative's phone call or fit in an extra playdate this weekend doesn't mean you should. Your ability to do it all is there, no doubt about it, but that doesn't have to be the deciding factor. What is the deciding factor, you might ask? Checking in with yourself to see what you need before adding more balls to your juggling routine. Using discernment to sort out what belongs in your busy day is a true act of self-love, so remember, just because you can doesn't mean you should.

Take the phrase "Just because you can doesn't mean you should" and use it in an area of your life that you'd like to shift. For example, if you're feeling overscheduled, try "Just because I have free time doesn't mean I should go."

Day Seventy-Seven:
A Favorite Child?

*Children mirror back the parts of yourself
you love and the parts you don't love.*

If you have more than one child, there's no question you love your children equally, right? It's impossible to love one child more than the other, but it is possible to *like* one child more than the other. That's a hard truth to admit because you may have one child that's more go-with-the-flow and it makes you feel like a great parent, and then you have another child that doesn't make you feel like a good parent and you wonder if you're doing anything right. Here's what's happening on a deeper level: Your children mirror back parts of yourself that you love *and* they mirror back parts of yourself that you aren't too fond of. Tapping into this awareness can be a freeing experience, allowing you to feel less guilt or shame about not getting along with one child as much as the other and instead to dive deeper into the parts of yourself that are being reflected back to you through your child. So much in parenting comes back to the relationship you have with yourself, and this is great news because it's the one relationship you have total control over.

Today contemplate the question "What are the things I see in my child that I love or don't love in myself?" By asking this, you are becoming a more conscious parent: You're becoming aware of what you bring to the individual relationship with each of your children.

Day Seventy-Eight: Scripts for Resilient Kids

You can handle your child's feelings to the extent you can handle your own.

Of course you want to raise resilient kids. But the moment you see your child struggle or experience any type of failure, you probably have the urge to swoop in to save your child, which doesn't allow that resilience to be built. Why is it hard for you? Well, obviously you don't want your child to experience any pain, but often it's deeper than that. It's difficult to witness your child experience uncomfortable emotions—like sadness, disappointment, betrayal, and not feeling like they belong—because these are feelings *you* aren't comfortable dealing with in yourself. Naturally when they come up for your child, you're going to want to make it all go away. So here are four small scripts to help you and your child build resilience:

- "This feeling is normal."
- "I get why you don't like this feeling."
- "I've felt this way too."
- "I am going to be here with you while you go through this."

You're not only building their resilience, but you're also building your own. This is the beauty of parenting: You can teach your children things as you learn them too.

Take a second to note a feeling you feel comfortable navigating with your child. What's allowed you to feel confident about sitting in that emotion? Is it an emotion you've learned to handle in yourself? You're able to do so much more than you realize!

Day Seventy-Nine:
How to Handle Your Feelings

Most of motherhood is learning how to handle your own emotions.

Like most mothers, it's likely you weren't taught to process your feelings in a *healthy* way. Rarely was it intentional, but you probably learned to minimize them, ignore them, or just push them away with being busy. So now that you're a mother, it's becoming more apparent that you need to find not only new ways to be comfortable with your emotions, but also how to be comfortable with all your child's emotions. The good news is that these two things are one in the same and you can become more comfortable with your feelings by validating what you feel, when you feel it. Each time you have an unpleasant feeling you can ask yourself, "Does it make sense that I feel this way?" You will generally be able to say, "Yes, it makes sense I feel frustrated because XYZ just happened." It may seem small, but these tiny validations allow you to stay in your feelings longer, creating a greater tolerance that will increase over time and allow you to stay present in your feelings as well as your child's.

Next time a difficult emotion comes up for you, ask yourself, "Does it make sense that I feel this way?" By practicing handling your feelings, you will understand that the emotion is warranted and therefore allow it to hang around just a little bit longer so it can be felt and released.

Day Eighty:
Avoiding Eggshell Parenting

The further you distance yourself from a feeling,
the harder it becomes to tolerate.

Have you ever tiptoed around your child to avoid them experiencing certain feelings? Maybe because you're not sure how to deal with those feelings or you're generally scared to make your child upset because it's difficult to calm them down. Walking on eggshells doesn't feel great, but it's the only way you've discovered how to get through those tough moments. Here's the thing: As much as you love your child and believe this special treatment is in their best interest, eggshell parenting unintentionally reinforces the feelings you so badly want to shield your child from. The further you distance your child from a feeling, the harder it becomes for your child to tolerate. It also exacerbates your belief (and your child's belief in themselves) that they can't handle these feelings. The first step in shifting this dynamic is finding a new belief about your child's ability to handle natural human emotions. Think about how you handle the feeling within yourself: Can you share that coping skill with your child? Trust yourself that no matter how big your child's feelings get, you'll be able to make it through with them.

Create small moments for your child to learn to tolerate the feeling you often help them avoid. You can do this through role-playing or through real-life experiences that you create simply to help your child build their confidence in handling this newly experienced emotion.

Day Eighty-One:
Handling the Silent Treatment

*The silent treatment is one of the loudest forms
of communication; listen carefully.*

If you've ever tried to have a conversation with your child and they've blurted back, "I don't want to talk to you!" you know that doesn't feel the best. Yet if you were to put your child in the shoes of an older adult who had the maturity to say, "Hey, right now isn't a good time for me to talk; can we talk later?" you'd have a better response, be more understanding, and not feel disrespected. This is why it can be helpful to take a step back and ask yourself, "What feelings are powering my child's response and how can I teach them to express what they need?" As much as you want your child to respect you, you have to give them the language to do so rather than shut them down for their delivery. Keep this in mind the next time your child does something that feels disrespectful so that you can respond in a way that supports your child learning more effective, healthy communication strategies.

One of the most effective ways to correct your child's behavior is to truly understand how they're feeling. Next time your child gives you the silent treatment, try putting yourself in their shoes, imagining yourself in the same situation. For example, can you recall a time you were upset and someone wanted you to talk when you weren't ready?

Day Eighty-Two:
Giving the Benefit of the Doubt

*The best way to connect to your child is to
give them the benefit of the doubt.*

One of the easiest ways to feel disrespected as a mother is to confuse your child disagreeing with you with your child not complying with you. It's likely a daily occurrence for your child to not agree with you, but often it's lumped in with your child not complying. The truth is, your child not agreeing with your opinion is not only normal, it's also pivotal in their development to be able to assert themselves and share their point of view with confidence. So next time, give your child the benefit of the doubt and understand that their intention is not to be disrespectful, but rather to express their differing opinion. Try this: Confirm with your child that they are allowed to disagree with you, saying, "Hey, it's totally okay that you don't agree with my decision to change curfew." And then note the difference between agreeing and complying: "While you don't agree with me, we still have to move forward with this new plan." Separating the two will help you see it's less about being disrespectful and allow you to respond rather than react.

Anytime you give your child the benefit of the doubt, you free yourself from taking their behavior personally and reacting defensively. Today ask yourself, "How can I give my child the benefit of the doubt and assume their best intentions?"

Day Eighty-Three: Handling Food Battles

Children learn to be respectful by being respected.

Okay, let's be honest: If you've spent your precious time cooking a meal for your family only to have your child push their plate away and yell out, "I don't want to eat this!" it's absolutely understandable that you would feel upset. Does it feel like your child is disrespecting you? Yes. Is your child actually trying to be disrespectful? It's unlikely. It's tough to swallow (pun intended), but as in many situations in motherhood, this isn't personal to you; it's personal to your child. Just like you have cravings and aversions to foods at different times, so does your child. Remembering this will help you respond with less rejection and keep your parent-child connection. Instead of writing off your child's behavior as disrespectful and taking it personally, you can look deeper and ask yourself, "Have I ever been there before?" When you do this, you're teaching your child what respect looks like.

Having a plan beforehand is helpful, so today take a moment to craft your response the next time your child won't eat what's for dinner. Here's an example: "I don't always like what's for dinner either. You can still give it a try or you can have the usual optional PB&J."

Day Eighty-Four:
Discussing Difficult World Events

You can't control the world, but you can control how you respond to it.

Here are three things to guide you in discussing difficult world events with your child. First, remind yourself that as uncomfortable as it may be for you to talk to your child, it's important that your child hear about difficult topics from their most trusted, loved source. That way when your child hears about these topics at school or with friends, they already have a foundation and feel safe in understanding something that's typically difficult to understand. Second, ask your child, "Have you heard about this before?" That way you know what you are walking into and you can help your child understand what they've already heard. It also prevents you from oversharing too much information your child may not be ready to receive. Third, remind your child that in tough moments there are always good people helping out. This shows your child that even in hard times, change and comfort are available. These three points will help you stay grounded when speaking to your child about the tricky reality we all live in.

Remember, you won't always have the answers. When you're unsure how to answer, it's okay to say to your child, "That's a good question. I want to give you the right answer, so I am going to think about it and let you know when I find that answer."

Day Eighty-Five:
When You're Triggered by Your Child

*You're not mad at your child; you're mad at
the feeling they've forced you to feel.*

Have you ever not liked the way you've reacted to your child? Here's an important reminder for you (because you don't deserve to go down the mom-guilt spiral). The way you respond to your child when you feel triggered is not representative of who you are, but it is representative of who you have *learned* to be. A trigger is really someone, in this case your child, tapping into a painful part of yourself that you have not yet healed. So your response is really just a way to defend and prevent yourself from feeling more pain. Rather than spiral into guilt or try to control everyone around you, you can actually learn more about your triggers. You can understand them, find compassion for them, and eventually disarm them so they aren't controlling your every move. Understanding and healing your triggers is a long-term process where you slowly uncover what vulnerable feelings lie beneath the surface of your behaviors. Go easy on yourself as you discover more about your triggers; you're doing important, healing work.

The next time you feel "triggered" by your child, try replacing judgment with curiosity. Instead of "How could I have yelled like that?" ask yourself, "What was my yelling trying to protect?"

Day Eighty-Six:
Find People Who Lift You Up

*Mothers deserve people who will lift them up
just as much as they lift their families up.*

Close your eyes and think about someone who instantly perks you up, who makes you feel alive and boosts you with their energy almost like an espresso . . . a human espresso. They're warm, strong, and full of life. It could be your child, your spouse, a family member, or a friend, but whoever they are, it's important to designate the individuals in your life that lift you up. Why? Because when life throws its curve balls at you, knowing who to reach out to without a thought creates a solid foundation of comfort and support. If your human espresso is your child, of course you would never give your child the responsibility to solve your problems, but it's helpful to note that your child's energy is what fuels you, lifts you up, and breathes life back into you. Knowing who you have in your life to lift you up (or calm you down) is essential as you navigate motherhood.

Right now, open up messaging on your phone and send your human espresso a text message to let them know how lucky you are to have them in your life. Sing their praises and share your gratitude. This won't just make their day, it will make yours too.

Day Eighty-Seven:
Deactivate Your Buttons

*The more you understand your own emotions, the more
you show up as the parent you want to be.*

"My child really knows how to push my buttons." If this phrase resonates with you, you're not alone because children do have this incredible ability to "push their parent's buttons" without even knowing that they're doing it. Asking, "Why does my child push my buttons?" doesn't help you get rid of any of those buttons, but these more helpful and productive questions will:

- "How did this button get here?"
- "What happens when I push this button?"
- "What would it take for me to deactivate this button?"

The only way to get your child to stop "pushing your buttons" is to deactivate those buttons so they no longer work. Start deactivating your buttons by diving into the questions in this entry; it's the realistic and approachable way to find more peace and calm in parenting, because the more you can understand your own emotions, the more you can show up as the parent you know you are and want to be.

Acknowledging the reality that you will get frustrated with your child will help you while you work on deactivating the buttons that are creating disconnection in your parent-child relationship. Next time your child gets on your nerves, give yourself some grace as you work through it.

Day Eighty-Eight:
When You Need Your Kids to Listen

*Your children's resistance might be their way of creating
a boundary; get curious, not judgmental.*

Why is it that when you're *desperate* for your child to listen to you, they absolutely don't listen? It is likely that your child is aware that you need them, instead of the usual, healthy environment they live in where they need you. In other words, it can make your child feel uncomfortable that you are depending on them for you to be "okay." So then how do you get your child to do what you need them to do? It's likely you're not just focused on the task you need them to do, you're also five steps ahead thinking about getting in the car on time, being in traffic, and then getting to your appointment on time. Because of that, your child isn't just doing a task; they also have the pressure of all the worries you've packed into them doing that task. Realizing this will allow you to see that your child's resistance isn't about compliance; it's about resisting all that pressure unintentionally placed on them. Your child is creating a boundary for themselves that says, "All this pressure on me doesn't feel safe, so I'm not going to assume that responsibility."

The next time you find yourself in this situation, pause and ask yourself, "How can I detach this moment from all the things I'm thinking about in the future?" so that your child doesn't feel that added pressure and instead they can focus on the task at hand.

Day Eighty-Nine:
Navigating School Struggles

Just because your child came from you doesn't
mean they're exactly like you.

You knew the school years would be challenging, but what you probably didn't realize was how much your child's school experience would bring up feelings from your school years. When you're worried about your child's struggle at school, the only experience you have to draw on is your own. And what tends to happen is you confuse your past feelings and outcomes with what is happening with your child—leading you far from the present moment. So naturally it's important for you to create a healthy separation between what your child is experiencing versus what you once experienced. While it may feel eerily similar, your child has a completely different life: a different temperament, different friends, different teachers, and most importantly a different parent, one who is actively learning how to guide their child through life without letting their own feelings and emotions get in the way.

Take a moment to identify what similarities you've noticed in your child's struggles at school with your own. What have you assumed is the same, and how can you see that the situation is in fact very different? Your support as a mother is a positive and crucial differentiator.

Day Ninety:
Connection Breeds Cooperation

Just because something is familiar doesn't mean it's effective.

If your spouse was angry at you, snatched your phone out of your hand, and said, "That's it! I'm taking this phone away from you until you listen to me," would you feel inspired to listen to them? You wouldn't feel good about it, but maybe you'd listen out of fear because you don't want them to take away things you love again. It's no different with your child, but because this is how things have always been done, it's a normal way to parent—get your child to do what you want by using the fear of taking away things they love. It sounds icky even reading it, doesn't it? But this is a prime example that just because something is familiar doesn't mean it's effective. Fear isn't the best motivator, but connection, that's what breeds cooperation. So think about it: What makes you more likely to listen? It's probably something like feeling cared about, understood, respected, or listened to because that person is connected to you. Remember this the next time you want to use threats or punishments: Connection breeds cooperation.

You're probably thinking, "I'm not getting rid of threats and punishments; they actually work," and you're right. They can "work," but if you want a stronger parent-child connection, reread this entry and see how you can find more ways to connect before using your go-to.

Day Ninety-One:
When Your Child Calls You Out

Encouraging self-trust is one of the greatest
gifts you can give to your child.

There are moments in motherhood where you are trying to be present and for whatever reason you just can't . . . and then your child calls you out: "Mom, you're not watching my dance!" or "Mom, you don't even care enough to remember my friend's name." In that moment you have two choices: to deny what your child has noticed or to own up to it and apologize. Here's why you should choose the latter: You want to strengthen your child's confidence in trusting themselves, that what they witness and feel is real. As much as it hurts you to admit that you weren't paying attention, honesty and authenticity will give your child so much more than denying their experience, leaving them hurt and confused. Allow yourself to make mistakes so that you can repair and move forward. Not only will you feel more connected to yourself, but you'll also feel more connected to your child.

The next time your child calls you out, it's okay to add in a little silliness by asking for a redo and pretending to rewind yourself in slow motion. Repairing doesn't have to be so heavy, it can be playful and fun too!

Day Ninety-Two:
Relationships Are Built

You are the foundation of your parent-child relationship,
so make sure you get all the love and support you need.

You are building a relationship with your child every day, and it's similar to building a house. You are the foundation upon which you construct the parent-child relationship. And because you've been around decades before your child, that foundation of yours has been through a lot. It has weathered its share of storms and has its imperfections. Yet it's not until you begin to build this strong, secure, and safe relationship with your child that you notice there are some cracks in that foundation, like not being able to tolerate the unknown or being uncomfortable with certain feelings. Whatever cracks you've begun to notice, know that they have nothing to do with your ability to love your child enough, but they do have a lot to do with you learning to love yourself enough. You are capable of tending to them and patching them up while you're on your parenting journey and you can do so with a mix of curiosity and compassion for yourself.

Ask yourself what parts of your foundation you would like more support with. How would you imagine that support helping you in your parent-child relationship?

Day Ninety-Three:
How Are You *Today*?

*Small doses of honesty and vulnerability breed
true connection to others and to the self.*

Everyone needs a deeper sense of connection in their lives. There is one word you can use that will truly help you deepen the connection you have with your child, your spouse, your friends, and really anyone. Instead of asking, "How are you?" ask, "How are you *today*?" Adding that one word, "today," shifts your loved one from the usual automatic answer where they just reply that they're "good" to allowing them to reflect on how they feel in the present moment. Asking, "How are you doing today?" can take your friend from telling you she's "fine" to actually telling you how exhausted she is from being up all night with her toddler. Doing this allows you to connect to the real true parts of your loved ones—especially with other mothers. The more you share your true self and feelings with others, the more you're connected and have a sense of belonging—something we all really need. So the next time you speak to a loved one, ask them, "How are you *today*?"

Pick a one loved one to call to ask how they are doing today and pick two loved ones to text asking how they are doing today. It can also help to mention a situation you know they've been handling to invite them to have a loving space to open up, share, and be heard.

Day Ninety-Four:
Turn Your Guilt Into Good

Healthy guilt is an emotion that moves you closer
to where you truly want to be.

Here's how you're going to take guilt and turn it into something good. First, know that there are two types of guilt:

1. *Functional, healthy guilt* that says, "I don't like what's going on here and I want to change it."
2. *Unhealthy guilt* that says, "No matter what choice you make, you'll still feel guilty."

Regardless of the guilt you have, the way to take it and make it something good is by playing the full movie of that guilt. For example, you feel guilty that you're not playing with your child right now. Playing the movie through would look like "If I were to stop and play with my child right now, would that feel true to what I want to do right now?" If your answer is yes, then that *healthy guilt* will help you move forward and grow. If your answer is no and you think, "I know I've spent enough time with my child—that's an old narrative that's making me feel bad even though I know it's not what I need to do right now," great! You've identified *unhealthy guilt* that doesn't serve you. The goal here is taking the guilt and asking yourself, "Is this guilt moving me closer to where I want to be?"

Take a moment to think about the most common guilt loop that circles in your head. Are those guilt loops healthy guilt or are they unhealthy guilt?

Day Ninety-Five:
What You Love Most about Your Child

*There are few constants in life, but one for
sure is that your child is forever loved.*

You love so many things about your child, but today take a closer look at the characteristics you love most. Think about what makes your child who they are. What about their temperament do you admire? What about the way they wonder and think do you love? What parts of your child do you wish you could bottle up and keep forever? The love you have for your child is clear, but taking a moment to really see your child—separate from the day-to-day—through the lens of their most precious qualities is a way to reconnect to your child even when you're not near them. While you can't sit and ponder the goodness of your child every moment, taking the time to savor all that you love about your child can be a beautiful way for you to calm the noise of the world around you and sink into what you love most.

Zoom out from day-to-day life today to see the big picture of your life. This can help de-stress you in the moments that feel like they will never end and remind you that it's a moment in time and the love you have for your child will always be constant.

Day Ninety-Six:
Catch Them Being Kind

*When you feel better, you do better, and
when you do better, you feel better.*

You deserve to enjoy your child more. Your child deserves to enjoy you more. One way to spark a new cycle of enjoyment in your family is by trying the Catch Them Being Kind Challenge for three days. Here are the three simple steps to get started: One, catch your child being kind; catch them doing good. Two, savor that moment; take it in. Three, let your child know what you just saw. Here's why this works: Catching your child being kind helps you reroute your brain from only focusing on the negative, which is what your brain is hardwired to do to keep you safe from danger. You start seeing more good, you start feeling better around your child, and then your child eventually starts feeling better about themselves. And when you feel better, you do better: This is a cycle that your family can absolutely benefit from, so give it a try for the next three days and see how it not only shifts you, but shifts your child.

When you catch your child being kind, don't get too worried about "overpraising" them. It's rare we compliment or notice every act of kindness our child displays. A higher concentration of love, appreciation, and recognition can go a long way in shifting your parent-child dynamic.

Day Ninety-Seven: Avoid Absolutes

The one thing you can be certain about in motherhood is that you won't always be certain!

When you think about bad words, the words "always" and "never" probably don't come to mind. But in parenting, when you speak in absolutes, it traps you in unrealistic expectations. The truth is, no one does something all the time, because we are not an "always" or "never" species. We are constantly changing and evolving—as we should be. While it can feel safer to live life in absolutes where everything fits in a box—good or bad, black or white—life is somewhere in the middle. So while declaring things like "I never yell at my child" is the goal, knowing that you need wiggle room to be human is best to be taken into consideration. Using words or phrases like "sometimes" or "most of the time" can help set more realistic standards, and not only will it free you of added, unnecessary stress, it will also model for your child what it's like to be human, where things are "most of the time."

Think about one thing you can laugh about that you said you would "always" or "never" do before having children—but now have totally changed your position on. It helps to add a little lightheartedness to motherhood whenever you can!

Day Ninety-Eight:
The Stories of Who You Are

*One of the quickest ways to see a change in your child
is to change the way you see them.*

The stories you were told about yourself as a child tend to stick: "She was always such a difficult baby" or "She was just the most perfect child." Why? Because the source of all your love and survival is the one telling you those stories, over and over again, and they become the story we're told of who we are. Knowing this shows you how powerful your words and your thoughts are about your child. This is why when you are struggling with your child, rather than create a story that says, "Something is wrong with my child," you can shift it to "My child is struggling and I am here to help them." Rather than assigning a permanent characteristic to your child of being difficult or perfect, start seeing them as whole—a whole individual who is looking to you for guidance navigating life. When you change the way you see your child, your child will change.

What was a story you've heard over and over again about yourself as a child? What feelings come to mind when you think about that story? Is it how you still see yourself now?

Day Ninety-Nine:
Raising Strong Children

Everyone wants to raise a strong child until your child uses their strength "against" you.

If you've tried to raise a strong child but wonder if you're on the right path, a good way to assess is how strong your child is with *you*! When your child's strength shows up in a way that makes you feel less than, it can be a strange experience. You want your child to embody their courage and confidence, but when that's used "against" you, you're unsure how to process it all. Strength in your child sounds like honesty, even when it doesn't paint a wonderful picture of you. Strength sounds like a disagreeing voice, even when it's not the popular opinion. Strength also looks like your child trusting themselves more than you. These are difficult moments to navigate as a mother, but they are moments you're navigating with a strong child. The urge to squash their strength can come in the form of questions like "What will others think?" or "What if they're too honest?" or "What if they're too confident?" As a parent, you'll help your child fine-tune their strength by giving them the tools to deliver their truth with tact and openness. As an individual, your challenge will likely be learning to be comfortable with what makes you feel uncomfortable.

Ask yourself what you admire most about your child's strength. What has your child's strength taught you about yourself?

Day One Hundred:
Authenticity Radar

Authenticity breeds connection and trust.

If you haven't noticed, your child has a built-in radar for authenticity. If you've ever been uncertain about a new parenting strategy or not fully confident in a choice you're trying to convince them of, it's likely your child rejected it. Your child can tell when you aren't being truly authentic, and that's because they are so truly themselves. Your child has just come into this world, and they only know how to be themselves. Therefore, when you aren't being your true self, it's obvious and they aren't buying what you're selling! So how do you navigate the many moments in life when you aren't 100 percent sure about something but need your child to cooperate? *Appropriate honesty*. If you are trying a new parenting style or implementing a new house rule, it's okay to say, "This is a new thing we're trying out here; it's different and it will take time to get used to and that's okay" or "I don't like how that went; let's try again." Your authenticity will create the connection and trust you want in your parent-child relationship.

Can you remember the last time your child wasn't buying what you were selling? How can you use appropriate honesty with your child next time?

Day One Hundred and One:
When You're Embarrassed by Your Child

You can never gain control by losing control.

Have you ever felt embarrassed by your child? You're out in public, and your toddler starts having a tantrum or your teen starts yelling at you and now everyone is looking at you. It's not a good feeling—you feel embarrassed and totally out of control. At that moment, your ego is in control and all you can think to do is regain control so you can feel okay again. What do you normally do? You yell, you threaten, and you do things you wouldn't normally do. But in those moments you have a choice: You can resort to the old-school idea that a good parent is one who has dominance and control over their child, or you can use the newfound idea of control, which is control over the self. Tell yourself, "I have control over myself, and whatever is going on with my child, I will help them figure it out." Then block out what you're imagining everyone is thinking and drop into a vacuum that's just you and your child. You do that by connecting to them, by being concerned, by having compassion, by having empathy, and by remembering that resorting to those outdated ways of parenting ultimately won't work and will instead make you and your child feel further disconnected.

If you feel like things are getting out of control with your child and you feel the embarrassment rising, remember that compassion and connection are more likely to get your child to calm down than anger and force.

Day One Hundred and Two: Care Without Carrying

Caring about someone doesn't mean you also have to carry them.

A lot of mothers tend to confuse the idea of *caring* for another person with *carrying* another person. Meaning when you love and care about someone you also equate it with carrying them and carrying their responsibilities—mental, emotional, social, or financial responsibilities. Your internal voice says something like "I love this person; they're my family, so I should also do everything in my power to make sure they're okay." Perhaps at one time in your life you could carry that person, but now that you have a child and your own family, you've realized the toll it takes on you. The solution here isn't to just stop doing things for others or stop caring for them altogether. The solution is to separate the two by asking, "What is me caring and loving someone else and then what is me carrying things for others that are simply not mine?" A good start can be to ask yourself, "Am I supporting someone because I want to and I can?" or "Am I carrying someone because I 'should' even when I feel overextended and resentful?" This shift can create a big change in your life that frees up more of your time and energy.

Are you carrying family members, parents, grandparents, or siblings? Use the questions in this entry to begin making small changes so you can care about them without always needing to carry them.

Day One Hundred and Three: Parenting Isn't Easy

Loving your child is easy, but parenting them is not.

Have you lost it on your child this week? The reason you've lost it on your child has nothing to do with how much you love them. Being a parent is not magically separate from the person that you are, so when you've yet to handle frustration when things don't go your way on your own, that same frustration will show up when you parent . . . only tenfold! You've come to the parenting table with a whole history of ways you've learned to deal with life, your emotions, and other people—and all of that comes with you into parenting. Rather than bang your head against the wall because you've read all the parenting books and you try to remain calm and gentle and yet you still don't feel like a great parent, know it's not about you being a great parent; it's about being great to yourself. Take time to learn why you are the way you are. The best investment you can make in your family is the investment in becoming more connected to yourself.

Ask yourself what the easiest part about loving your child is. What's the hardest part about parenting your child?

Day One Hundred and Four: Scaffolding Parenting

Your child may not always need you there, but hopefully they'll always want you there.

If you've ever walked in a city, you've most likely seen a building with scaffolding around it. The scaffolding is there to support the building as it is under construction or being renovated. And when you think about it, motherhood is just like scaffolding. In your child's earliest years, you fully support your child with every need they have. As your child grows and gains more independence, you slowly start to remove support, like the scaffolding, because your child is able to do more on their own. When your child becomes an adult, you remove your scaffolding completely—a bittersweet experience to say the least. But here's the thing: Just like buildings need renovations, so will your child—they'll need you to step in throughout their life. So if you ever feel emotional about how quickly your child is growing, it means you've done a great job. And because of that, they'll still very much want that support even when they may not necessarily need it.

What's been a bittersweet moment for you in motherhood this week? Give yourself compassion for the parts that are bitter and allow yourself to savor all that is sweet.

Day One Hundred and Five: Confidence Is Self-Trust

Teaching your child to trust what they feel is teaching them to trust themselves.

Confidence is a deep trust in oneself. If you've ever wanted to help your child build confidence, there's a way to do so that doesn't require winning trophies or acing tests. While it's simple in theory, it takes time to put it into practice: Be with your child through their feelings. Yes, be with your child in their most difficult moments and tell your child their feelings are valid. When you stay with your child, you're showing them that their feelings aren't too big. When you validate your child's feelings, you're telling them that what they feel is real and to trust what they feel. This is a basic level of trust, and it is one of the most foundational gifts you can give to your child. When children learn to trust themselves, to believe in themselves, and to rely on themselves, they develop a layer of confidence that cannot be taken away from them.

Being with your child in their big feelings can be exhausting. Take care of yourself after by tapping into and validating what feelings came up for you during their tricky moments.

Day One Hundred and Six: Will Your Child Be Embarrassed?

You can't prevent your children from feeling pain, but you can give them tools to navigate it.

Have you ever seen your child do something you've deemed embarrassing? If so, you may have struggled with whether or not to intervene. While your child is perfectly happy, being themselves, you can't help but think about preventing them from experiencing hurt. For example, let's say your child puts on an outfit you worry they could be made fun of for wearing. You may want to say, "Don't wear that, you'll stand out!" But, on the other hand, you don't want to crush your child's spirit. In moments like these, gently realize this is more of a *you* thing; yes, you've taken your past experiences and inserted them into your child's world. Even when you think you're coming from a place of love (I love my child; I don't want them to be embarrassed), you may actually be coming from a place of fear (I'm so afraid they'll be hurt, I have to prevent this). There isn't a mother in the world that doesn't want to protect their child from pain, but your job isn't to prevent your child from experiencing pain; it's to make sure they have a safe, loving environment to move through their pain.

This is a tough one to navigate. Here's a question to help you decide whether or not to intervene: "Will I be unintentionally causing my child pain when I tell them what they're wearing or doing is embarrassing or not cool enough?"

Day One Hundred and Seven:
Accepting the Good in You

If you want your children to be proud of themselves, you can show them what that looks like when you celebrate how proud you are of yourself.

The fact that you are here, reading this book, says so much about the mother you are: You not only care about your child, you also care about yourself. You're taking time in your busy day to support yourself; that in and of itself is a beautiful gesture of self-love. This brings up the relationship you have with all the good inside you: How often do you feel good about yourself? How often do you stop to appreciate your accomplishments? If the answer isn't easy to come by, that's okay. Practice noticing the good in you right now by acknowledging that you're doing something pretty special by committing to and reading this book. Accepting the good that you do in small ways is a beautiful way to pat yourself on the back. And the best part is, by doing so you will be modeling a healthy relationship with the self for your child to see and learn from.

If it feels silly to feel good about something small, like reading this book, pick something you do feel good about. Watch for any judgment that pops up and try replacing it with curiosity as to why you shouldn't be allowed to celebrate any small win. Because you absolutely are allowed to soak in all the good you do!

Day One Hundred and Eight: Is Your Child Too Honest?

Your honesty is appreciated, but your delivery is not.

You want to encourage your child to stand up for themselves. You want your child to speak their mind. You love that your child is comfortable speaking their truth with you, but there are times when your child does so in a disrespectful, unkind manner. You've done a great job creating an environment where your child feels safe to be themselves, but now it's time to help them shape how they express their confidence. This is when you can step in with *appropriate honesty*: to be honest about how you love their strength, but to also be honest about how their delivery makes you feel. Try saying, "Your honesty is appreciated, but your delivery is not." Helping your child express their truth in a healthier way won't deter them from being confident in expressing their thoughts or feelings because you're bringing your confidence to the conversation to assure them you aren't squashing their truth; you're helping them make that truth deliverable: "Listen, I love that you're telling me how you feel, but when you speak like that it makes me not want to listen because your words are unkind."

The next time your child uses a rude tone or harsh words to share what they want: Before you snap back at them, take a breath and tell them you hear what they're saying, but the way they're saying it makes it tough to get their message through. Then model a healthier way.

Day One Hundred and Nine: Disassembling Mom Guilt

When you've held yourself to a higher standard than others, it's a clue that your guilt is unfounded.

If you are so over mom guilt because it is sucking the joy out of your life, here are three questions that will help you disassemble the mom guilt. The first question is "Would I hold a friend to the same standard I hold myself to?" If you feel guilty for taking time away from your child and if your friend told you the same thing, you'd probably say something like "No way, it's an amazing thing you take time for yourself; you need it!" When you spot that you've held yourself to a higher standard than others, you can see that your guilt is unfounded. The second question is "Where did these thoughts come from?" Are those thoughts really yours? Most likely they're not, and when you start getting curious about where those thoughts came from, you realize they've come from somewhere else. The third question is "Is this healthy guilt?" Healthy guilt tells you that you want to do something differently; unhealthy guilt typically doesn't make sense. The more you can poke holes in your mom guilt, the more you can free yourself of it.

Anytime you feel guilty today, take a moment to label it as healthy guilt or unhealthy guilt. This will help you shed some of that unnecessary, unhelpful, unhealthy guilt.

Day One Hundred and Ten: No One Is Prepared

As you figure out motherhood, the best sidekick you can bring along is compassion.

Just in case you are feeling like you're the only mom out there who doesn't have this parenting thing figured out, let it be known that no one is fully prepared to have children. Sure, maybe you took all the classes and read all the books and you knew you were going to be tired. But no one knows exactly what is in store for the *emotional* component of motherhood—all the feelings that come up raising a child and then realizing you also have to raise yourself right alongside your child. So just in case you're beating yourself up for not having it all figured out, know that every mother is figuring it out as they go. The best thing you can do is figure it out while giving yourself compassion and giving your child that same compassion as you both figure out this most important relationship of your lives.

What part of motherhood did you feel most prepared for? What part of motherhood would you have liked to have more preparation for? Take that answer and allow yourself to explore how you can get support for it now because it's never too late.

Day One Hundred and Eleven: Playdate Survival

*Just because your child made a new friendship doesn't
mean you have to make a new one too!*

How wonderful would it be to hit the playdate parent jackpot? You know, when your child makes a new friend and that child's parents are not only wonderful, they also live close to you and have similar schedules (it's beautiful!). But let's be honest—it doesn't always happen that way, so here are some guidelines to help you survive a new playdate:

- One, get comfortable with silence, because it is so much effort to keep a conversation going for an hour or two with someone you don't know or aren't really clicking with. It's okay to watch the kids play or to look around—silence is okay.
- Two, most people love to share about their lives, their kids, and their jobs, so ask more questions—it's a great way to get to know the family your child is spending time with.
- Three, take the pressure off yourself. It may seem like everyone else has the best little mom groups, but that's not always possible. Instead put the focus back on your child. You are there for your child to foster and grow a friendship, not necessarily for you to foster and grow a friendship.

There are so many awkward moments in parenting (like playdates) and it can help to laugh at them, so take a moment to remember one and even share it with a friend later today.

Day One Hundred and Twelve: Stop Forcing Gratitude

You have to embody the qualities you want your children to embody.

Every mother wants to raise a child who is respectful and grateful. So when your child behaves in the exact opposite way, a normal response to correct that behavior usually sounds like "You should be grateful." Think about it, though: If someone said that to you, you might hear what they're saying, but it's very unlikely you're going to magically feel gratitude. How you learn to feel a certain way is to experience that feeling in another person, to watch what it's like to be grateful or feel what it's like to receive respect. So the next time you want to tell your child to feel a certain way, remember it's not actually possible to feel on demand. Instead ask yourself, "How can I model this? How can I show my child what this looks like?" It always starts with you. And yes, it's one more thing you have to do! It would be so much easier if you could just snap your fingers and your child could automatically embody those feelings. But the truth is, you have to embody the very qualities you want your children to embody.

A great way to encourage respect and gratitude is to point it out when you see it in your child or in others. Today try to find moments to point out to your child. For example, "Wow, you feel so grateful grandma gave you that stuffed animal" or "That was so respectful when you gave your sister her toy back because it was hers."

Day One Hundred and Thirteen: When You're a Good Mom in a Bad Mood

Good moms have bad moods. Period.

Are you ever in a bad mood, but still have to show up and be a mom? You're not alone, so it's important to remember that good moms have bad moods. Here are three ways to keep being a good parent in a bad mood. First, tell your kids, "Hey, I'm in a bad mood. I'm cranky and I don't like it, but it's my problem, not yours." This tells your child it's not about them, it's not their responsibility, and it's up to you to figure it out. Second, don't judge yourself for a bad mood; you're human and it happens. Along with no judgment comes not judging the actions you take to help you get through the day—extra screen time, less quality time—it's all about supporting yourself through this temporary rough patch. Third, remind yourself this is temporary; you won't stay in this bad mood forever. It comes and goes; tomorrow is a new day. Accepting this can help you let it go. Resisting it or punishing yourself for it is only going to make it worse. So when you're in a bad mood, take accountability, do what you need to do, and let it naturally fade away.

The next time you're in a bad mood, don't be afraid to share that with your child so they know it's not about them. When your child sees you at your best and your worst, they'll know it's okay to be human.

Day One Hundred and Fourteen: Be Honest with Your Anger

Being honestly angry is much better than being dishonestly detached.

If you've ever heard that it's not okay to share your feelings with your child, it's important to separate what is an unhealthy, burdensome expression of your feelings and what's a healthy, authentic expression of your emotions. For example, think about how many times your child has asked you, "Mom, are you mad at me?" Here are three reasons why it's healthy to be honest about how you feel:

1. Reason one is to normalize human emotion: "Mommy gets mad just like you."
2. Reason two is to show your child you can have emotion and be accountable for those emotions: "Yes, Mommy is mad, but that is my responsibility to handle, not yours."
3. Reason three is that your child learns to trust what they are feeling. When you deny that you're not mad but your child can see that you're upset, they can get confused about trusting you and their emotions.

It can be hard when you're upset, but it's so much better to be honest so that you can normalize anger. Show your child how to take accountability and that they can trust that you will always tell them the truth.

You are going to get mad at your child, so when you do, separate what your child did and your ability to cope with your feelings. This makes you a conscious parent: You are aware that you have a good reason to be upset, but realize that your child isn't responsible for making you feel better.

Day One Hundred and Fifteen:
Break the Defensive Mom Mode

You always have a choice: to instantly react or to pause and respond.

It's easy to get defensive when your child is saying things like "I don't like you!" Even though you know you don't *actually* have to defend yourself against your child, it sure feels like it. Being on the defense leads you to *react* instead of *respond*. Reactions sever connection rather than repair it, which is the exact opposite of what you want to do! But have no fear, a simple self-check-in can reroute you in these moments: "What is the vulnerable story that comes up for me at this moment?" While no one wants to be told they're not liked, hearing it makes you feel not just sad or angry, but rejected, unloved, or unappreciated. These feelings have deeper roots beyond your role as mom, extending to your role as spouse, sibling, and daughter, and those feelings tell a story: No one appreciates me, no one cares about all I do, and so on. When you pause to see the power that story has over your reaction, you can assess whether this story is true at the moment or if it's an old story that doesn't serve you anymore. As you clear away the old stories that keep you defensive and reactive, you'll start to notice more space for you to respond in a more calm, confident, and controlled manner.

Today if you find yourself on the defense, remember it's a sign to stop and assess what story is being told. Knowing this will help you regain control over yourself to be responsive instead of reactive.

Day One Hundred and Sixteen: Your Child Knows Their Worth

It takes a strong parent to see their child's truth as a strength and not an attack.

Imagine there being a downside to raising your child with respect. Technically there isn't, but it can be difficult when you've had a rough moment and end up yelling at your child. Why? Your child is so used to being treated as a respected member of the family, they totally call you out for yelling. It would be easy for you to turn it around on them and call them disrespectful for speaking against you. However, what's truly happening is that your child *knows* what it feels like to be treated right because it's how you treat them most of the time. So when they *aren't* treated kindly, they're incredibly aware, even when you're the culprit. It's a pivotal moment: to either see that your child is reflecting back to you a very beautiful display of self-worth or to allow your ego to take over and squash what you've worked so hard for your child to build. This is *a lot* to think about, so take a moment today to see where you can allow your ego to take a walk and let your connected, loving self enter the building to validate your child's experience.

Take a moment to be proud of yourself for raising a child who knows their worth. You're doing big things for your family.

Day One Hundred and Seventeen: Making Mistakes

Making mistakes doesn't weaken your parenting; it strengthens it.

Making a mistake in front of your child is a good thing. Yes, making mistakes and then handling it in a healthy way doesn't weaken your parenting; it strengthens it. Here's why: Instead of doubling down and justifying your mistakes, *own up to them*. You admit and then right your wrongs. Your mistake becomes a valuable life lesson where your child learns that making mistakes is a normal part of being human and you can take accountability and not beat yourself up over it. While using your own words is best, here are a handful of phrases you can borrow the next time you make a mistake: "I don't like how I spoke to you"; "I shouldn't have said that"; "I am so sorry for what I said"; "Can we have a do over? I don't like how I handled that"; "Let's rewind and try again." The next time you feel guilty or shameful about your mistake, remember, you can turn this into a beneficial learning experience for your child.

Owning up to your mistakes can benefit all your relationships. Let this flow over into your marriage, relationships, friendships, and more. Today intentionally highlight a mistake you make and take accountability so you can build trust and strength in your relationships.

Day One Hundred and Eighteen: Navigating Friendship Troubles

Facilitating your child in problem-solving takes them further than just solving their problem.

Has your child ever shared about a friend or schoolmate being mean to them? Did your blood start to boil? Most mothers want to go full mama bear mode when they hear anyone is being mean to their child. Here is something to remember: The fact that your child comes to tell you something is going on is huge and you want to preserve that. You can preserve it by not letting your fears and your emotions interfere with your child's experience. Instead of telling your child, "Well, don't be friends with them," you can ask your child questions so they can trust how they feel to make that decision. When you have a strong opinion on what to do and your child chooses otherwise, they might not feel safe to come back to you again. Now, of course there will be times where it is necessary for you to intervene, but for all the other times, remember, the goal is to keep the line of communication open. The best way to do that is to make sure you keep your feelings separate from your child; this is yet another way you're doing an amazing job at building the trust and connection in your parent-child relationship.

In these tricky situations, try asking your child questions instead of telling them exactly what to do. Reflect back what they tell you by using as many of their own words as possible. This will let your child work through their emotions with you by their side.

Day One Hundred and Nineteen: Escaping Orange Juice Mothering

*Just because you've always been one way
doesn't mean it has to stay that way.*

If you hold an orange in your hand and squeeze hard enough, juice will come out. Your hand is the force squeezing out the juice, but your hand didn't make the juice. The juice was already inside the orange, right? This is how you can look at the experience of feeling "triggered" by your child: Your child is certainly the squeezing force when you feel irritable, but what comes out . . . that was inside you. This analogy is a building block for you to understand that the experiences you have with your child are real: that they can be frustrating, upsetting, and infuriating, but that what comes out of you was already there, and it's for you to handle and heal. The next time you notice the "juice" that comes out of you isn't how you want to respond to your child, it will be an opportunity to understand yourself better: What about your response are you consciously choosing and what about your response feels like an automatic, knee-jerk reaction? Getting curious about the latter will allow you to slowly drain that "juice" and move closer to the intentional, connected communication you want with your family.

Today reflect on what it feels like when you consciously respond to your child versus when you unintentionally react to your child—with less guilt and more curiosity, ask yourself what about the situation made you feel under attack.

Day One Hundred and Twenty: Defusing Bedtime Battles

A child can learn to care about your feelings, but should never learn to be responsible for your feelings.

Does it ever feel like on the nights where you *really* need your alone time, the evenings where you are desperately dreaming of your bed . . . that those are the nights your child coincidentally is the hardest to settle down? It might not be a coincidence at all. You've given your child a healthy relationship—one where they rarely feel responsible for you, your moods, or your feelings. Yet there are moments, like when you're desperate for sleep, that your child can feel the weight of responsibility for you: "I need you to go to bed so that I can be okay." Of course this is not what you're saying to your child, but energetically they can feel the shift in your usual approach. This is unintentional and it can be easily fixed through appropriate honesty. The next time you are at your wit's end and need your sleep, be appropriately honest with your child: "Oh, I am *soooo* tired . . . What can we do to get you ready for bed because I can't wait to sleep!" The more you can get your child involved in an unpressured, playful manner, the more you and your child can connect and move forward with bedtime.

Think about how you'd feel if someone demanded you do something with the pressure of their happiness or well-being on your back? Not great, right? But if they said, "Hey, I really need XYZ; can you help me figure it out?" you'd probably feel way more inclined to want to participate.

Day One Hundred and Twenty-One: Making Room for Motherhood

You don't lose yourself in motherhood; you find who you really are.

There is so much to be proud of for the woman you've become. There is also so much to be proud of for the mother you've become. Yet entering motherhood can be challenging when you try to hold on to the exact woman you were before having children. While you don't become someone completely different, you will relate to your life differently. If you once were at the beck and call of your family of origin or your friends, being able to fulfill that same role will be difficult. Part of this struggle comes from the fact that no one ever gave you permission to allow this natural change. Know this: You are allowed to shift, change, and grow into motherhood. You're responsible for tiny humans who truly need you, which means you'll have less capacity and desire to be the old version of yourself. You may feel guilty, you may get pushback, but this is the truest version of yourself because it's abundantly clear that you know where and who you want to be there for: You and your child are priority number one.

It's rarely talked about how the transition from your primary role from daughter to mother, sister to mother, or wife to mother can be confusing. Today just acknowledge that you've had to make these transitions. It's not always easy and you deserve a pat on the back.

Day One Hundred and Twenty-Two: Rise Above Unnecessary Suffering

You can experience pain without turning it into suffering.

There is a big difference between pain and suffering, and understanding that difference can help you in the moments when you're upset with your child. The parable of the two arrows tells us that when you experience interpersonal pain, there are two arrows. The first arrow that hits you is the actual event, and it's a natural human experience to feel pain when someone hurts you: "You're the worst mom ever!" Hearing that is bound to cause you some pain. The second arrow that hits you is suffering, another very human thing, which you *unintentionally* bring upon yourself. Suffering comes from twisting the arrow over and over again about why you were shot with it, with judgments, assumptions, and stories that exacerbate the pain and turn it into suffering: "My child says I'm the worst mom ever; what have I done so wrong? I never get anything right. I'll never be good enough no matter how hard I try." So avoid causing yourself unnecessary suffering and start spotting the second arrow. You can't stop the first arrow, but you can stop the second one.

When you spot the second arrow, ask yourself where you learned those stories from. How have they helped you and how do they hurt you now? The more you get curious about yourself, the more you can free yourself from stories that no longer serve you.

Day One Hundred and Twenty-Three: Leaning Into Bedtime

When you meet your child where they are, you aren't minimizing or maximizing their state; you're simply allowing it.

There are times when children just simply aren't ready to go to bed. You've probably had those nights where you're in your usual bedtime routine, but your child is full of energy, bouncing off the walls, and looking for a way to get that energy out. In those moments, you have a choice: You can resist that energy to make bedtime happen on your terms, which tends to require a lot of *your* energy and can be generally unpleasant for all. The other option is to lean into your child's energy, utilize their energy, and use that time for connection. It may be another ten minutes of bedtime, but when you meet your child where they're at (which doesn't mean to raise their energy, but rather simply to allow it), you can actually use their energy as a tool to connect and have fun. The energy that the second option requires is a different type of energy from resistance, fighting, and yelling. It's always these tiny shifts you can make that will change the dynamic of your parent-child relationship, and it always starts with a little curiosity: "How can I get this story to end differently?"

If you're worried that if you give your child an inch, they'll take a mile, it's worth challenging that belief with the fact that the inches you are giving are needed because you're attuned to your child's needs; when you meet those needs, that mile won't be needed.

Day One Hundred and Twenty-Four: Flip Your Battery

*Two wrongs don't make a right, just like two
yelling parties won't end a fight.*

In motherhood we have to laugh at how we model the very behavior we want our child to stop. One of the ways you may do this is when your child is yelling and screaming, you yell and scream to get them to stop. The irony! Of course this is unintentional; it's a knee-jerk reaction, so here's a story to help you in those moments. Let's say your child has a new toy that requires two batteries. If you take the two negative ends of the batteries and put them together, the toy isn't going to work. If you take the negative side of one and the positive side of the other, the toy starts working. This can be said for your child's "negative" behavior; as much as you may want to match yelling with more yelling, it often won't work out the way you had hoped. But if you meet your child's yelling with your "positive" behavior, you are modeling healthy behavior your child can use and it's much more likely to get your relationship up and running again. So the next time you realize you're modeling the very behavior you want your child to stop, remember to flip your battery!

What ways do you already flip your battery? It is likely you're already doing this with your child, and it's important to make note of that win so you can apply it in other areas down the road!

Day One Hundred and Twenty-Five: Aligning with Yourself

Nothing is more powerful than the shift from aligning with others to survive to aligning with yourself to thrive.

Whether you're aware of it or not, right now you're on a very important journey learning to align with yourself. For most women, our lives are rooted in aligning with others to survive, yet here you are now, choosing to align with yourself to move past surviving and actually build a life where you're thriving. However you've found your way to this book, it's a testament to the belief you have in yourself that you want to show up differently and you are choosing to show up differently. It's not uncommon for most people in your life to not understand the path you're on; don't let that deter you. It's not indicative that you're on the wrong path, but instead that your change may be shedding light on parts of their lives they may want to change too. Just know there is a community of women just like you reading this page and that collective is here supporting you as you hold this book. Each small step you take in daring to look at yourself more deeply is one big step you take to connecting to your most true, authentic self. Keep going and trust in the power of you.

Share your light by reaching out to a mom today that you feel proud of. Share your light with her and watch how your light will shine even brighter.

Day One Hundred and Twenty-Six: Embracing the Inconvenience

The hardest part of parenting is the idea that it shouldn't be hard.

There's this idea in society that you should get your child under your command and on a routine so you can get back to your life, avoiding as little inconvenience as possible. And what an unrealistic standard for you to live up to, that your goal as a supreme parent is to get your child to fit into your life by any means necessary. This idea keeps you in a struggle trying to make your child fit the mold of you, and it also doesn't yield truly happy, healthy children. So, what if instead of parenting being something to "figure out" so it's not an inconvenience, that parenting was exactly where you needed to be? That parenting was the necessary path to creating a better relationship with the present moment, where you welcome your life rather than rush through it? That very well may be your reality today. You already know parenting isn't always a walk in the park, but that walk that you're already on is what will bring you to a more accepting, comfortable relationship with yourself and of course with your child.

Ask yourself what lesson you are most grateful for having learned in motherhood that you had no idea you even needed to learn.

Day One Hundred and Twenty-Seven: The Good Old Days

In motherhood, you know you're in the good old days before you've left them.

Has anyone ever said to you, "You're gonna miss these days"? It usually comes from the best intentions, someone reflecting back on how fast the time goes. However, it *really* doesn't land for a mother who is struggling to get through the hundredth day of interrupted sleep or the mother who is in a constant power struggle with her child. You obviously know how precious your time is with your child and that these are the "good old days," but that doesn't make the pockets of tough times feel any less tough. But here's something that knowing you're in the good old days will do: It will make looking back sweeter, because you're able to savor that *you made it through.* That you made it through the toughest and sweetest of moments. So if you feel like guilt is trying to take the reins by telling you that you haven't been enjoying the good old days, enjoy and savor the fact that you've made it through and you're continuing to make it through. And always remember, you're doing so much more right than you're doing wrong.

What part of motherhood that you're in right now would you like to bottle up and save forever? Let yourself savor that special part today.

Day One Hundred and Twenty-Eight: Family Fun

It's great watching your child have fun, but watching your child have fun because they're having fun with you, that's the good stuff.

We forget play isn't just for kids, it's for moms too. So if you feel like your family has been lacking in the fun department, here's a game to play that will get everyone laughing. Ask your child to imitate you: "You are going to pretend you are mommy talking on the phone" or "Pretend you're mommy getting everyone ready for bed." You can also play a game of family charades, where you try to act out other members of the family. You can encourage even more silliness by letting your child dress up from your closet. What your child will come up with will be absolutely hilarious and is guaranteed to light them up. Sometimes it can feel like you have to be away on a vacation or spend money visiting a special place to create memories with your family when really you can carve out a small amount of time to intentionally interact with your child. Use today's entry as a reminder that you deserve to have fun and enjoy motherhood too!

What fun little games from your childhood have you yet to share with your child? Think about the fun you used to have and see what your child thinks of it. To name a few: freeze dance, Simon says, I spy, four corners, charades, and hide-and-go-seek.

Day One Hundred and Twenty-Nine: Gentle Parenting for Parents

Be a gentle parent to yourself first.

Gentle parenting has become a popular approach in motherhood. Gentle parenting is when the parent gives their child respect, compassion, empathy, and understanding rather than the traditional approach that demands all those traits of the child . . . without ever having modeled them. If you've tried gentle parenting techniques—like staying calm, speaking softly, and not using punishment—only to find yourself right back where you started, you're not alone. Often the missing puzzle piece to gentle parenting is the parent being able to give *themselves* compassion, empathy, and understanding. It is difficult to give your children patience and kindness when you rarely give those same things to yourself. So if you've fallen short on the gentle parenting train, don't beat yourself up. Instead start parenting yourself that way first. Give *yourself* more compassion when you've messed up; give *yourself* more understanding when you have a big feeling. The more this becomes your own personal practice, the more it will naturally flow over into your parenting practice.

In what ways are you most gentle with yourself? Where did you learn to give yourself that grace? Take time today to think about how you show up as a gentle parent to yourself and let yourself be proud of that big win.

Day One Hundred and Thirty: Using Replacement Behaviors

You give your children the instruction manual for life.

"Stop jumping on the couch," "Don't hit your sister," and "You aren't allowed to talk to me that way." As a mother, you are always responding to your child's behavior, and it can feel like most of the time you're only *stopping* behavior. Not only do you feel like a broken record, but it's also ineffective when a replacement behavior isn't given. Anytime you are responding to your child's behavior, keep in mind what you want your child to do instead. Your child is much more likely to change their behavior when you give them a replacement behavior. Why? Because you're modeling exactly what they *can* do rather than just telling them what they *can't* do. So next time you want your child to stop doing something, let them also know what they can do: "You can't jump on the couch, but you can go outside to jump on the trampoline"; "You can't hit your sister; if you're mad you can let her know or you can go hit the pillow in your room"; "You can't speak to me that way so when you're mad you can let me know you're angry without using hurtful words."

Let's get you ahead of the game: Write out the most common behavior you ask your child to change and then write out three other options (aka replacement behaviors) that they can choose from.

Day One Hundred and Thirty-One: Don't Suppress; Acknowledge

Go easy on yourself; you're learning how to handle your feelings alongside your child.

Have you ever had a cough and bought a cough suppressant to feel better? That medicine didn't get rid of your cough; it suppressed it, right? It helped you for a bit, but it didn't actually heal the cause of your cough. The same can be said when you promise yourself, "I'm not going to yell anymore." That's like a cough suppressant. Sure, you can say you're not going to yell for a period of time, but there are still feelings swirling around inside you that are *causing* you to lose your cool. When you feel frustrated or angry, say out loud to yourself exactly how you feel. This may feel silly, but it is imperative that you appropriately acknowledge and validate what you feel. Why? This replaces the ineffective promise of "I won't yell" with something you can do instead: Say exactly how you feel instead of push down how you feel. Once you get comfortable with how you feel (be patient with yourself because this is a brand-new practice), you won't resort to yelling to process your feelings. You can instead *understand* your feelings, feel in control of them, and choose a response that keeps you and your child connected.

Do not think that suppressing your feelings is a character flaw; you are learning for the first time how to have a healthy relationship with your emotions. Go easy on yourself and know that as you are teaching your child to process their feelings, you're teaching yourself to do the same.

Day One Hundred and Thirty-Two: Lend Your Understanding

You don't need to correct your child's feelings;
you need to validate them.

If you have a child who is hard on themselves, yet you have made a conscious effort to *not* be hard on them, you may be confused as to why this is happening. First, know you've done a wonderful job intentionally not making your child feel like they need to earn their love through their achievements, grades, looks, beauty, and so on. Because of that, your child doesn't need to be corrected; they need your understanding and guidance. When your child is hard on themselves, rather than try to make them feel better by saying, "No, you're so smart, don't say that," try validating their feelings instead: "It must be tough to work so hard and feel that way." Try asking more questions to find the best way to support your child. If you know what it feels like to be hard on yourself, you can absolutely relate to that feeling. We always want the cause and the solution right away, but we forget that so much of the "solution" can be found right here within our experience, so take your experience and lend it to your child because you have so much more wisdom than you may give yourself credit for.

Many times it's not how harsh, judgmental, or critical you are on your child, but how harsh, judgmental, and critical you are on yourself. Take a moment to reflect on where you are hard on yourself; however you would guide your child, guide yourself that same way too.

Day One Hundred and Thirty-Three: Fine-Wine Motherhood

Time is a main ingredient in becoming the mother you want to be.

You have so much information being thrown your way in motherhood. It can be easy to feel bombarded, but also disappointed that all that information isn't so easily implemented. This is where you have to remember that you are just like a fancy, fine wine being aged in a French oak barrel for years. It takes time to let all the knowledge soak in to give you your unique, well-rounded motherhood quality. So the next time you get upset that you haven't "mastered" motherhood or that all the things you've been reading have yet to come to fruition in your day-to-day life, remember that slow and steady wins the race. The tough moments you have are an opportunity to reflect on and see what areas you want to focus more on fine-tuning. You're worked so hard, so trust the process and give yourself time; what you're creating is a quality, fine-wine motherhood.

Motherhood takes lots of practice—which means getting it wrong a bunch before you get it right—before you feel confident in how you handle yourself. Find a moment today where you don't get it right and use that as a way to reflect how far you've come.

Day One Hundred and Thirty-Four: Avoiding Emotional Quicksand

It might not always feel like it, but your child's feelings are normal and temporary.

You know those moments when your child is inconsolable? Think of those moments as emotional quicksand: Your child is angry or sad, you reach in to help them, but then *you* start to sink into those feelings and believe that they won't be okay. And now *both of you* are drowning in those unpleasant feelings. . . . Here's how you can change that. You intellectually know feelings are normal and temporary, but at that moment it sure doesn't *feel* that way. So think back to a time when you felt crappy: It was normal and it was temporary because right now you aren't feeling that same way. The more you can establish this truth with your own experiences, the more you can provide that security to your child in their tough moments. You are your child's anchor. Even when your child is certain they can't get through their big feelings, you are that anchor of certainty for them. Go easy on yourself the next time you feel like you might get sucked into your child's emotional quicksand, and anchor yourself in remembering these feelings are normal and temporary.

Today think back to a time in your life that you thought would never end, but did eventually pass. Walking yourself through proof that your feelings are temporary will give you confidence to be an anchor when your child is in the thick of their feelings.

Day One Hundred and Thirty-Five: Good Moms Have Good Kids— Who Don't Always Listen

What if the answer wasn't being harder on yourself, but instead being softer on yourself?

How great would it be if there was a way to make sure your child listened to everything you said? You ask your child to do their chores, and they do them without a peep! You tell your child to stop bothering their sibling, and they never do it again! This is absolutely impossible, but would you have so much less stress about being a good mother if your child always listened? Think about that answer for a moment because it defines your view of what it's like to be a good mom. If you've been defining yourself as a good mother based on your child's level of obedience, let's try a new way. What if being a good mom was way less about how your child behaves and way more about how you treat yourself in the moments that they don't listen. You'll always be adjusting to motherhood as your child increases their autonomy (and therefore tests your authority). So the next time your child isn't listening, first mark their rejection as part of childhood development—it's normal to test boundaries. Then turn inward and comfort yourself, and rather than be hard on yourself, be softer on yourself—because it is *hard work* to hold boundaries, but you're doing a pretty great job at it.

In any parent-child interaction, there are two parties at play. Rather than focus on how your child's behavior is a reflection of you, focus on how you are treating yourself in those moments.

Day One Hundred and Thirty-Six: Stop Resisting Resistance

What you resist persists; what you allow flows.

Is it the most frustrating thing when your child doesn't listen to you? Yes. Is there a way you can always get your child to listen? No. Is there a way you can make your life easier when your child doesn't listen? Yes. The first thing you can do is to *stop taking it personally.* Your child is not saying no to you; they are saying no to the thing you are asking them to do (or stop doing). The second thing you can do is to *stop resisting their resistance.* Instead drop your resistance and meet them with acceptance of their feelings. You aren't accepting their actions; you are accepting that what they feel is real. By doing this you are making space for your child to feel *all* the feelings of not wanting to do something, of being too tired, of being too unhappy, and so on, and you are still continuing to hold the boundary. The goal in these moments is to depersonalize your child's resistance so that you avoid exacerbating the tension and instead prioritize a solution.

The next time your child doesn't listen, try to separate their behavior from their feelings. This will help you move away from taking your child's behavior personally and move toward helping them through their resistance.

Day One Hundred and Thirty-Seven: Meet Yourself Where You're At— Period Parenting

When you don't feel 100 percent, you can't give 100 percent.

When you have your period and you do not feel your best, use your wonderful ability to connect to yourself by meeting yourself where you are at. Yes, if you are feeling cranky and tired, acknowledge it; don't try to pretend you're not. Why? When you do not feel 100 percent, you cannot give 100 percent. Parenting more consciously isn't just about connecting to yourself in the good moments, it's also about connecting to yourself in *all* moments so that you can approach motherhood in a realistic, doable way. Of course you still have responsibilities and obligations, but if you aren't willing to acknowledge what your mind and body need, it's likely no one else will either. So next time you're in the hormonal trenches, remember it's okay to let go of your normal standards and expectations and meet yourself where you're at.

Just a reminder that there are chemical and physical changes in your body during your cycle, so when you're not feeling your best self, acknowledge the very real shift that's occurring and take it easy on yourself.

Day One Hundred and Thirty-Eight: No One Needs a Perfect Parent

Your child doesn't need a perfect parent;
they want a connected parent.

If you grew up in the role of the perfect daughter, a little girl who did everything right, rarely got in trouble, and was praised for being an easy child, motherhood can be challenging when you realize no matter how hard you try, you can't be the perfect parent. The good news is that your child doesn't want a perfectly curated version of you. In fact, your child may even reject that version of you. This is because your child is one of the most authentic humans you know; therefore, the more closely connected you are to yourself, the more closely connected you can be to your child. Knowing you won't always be able to make your child happy will be a learning curve for you, but this is a beautiful invitation to step out of the role of people pleaser. Take small steps as you sit with the feelings of discomfort when you can't please everyone and know this is the path to not only being more authentic and connected to yourself, but also more connected to your child.

Motherhood has a way of helping you become more true to yourself. Today think about one people-pleasing behavior that motherhood has helped you shift away from.

Day One Hundred and Thirty-Nine: Tantrum for Two

Things shift the moment you realize you've been having your own tantrum amid your child's tantrum.

You're getting ready to leave for school and your child loses it. They're crying, yelling, screaming, kicking, and resisting anything you do to try and calm them down. You remained calm as long as you could, but you felt your blood boiling and you started having your own mini tantrum too—you're not open to new ideas; you're stuck in your feelings and you're seeing red. Does this sound familiar? Here's the thing: The moment you realize you've been having your own tantrums is the moment you see there's room to grow. You've lived your life handling emotions the only way you've known how, and now that you're a mother you're realizing that how you cope with anger, disappointment, or frustration isn't as healthy as you want it to be. This is a powerful realization that you shouldn't take lightly. If you are aware that you want to shift, that awareness will take you far. The next step is compassion, yes, compassion for yourself. Compassion means you understand this process is difficult (shifting decades worth of coping skills) and you replace judgment with curiosity.

If you're feeling brave, ask yourself what about being angry is uncomfortable for you. What other feelings are beneath your anger? This discovery will show you that your anger has really been keeping a more vulnerable, tender feeling safe.

Day One Hundred and Forty:
Slow Down

*Your child calls you to the present moment.
Don't be afraid to pick up and answer.*

You've heard the phrase "The days are long, but the years are short," and my goodness, are the days long when you have a little one taking their time and asking for "just one more minute." While of course you have to keep your child on some sort of schedule, there is something to be said for leaning into the ways your child calls you to slow down. The younger your child is, the more they live in the present moment and summon you to do the same. The next time your child calls you to watch them play while you're cleaning up the kitchen, know it's okay to slow down and enjoy that moment. You'll probably feel the pull to get back to regular programming, but you might also feel another part of you that longs to be more like your child. Motherhood is finding a balance of those two and taking the cues from your child that slowing down might just be a little more of what you need.

Today make it a point to answer your child's call to slow down and enjoy the moment they're enjoying too. It doesn't have to be too long, just long enough where you can truly slow down.

Day One Hundred and Forty-One: Guilt Can Be Fuel

Guilt is an alarm that signals change is needed.
Use it to your advantage.

If you've ever yelled at your child and afterward you felt awful, this is a good thing! Yes, you feel awful because you're feeling guilt. And that guilt is telling you that you don't like how you feel and you don't like how you acted. Your guilt can be used as fuel, but it's up to you where you're going to use that fuel. You can take the fuel and put it in the tank in your mind that says, "See, I'm such a bad mom!" or you can put it in the tank that says, "I'm a good mom. This doesn't feel good to me—I want to change; I want to do something differently." Don't let that awful feeling go into the tank that fuels negative stories that don't serve you; use that fuel for good and fill up the tank that wants you to grow, knows you have the best intentions, and is ready to look at different ways to deal with your emotions so you can also help your child learn to deal with their emotions. Today's the day you're going to use your guilt to your advantage!

Don't let your guilt go wasted. Make a note today to use guilt to your advantage and thank your guilt for showing up for you to alert you that change is needed.

Day One Hundred and Forty-Two: Are You Self-Centered?

Your child's behavior is less about you and more about them.

As a mother, one of the last ways you'd describe yourself would probably be self-centered. But would you laugh if this entry showed you otherwise? Okay, you aren't actually self-centered, but as a mother it's common to unintentionally and unconsciously believe that everything about your child reflects back on you. When you've asked your child to get dressed for school for the third time, you may think, "No one cares about me around here," or if your child talks back: "No one ever respects me." If whenever your child doesn't comply or behave to your standards, you make it about you, you're not only dragging yourself through unintentional pain, it's also simply not true. Most of the time, your child's behavior is about their wants and needs. When your child doesn't rush to get dressed for school, it's more likely because home is way more comfy. When your child talks back, it's more likely that your child is frustrated and trying to get their way. Realizing your child's behavior isn't always personal to you can help you show up less reactive, more understanding, and more powerful in reshaping your parent-child relationship.

Is there a specific behavior of your child's that feels like it's a personal attack on you? How can you poke holes in that belief to see how it can be more about your child?

Day One Hundred and Forty-Three: Savor the Good

Savoring the good will help you endure the not-so-good too.

Sometimes it can feel like you're focused on the negatives in motherhood: what your child is doing wrong, who isn't listening to you, and what isn't going right. Did you know that your brain is hardwired to look for the negatives, the threats, and the potential risks? Yes, your brain's job is to protect you from harm. Over the years, your body has adapted to look out for specific threats that have ignited unpleasant feelings. So now that you're a mother, of course you're going to be looking out even more to protect your child. However, sometimes this can lead you to *only* seeing the negatives and *rarely* experiencing the positives. Making a note to look for and savor the good will not only bring more joy to your awareness, it will help you endure the not-so-good too. There is so much value in being prepared to handle the hard times of motherhood, and there is equal value in allowing yourself to enjoy the good too.

Today think about one part of motherhood that you'd like to savor more of. Take some time to linger in that aspect of being a mother.

Day One Hundred and Forty-Four: When Your Child Tells You No

*Taking the time to understand your child's
no can set you free from reactivity.*

Has your child ever looked you straight in the eye and said, "No!"? Most likely this made you angry and reactive. You likely no longer focused on the task you wanted your child to do; your attention was rerouted to your child being disrespectful. What if your child said no and you didn't feel the need to rage back? What if you didn't view that no as a sign of disrespect and instead as an invitation to check in with your child's feelings? You can create this reality for yourself by helping you and your child separate their feelings from their behaviors. This doesn't mean that all behaviors are accepted or that just because your child doesn't intend to be rude, they aren't rude. Instead this is opening the door to understanding what your child is experiencing before deeming their behavior disrespectful. This change will give you the comfort to respond rather than react because you are deactivating the trigger of disrespect.

The next time your child tells you no, don't take the bait that will drag you into a power struggle. Instead take a moment to understand and you may be able to proceed feeling more in control of yourself.

Day One Hundred and Forty-Five: Family Mission Statement

Your family is the greatest investment you'll ever make.

Corporations spend millions of dollars helping their leaders develop corporate values and create company mission statements. They do this to make sure that they meet their goals and that every decision made is aligned with those goals. If these big companies are taking the time and money to invest in setting goals, why can't mothers do the same for their families? You've likely been raising your family according to your values. So intentionally taking time to think about, discuss, and evaluate your family values and goals will be a beautiful exercise to affirm the direction your family's headed in. Some questions you can discuss as a family:

1. "What is our goal as a family?"
2. "What are our family values?"
3. "How can we make sure that when we make decisions for our family, our decisions are aligned with our family values and goals?"

Answering these questions will help you create a family mission statement. Here's a sample: "The Martinez Family values hard work, respect, compassion, and fun, and each family member will feel supported, loved, and successful in every aspect of their life."

Schedule time this week to create your family mission statement by answering the questions in this entry. Using the Notes app on your phone, jot down what comes to mind and allow the other family members to contribute what matters most to them as well.

Day One Hundred and Forty-Six: Congratulations Are In Order

In motherhood, the little things aren't so little at all.

Sometimes the things that matter most in motherhood are the things that get the least recognition. The evenings you sat with your child through never-ending meltdowns, the time you've taken out of your day to read a book to help you show up as a better mother—those moments aren't the ones you get praise for, yet they're the ones that matter most. The world may pat you on the back for your child getting the honor roll or the lead role in the play, which are absolutely moments to be proud of. But today is the day you take time to acknowledge the parts of motherhood that no one sees—that don't receive a trophy—but that have been an important contribution to your child's life.

It's easy to forget the little things you do for your child, so today what's one little thing in motherhood you've made a point to do that you know isn't so little after all?

Day One Hundred and Forty-Seven: Parenting Explosions

The best gift you can give to your child is investing in the connection to yourself.

Ever wonder why you explode on your child over something so seemingly insignificant? Think of your body like a soda bottle, a soda bottle that existed way before your child entered the picture and has been shaken up by the many experiences of your early years: by learning to not trust your feelings and disconnecting with yourself so you can fit in with your loved ones. All of that shaking builds up pressure. Then you have a child, and that new experience adds more pressure to the bottle. Eventually that bottle reaches its capacity. This is why the one small thing your child does is what screws off the cap and then, boom: All that built-up pressure explodes all over your child. Your explosion has nothing to do with how much you love your kid, with your effort, or with your willpower. It's about the connection to yourself. This is why learning to connect to yourself is the best gift you can give your child.

You deserve to let pressure out of the soda bottle that is your body. Use one of these practices today to see which works best to help you let out your feelings: journaling, sending a voice note to yourself or a friend, meditation, walking meditation, therapy, coaching, or noting (naming what you feel when you feel it).

Day One Hundred and Forty-Eight: Learn How Your Child Connects

The more you learn about your child, the more you'll deepen the love with your child.

Have you ever been rejected by your child? You went for a hug and they didn't want one, or you were looking forward to hearing about your child's day only to get a silent car ride home? After you silently weep at their rejection, remember that your child might like to connect differently than you do. Conversation or cuddling may be your preferred way to connect, while your child prefers your undivided attention or quality time. So, what if you asked your child, "How do you know I love you?" It may sound like a strange question, but the range of sweet, heartfelt, and silly answers you will receive from your child will open your eyes to how your child views love. The next question is even better: Ask your child, "How do you want me to show that I love you?" Again, these answers can range from "I want more alone time with you" to "Giving me more allowance." . . . Take the answers as they are, but the next time your connection is rejected, remember what you heard from your child and try that instead.

Did your parents show you love in a way that was different from what you wanted or needed? Did they ever ask you how you wanted to be loved? Asking your child about how they want to be shown love is yet another opportunity to see what a wonderful mother you are.

Day One Hundred and Forty-Nine: Honesty and Accountability

When you've made a mistake, remember that honesty is best paired with accountability.

When it comes to being honest with your children about how you feel, it is best paired with accountability. What does that mean? It means that if you are frustrated with your child for not putting away their laundry, you can be honest about how you feel. Accountability comes into play when you make it clear that your behaviors, actions, and how you handle your feelings are 100 percent your responsibility; you aren't weaponizing your frustration as a rationale for yelling. A response using honesty and accountability would sound something like "You're right, my love, I am so frustrated that your laundry still isn't put away, but that doesn't mean I should have yelled, that wasn't okay. Let's talk about how we can make laundry easier for both of us." If you want your child to be honest and accountable, you will model it for them by remembering this two-step process: Honesty is best paired with accountability.

Think about if your spouse, partner, or family member was able to be honest with you about how they felt, but also took accountability for their actions. That would feel like a pretty healthy relationship, wouldn't it? Practice this in all your relationships; big shifts can happen!

Day One Hundred and Fifty: Your Child's Narrative

When you change the way you look at your child, your child changes.

There's something equally as important as what you say to your child; it's how you feel about your child. Well, of course you love your child, but what we are tapping into today are the narratives you have about your child: "This is my easy child," "This is my difficult child," or "Things don't come easy to my child." The narrative you have about your child impacts how you show up for your child, and it can be in a positive way or a not-so-positive way. The narrative of "Something is wrong with my child" truly prevents you from seeing your child as whole. For example, if your narrative is "My child never listens to me," you'd be unconsciously approaching every interaction with your child expecting a fight, which doesn't leave room for you or your child to change. Now, this doesn't mean you should "pretend" that your child is perfect, but instead change the narrative to "My child needs more support and guidance with directions." This shift helps you create a better approach with your child and helps your child see themselves in a different light, not as a problem, but as a child who can find solutions with their mother.

Think about the narratives you have for your child. Are there any narratives that aren't serving you and your child's relationship? If so, think about a narrative that helps you both connect to create a new path forward. (PS: It's usually one with compassion and understanding.)

Day One Hundred and Fifty-One: Daughters to Mothers

The magic of being a mother is that you can create and give what you never received.

There's this incredible thing we do as mothers: We create what we didn't receive as daughters and give it to our children. This is by no means a knock to your parents, but instead an acknowledgment that you're able to create new, healthy traditions for your family. Sometimes, though, when you're so focused on not carrying on an unhealthy family tradition, you become hyperaware of your child's needs. This means overextending yourself to make sure your child doesn't have your experience. Not only can this be exhausting, but it's an unrealistic expectation for you. So rather than try to right the wrongs of your parents or parent away your own pain, know that you can instead just parent the child you have in front of you—which is a child who has so much love from their mother. You are doing so much to show up for your child; all the extra small things you do—like reading this book—are proof that you're a committed and thoughtful mother. So don't you forget it!

What parenting practice of yours are you most proud of today? Think about one tradition or routine that works well with your family and soak in the love that's coming from your efforts.

Day One Hundred and Fifty-Two: Be Authentic to Be Connected

The more connected you are to yourself, the more connected you can be with your child.

Children are like the dogs at airport security; they can sniff out your authenticity and they know when you aren't being real. Yep, children know when you are full of it, don't mean what you say, and don't say what you mean. Have you ever tried to use a calm, gentle parenting script and your child looks at you like "Who are you and what have you done with my mom because she never talks like this?" This is because your child is basically the most authentic person you know and therefore they know when you aren't! This is why there is no quick tip or hack to create real connection with your child; you can't say the right thing to "connect" with your child. You have to *actually* want that connection and want to develop that connection to yourself. This means getting real with yourself: Be honest about how you feel, be honest about what role you've taken in your own feelings, and be open to choosing a new way to approach your relationships. The more connected and authentic you become with yourself, the more authentic and connected your parent-child relationship will be.

A great way to authentically promote connection with you and your child is by being honest about school. When your child complains they don't want to go or how hard it is, validate that with your own truth! Share about your school life or your work life and show them you have the same feelings they do. They'll love that realness!

Day One Hundred and Fifty-Three: Attention-Seeking Behavior

Attention-seeking behavior is really connection-craving behavior.

Listen, it can absolutely be annoying when your child is doing something for attention, especially when you've labeled that attention as something that is "bad" to want. So let's make those moments easier for you by unraveling what attention is: Attention is a need to be seen, heard, and connected with another. When you realize that the command for attention is really a call for connection, it probably makes you inclined to respond with a bit more softness and understanding, right? The key to eliminating negative attention-seeking behavior is to show your child how replacing that behavior will get them what they want; at first they get what they want immediately with that positive replacement behavior and then over time you can fade it out as your child learns that most of the time, their positive behavior gives them the connection they are seeking. The next time you see "attention-seeking" behavior, remind yourself that it's really the connection your child wants and that you can absolutely help them get that need met by modeling it in a healthier, effective way.

Today think about your child's behavior and what might be a call for connection. If your child yells loudly across the room for your attention, model what they would need to say to get your attention, like "Mommy, can we talk?" or "Mom, I need you, please." Have them practice and immediately give them your attention. Do this many times with instant attention to show them this new behavior is effective. Over time they'll see that this new replacement behavior is more favorable for them and you!

Day One Hundred and Fifty-Four: Fasting from Correction

When you look past behavior and see a feeling,
you've truly seen your child.

If you're exhausted from constantly correcting your child's behavior, please know that this exhaustion is a real thing. If you only hear yourself say "No!" or "Don't do that," you can really start to hate hearing your own voice (and it's likely your child is too). After a while, your words become a broken record and lose their meaning. If this sounds like you, here's an invitation to stop correcting your child for one day. Yes, instead of correcting your child's behavior today, get on their level and address their feelings in a concerned and caring way: "Hey, you must be really upset right now, what's going on? How can I help you?" Now, of course this doesn't apply to harmful behaviors; those have to be corrected. But for everything else, try separating your child's behaviors from their feelings. Fasting from the constant cycle of correction for one day will help you see your child in a different light and help you find a new path forward. When something isn't working, you can always try a new approach to switch things up.

Sometimes it can feel like nothing will ever change, so challenge yourself with that thought today: "What's one area in parenting that feels like it will never change and what's one way I can make a tiny shift?"

Day One Hundred and Fifty-Five: Being Flexible

There is strength in flexibility.

If you've ever seen a hurricane make its way through a tropical location, you may have noticed that the trees that can best withstand the storm are slender, flexible palm trees. When you look at them, you may think, "Those things are strong; look at them blowing around in the wind," but in fact it's their flexibility that gives them strength. In motherhood, there's something to be said about the strength flexibility gives you. Now, does being a strong mother mean you should bend every time your child asks for something? Oh, absolutely not! What it does mean is that when you notice the conditions in your family have changed, you have the strength in yourself to know you can change your routine, your rules, or really anything that will create a healthier experience for you and your family. Rather than hold on to an idea or practice out of principle or for consistency's sake, ask yourself if flexibility is needed. If you worry that bending the rules in one situation will cause you trouble, be clear about the exception and trust that your strength will support you through that next moment as well.

Is there one way you wish your parents had applied flexibility when you were a child? How do you show up in that area as a parent today?

Day One Hundred and Fifty-Six: Learning How to Be Sad

*Sadness is a normal, necessary, and temporary
emotion that every human feels.*

This may sound like a weird question, but did anyone teach you how to be sad? Most parents didn't sit their children down and say, "It's okay to be sad; cry as long as you want," so if your answer is no, you're with the majority. What's more likely is that your relationship with sadness is one that is pushed away, hurried along, or covered up. When you fell down and scraped your knee, were you given a lollipop to make it all better? When you didn't get what you wanted, were you told to stop crying and be grateful for what you did have? Did the adults in your life comfort you through your sadness? Exploring your relationship with sadness is necessary now that you're a mother because your child will experience sadness all the time, and how that makes you feel shapes how you can show up for your child. Sadness is a normal, necessary, and temporary emotion that every human feels. Remembering this will help you tend to your child with less fear and more calm. When your child is sad, pay attention to how you feel inside your body. If you have any particular avoidance energy with sadness, explore that to see where it comes from.

The next time your child is sad, remind yourself that feelings are a messenger system telling your child what they want. There doesn't have to be a negative or positive spin on sadness; instead let it just be a messenger for what your child needs or wants.

Day One Hundred and Fifty-Seven: Having a Hard Time

Your child isn't giving you a hard time; they're having a hard time and doing everything they can to show you how hard of a time it is.

Have you ever heard the statement "Your child isn't giving you a hard time; they're having a hard time"? If so, you may have rolled your eyes because your child absolutely has given you a hard time before. It's totally eye roll worthy when the premise for this statement isn't broken down, so let's do that today: The way you view your child shapes everything; it shapes how you treat your child, how you connect with your child, and how your child sees themselves. So when you deem your child's behavior an intentional slight against you, you're going to be on the defensive. Being on the defensive means you're not showing up as the parent you want to be—you can't because your body is protecting itself. So rather than pretend like your child is a perfect little angel having a hard time, why not see your child as a human who is absolutely having a hard time *and* doing what they can to show you how hard of a time they're having. Perspective shifts may seem small, but they can really shift the dynamic of your relationship. Try one out next time your child is having a hard time.

Have you ever been more "short" or snippy with your spouse or partner because you're hurt, sad, or mad? This is you having a hard time, right? But you're also showing the other person that through your behavior. Food for thought: Relate to your child by finding a similar experience.

Day One Hundred and Fifty-Eight: Running Late

Just because it's always been that way doesn't mean it's the right way.

You know when you need to get out of the house on time and your child just won't get it together? You put your gentle-parenting mask on for a few minutes, but then you rip it off because it's not working! So you yell, scream, and sprinkle in some threats to get the job done, and you finally get them in the car . . . but then you feel crappy, why? Because you had to sacrifice your connection for compliance. When this happens, go easy on yourself and know it's nothing an authentic repair can't patch up. But today let's look at what's packed into the idea of tardiness for you. While of course you don't want to disrespect someone else's time or be late, often there are many other associations packed into timeliness. If being late is a trigger for you, it can be helpful to explore the stories you've attached to being late: "I never have it all together," "I'm a bad parent," or "I am rude and disrespectful." Tap back into what you learned about being on time and ask yourself if that's something you want to carry on into the family you've created. Punctuality can be your goal, yet when it's not achieved, replace shaming yourself or your child with chalking it up to normal human error—or make small shifts to improve your routine.

If you want to create a new narrative around being on time, today's the day: Leave behind what doesn't work and add in what will help you and your family find your flow.

Day One Hundred and Fifty-Nine: Feelings Aren't for Fixing

Feelings aren't fixable; situations are fixable.
Feelings always need to be felt.

Moms are good at fixing things, and so it might feel like you need to fix your child's feelings. Your child is sad, mad, or any other feeling, and something comes over your body that says, "Make that go away!" Of course you don't want to see your child in pain, but the truth is, *feelings aren't fixable*. While the situation at hand can change, feelings will still be felt. Fixing others' feelings generally has a low success rate. A helpful question to ask yourself is "Do I need to fix their feelings or facilitate their feelings?" Most of the time, facilitation will be the answer, so here's how you go about it:

1. First, let your child know you 100 percent believe them in how they feel.
2. Second, avoid convincing your child to feel differently by saying, "Don't be sad."
3. Third, use less words and more presence. You don't have to fill every moment with conversation; you can allow silence, sitting, and room for your child to move through what they're feeling.

These are *hard* moments, but you can make them a bit easier when you don't expend all your energy on resistance and instead allow them to exist and naturally fade away.

Moms can be so quick to fix everything, so today before you rush to fix something for your child, ask yourself if they really need your fixing or if they need your facilitation.

Day One Hundred and Sixty: Holding Space

At the end of the day, every child just wants to be loved and accepted as they are.

What does it mean to hold space for your child? It means to accept your child without needing to judge, comment, fix, or correct them. It doesn't mean you have to agree, condone, or even understand them. The only thing you have to understand is that your child feels safe telling you about their experience and they want you to be there for them. It can be very uncomfortable to witness your child's feelings without being able to change them. Yet this simple act of allowing your child to share their feelings without the fear of being doubted or judged is powerful. A great way to deepen the connection between you and your child is to hold your opinion and instead hold space for your child.

Have you ever gone to a friend or a family member to share about your experience and you were met with advice, judgment, or a lecture? Next time be sure to tell your loved ones what you want: "Hey, I need to talk this out; can you listen?" or "I need an ear; can we talk?"

Day One Hundred and Sixty-One: You Are a Good Mom

Good moms wonder if they're good moms.

If you've ever stopped and asked yourself, "Am I a good mom?" the answer is yes. Why? Because good moms wonder if they're good moms. Good moms wonder because they care. Good moms mess up, make mistakes, and feel bad about it—because guilt is a healthy emotion guiding them back to where they want to be. Good moms work on having more compassion for themselves and their children. Good moms take time for themselves, just like you're doing with this book. Good moms have a healthy practice of stepping back and asking themselves, "What change can I make to feel better, do better, and enjoy my family more?" And finally, good moms take small moments to see all the good they've done and because of that, they know they're a pretty good mom.

Today you are going to take a moment to pick out the good you've done as a mom today, this week, or this month.

Day One Hundred and Sixty-Two: Catching Your Child in a Lie

The greatest lie you'll ever tell is that you've never told a lie.

Lying is a part of human nature, yet it never feels good to catch your child in a lie, and it certainly doesn't feel great for your child either. One of the ways to promote truth telling is to avoid setting up your child to lie, meaning don't ask a question you already know the answer to. For example, if you know your child didn't do their chores, have a conversation: "I noticed you didn't clean up your room; let's talk about how we can figure this out so it's easier on both of us." When you need to address lying behavior, create a shame-free environment by letting your child know "I know you're worried you will get in trouble, but you won't because being honest is what we care about most." Finally, rewarding honesty will teach your child that the truth is a better choice than the lie. For example, if your child has been taking cookies when they aren't supposed to, let your child know asking for a cookie is a better choice by giving them the cookie whenever they ask. Slowly over time you can fade out the instant cookie gratification, but it's important to build the skill of honestly asking so your child knows it's a beneficial option.

It's hard to be honest about something you might get in trouble for. So today, have a talk with your child, tween, or teen about an honesty-safe world. Together, pick a word that can be used when they're afraid to tell you the truth about something but don't know how to start. This will create an easier path to handle more difficult conversations.

Day One Hundred and Sixty-Three: Handling Negative School Feedback

Check your immediate assumptions; those are usually the least helpful in solving the problem in front of you.

Have you ever received feedback from your child's school that wasn't positive? Did you feel a wave of panic, fear, worry, and defensiveness take over your body? Here are some steps to help you through receiving that feedback:

1. First, check in to see what automatic assumption you've made: Are you immediately mad at your child? Mad at the teacher? See what your first thought is and know that your first thought is usually not the best.
2. Second, check in to see if you're unintentionally making this about you: "Where did I go wrong?" or "How could I have let this happen?" You may notice your own feelings are interfering with how you show up and handle this situation with your child.
3. Third, identify the difference between your feelings and assumptions and the information you were given.
4. Lastly, speak to your child with an open mind; let your child know you heard what happened and you want to see how they're feeling.

Once your child feels safe to talk about their school troubles, they'll be able to open up more about details without being afraid.

School is important, but it doesn't define your child. Think about what you're most proud of about your child. Remember how wonderful your child truly is—for their talents, characteristics, and skills—regardless of what current struggles they may be facing at school.

Day One Hundred and Sixty-Four: Working Through Transition Times

Mothers deserve realistic expectations; set them accordingly.

Whenever you have to get your family back on schedule, it can feel like quite the daunting task. Whether you're adjusting from being home after a vacation, you're moving into a new home, or daylight saving time has shown up to ruin your sleep schedule, moms tend to bear the weight of getting everyone back to the normal routine. One very helpful reminder that you might forget is that transitions are a necessary part of human life. You aren't a robot that can adjust immediately; you need time and so do your family members. Label these adjustments as transition times so that while you're trying to get everyone back to sleep on time or you're trying to get used to your new surroundings, you have the sign "transition time" mentally smacked on your forehead. Why? You deserve realistic expectations. Remembering that it takes time to get from point A to point B will give you and your family grace, allow you to laugh when it gets tricky, and have realistic expectations for when things go wrong.

What has been the hardest transition for you and your family? It can be anything from getting your toddler out of a crib and into a bed to switching schools—whatever it is, ask yourself if you set realistic expectations and if not, how would that have helped you?

Day One Hundred and Sixty-Five: Natural Consequences

"I told you so" is best replaced with "I told you I'd always be there for you."

Where do you fall along the spectrum of letting your child experience natural consequences? Do you tend to rescue your child? Do you tend to double down and reinforce the lesson they learned? Are you somewhere in the middle? Children certainly need to experience consequences so they learn how to function in the world, but they also need to feel unconditionally loved by their parents to feel safe in experiencing those consequences. It may be hard for you to step out of the way when you see your child about to experience a consequence, and other times you may encourage that consequence so they can learn. Wherever you're on this continuum, know that your role will always remain as a supporter and a guide. You will be there to support your child through their experience without adding guilt or shame and guide your child in how to make different choices, leaving them feeling more confident in themselves.

The next time you feel like saying, "I told you so," try replacing it with "I told you I'd always be there for you." You and your child will feel a whole lot more connected.

Day One Hundred and Sixty-Six: Bracing for Tornado Tantrums

You are the calm before, during, and after the storm.

Tantrums are treacherous grounds and it can feel like nothing you do will help your child, tween, or teen calm down. One of the most helpful visualizations for tantrums is envisioning a tornado. Your child is basically a tornado of emotions, violently spinning around, uprooting people, places, and things with their feelings. At times, their emotions get you riled up and you form your own tornado, swirling in all the feelings about how hard parenting can be. Eventually your and your child's tornadoes combine and it's not pretty. So, here's what you can do instead: Prepare for the tantrums in advance, right now. Imagine yourself firmly planted inside a shelter, safe and secure because you know that the tornado will pass. You're not trying to convince the tornado to stop or bribe it to slow down; you're just patiently, calmly, and confidently waiting for it to pass. This visualization will help you not get sucked into your child's tornado. It will help you remember that being a stable, sturdy, and safe place will not only keep you grounded; it will also allow you to be the comfort your child needs when they're ready.

Don't be shy to collect all your tantrum wins today: Did you not get sucked into your child's tornado? Were you able to weather the storm? That deserves a trophy, and the more you do this, the better you'll get at it, so keep at it!

Day One Hundred and Sixty-Seven: Self-Care Redefined

You can't spell "family" without an "I."

The next time you feel guilty doing something for yourself, just remember that you can't spell "family" without an "I." What does that mean? It means that you are an important part of the family; you're needed, you're essential, and quite honestly you're irreplaceable. Remembering your importance means that you take care of yourself in all the ways you can: physically, mentally, emotionally, nutritiously, spiritually, socially, and any other way that fills you up. The things you might have previously labeled as a luxury become a necessity when it comes to being a mom. So the next time you feel like you "shouldn't" get the babysitter, buy yourself a new pair of jeans, or go for a run, know that you very well might need to. Because the human who takes care of all the humans needs to take care of herself.

Think about one way you care for yourself that you're proud of. It's important to look for the tiny ways you show up for yourself; these encourage you to make showing up for yourself a necessary recurring practice.

Day One Hundred and Sixty-Eight: Easier, Not Easy

Motherhood won't be easy, but it can be easier.

Imagine if there was a parenting method, technique, or hack that would guarantee you an easy ride through motherhood; it would be like finding the fountain of youth! While motherhood will never be easy, it can be easier. Of course the catch is that to make motherhood easier, you have to do something that isn't so easy: Learn to cope with all your feelings—the icky ones, the scary ones, and probably ones you don't even know you have. Why would that make motherhood easy, you ask? When you aren't controlled by your feelings, meaning when you are accepting and you are allowing whatever feelings come and go throughout the day, you are less likely to react and more likely to respond to your child in a way that is connected to your highest self. The process of becoming more connected with your feelings and ultimately yourself can be done through therapy, coaching, and other self-focused reflection. If you've been on the fence about getting support for yourself, today may just be that nudge to invest in yourself; of course this will be wonderful for your family, but the best gift is truly doing it for yourself.

Today jot down two support options for yourself. These might not be doable right away, but verbalizing or writing what support you may want is a beautiful step: therapy, coaching, workshops, retreats, memberships, courses, books, support groups, and apps, just to name a few.

Day One Hundred and Sixty-Nine: You're Doing a Good Job!

There is always so much more you're doing right as a mother than wrong.

You probably don't hear enough how grateful your family is to have you. You probably don't get complimented enough for what a great mother you are. You deserve to hear that more, from others and from yourself. Not to inflate your ego or to pretend you're perfect, but to acknowledge that you show up, over and over again, and to allow the good that you do to be witnessed, praised, and appreciated. No matter how silly you may feel, take a moment to compliment yourself in the mirror. Yes, go walk over to a mirror after you're done reading this. (Don't brush it off; actually do it.) Out loud is the best way to tell yourself what a good job you are doing, but you can also say it silently. Whichever way you do it, take that moment to really believe what you're saying, because there is always so much more you're doing right as a mother than wrong.

Does this exercise make you cringe? You're not alone, but get curious about the feelings that come up. Also, what would you say to your child if they struggled to compliment themselves? Maybe you need to say that to yourself too.

Day One Hundred and Seventy: Selfless versus Selfish

You are many identities wrapped into one wonderful you.

If you ever feel confused about how to be a mom *and* also be your own self, that's because our society hasn't done a great job at creating a flexible narrative for mothers. It's almost binary: You're either a selfless mom or a selfish mom. You can be the selfless mom who lives her life for everyone else or the selfish mom who lives her life only for herself. Neither seems to paint an accurate picture of the mother you are or want to be, which is likely a little bit of both. Some days you are the selfless mom, so busy helping your family you don't even have the chance to even think about your own self, and then other days you take time to fill your own cup. You actually get to create your own identity, which is filled with the many aspects of you all wrapped into one. So the next time you feel like you must pick one of the extremes, know neither of the prescribed roles fits who you really are—you aren't either selfless or selfish; you're simply you.

Today jot down the many different traits of your identity. Allow them to contradict one another: This is what it means to be human, a woman, and a mom. You can be silly and serious; you can be driven and adore alone time to relax. All of this is who you are, and allowing this truth will give you a deeper sense of comfort in your own skin.

Day One Hundred and Seventy-One: Not Everyone Is a Superstore

When you can't find what you need,
it's something that exists inside you.

If there is someone in your life that continues to disappoint you, take a moment to ask yourself if you're treating them like a superstore. You know how superstores sell almost everything you want and need? Are you treating that person like someone who has all the things you need when really they just don't provide what you're looking for? That person might be more like a small specialty store; maybe they sell one or two things you need, but all that other stuff, it's just not in their inventory. This doesn't mean you shouldn't be sad, disappointed, and upset that someone you love is unable to give you what you need, but it does help you change where you shop. Maybe you have a parent who you wish would give you more support, but you've realized they just can't give that to you, so you feel all the feelings about it and also find that support in a partner, friends, or other family members. Even a superstore doesn't have *everything* you need, which is why you can work on providing yourself the things you need too.

Today think about who your go-to people are for support in parenting. How about support in relationships? Are those people able to give you what you need?

Day One Hundred and Seventy-Two: When You're Embarrassed

Your child's behavior does not qualify how good of a mother you are.

Do you feel like you're easily embarrassed by your child? You're not alone; it's normal to feel embarrassed when your toddler is making a scene disrupting everyone's peace or when your teen's new clothing style draws everyone's eyes to the both of you! However, if you feel like embarrassment is a recurring feeling, there may be a little more to the situation than meets the eye. Our world has done a great job to make you feel like your child is an extension of you, almost like your child is this living, breathing, walking resume of how great you are. It's set you up to attach your worth or image to your child's behaviors. So naturally, if how accepted you feel is based on something external—like a small human who is new to many of the experiences in this world—then yes, you would certainly feel constantly embarrassed, out of control, and probably a little angry. So the next time you feel embarrassed by your child, view that as an alarm that says, "I am making this about me when it's not" and then confidently use your compassion to guide your child because you've freed yourself from letting your own stuff get in the way!

A helpful reminder to jot down today is "It's not me against my child; it's me and my child against this big feeling they're having."

Day One Hundred and Seventy-Three: Family Boundary Bouncer

Saying no to others is often saying yes to yourself;
that's a no that's worth a lot.

Being a mother is pretty much like being a bouncer at a nightclub. You are in charge of who gets in and who gets access to your family. This isn't an easy job because there are a lot of people who believe they should get VIP access and enter whenever they want (often your or your spouse's family of origin). But let's think about an actual nightclub—the purpose of the bouncer is to keep the club safe; there can't be too many people or it's just not enjoyable or comfortable. The same can be said for your family: You are there to preserve the quality of your family's life. If you have too many plans and too many visitors, it gets overwhelming, and when everything hits the fan, it comes back to you to handle. So since you're the bouncer to the most important selective club you know—your family—allow yourself to use your judgment when it feels like it's too much. You are allowed to delay plans, cancel plans, or change plans as needed so that you and your family can have a happy, healthy, and safe environment. Saying no to others is often saying yes to yourself.

Today have a conversation with your spouse, coparent, or family members about your role as the family bouncer—it's important to explain that your selectivity isn't about being rude, but about putting your family's energy, time, and rest first.

Day One Hundred and Seventy-Four: Playing

Your children call you to slow down, let go, and have fun—answer the call.

Do you ever feel guilty for not enjoying playing with your child? It may be hard to admit, but many mothers feel this way, and there's good news for you: This has nothing to do with loving your child; it actually has very little to do with your child. Playing requires you to stop "doing," requires more "being," and requires you to be vulnerable and out of control: These are three things that are difficult for moms to do! So when your child says, "Mommy, come play with me," it's not your child you are resisting; it's how play makes you feel. It's hard to slow down and start to feel things that are usually pushed down by being so busy. Think about when you try to play with your child; you try to focus, but then all these thoughts and feelings pop up because you're so programmed to be busy! So the next time you think, "I should play with my child," don't do it for your child, try it out for you—the more you can let yourself "be" without judging yourself for not being productive, the more you will slowly lean into play and maybe, *just maybe*, enjoy it!

Think about one way you loved to play as a child. Did you have a favorite game? Tell your child about it and ask them to join you in some old-fashioned fun (okay, not that old-fashioned, but you get it)!

Day One Hundred and Seventy-Five: Rethink Multitasking

In a world of habit stacking and hacks, take a moment to simply enjoy what you're doing.

If you're a mom, you're a multitasker; the two go hand in hand, don't they? You're washing the dishes and breaking up a fight; you're sending an email and heating up dinner. Sometimes you have no choice but to do two or three things at once. Yet with multitasking come feelings of not-enoughness and lack of connection. Multitasking gets things done, but it doesn't leave you feeling fulfilled. This is because when your body has to switch back and forth between tasks, your nervous system is heightened and you can't fully sink into the present moment. By no means is this entry suggesting you stop multitasking, but it is suggesting you allow yourself the freedom to not multitask just because you can multitask. Rather than do two things at once, let yourself do one thing and then the other. See how you feel when you intentionally allocate five minutes to each task instead of cramming two tasks into ten minutes. It may feel foreign, it may feel wrong, but your body and your mind will thank you for it.

Tonight intentionally pick one task to do on its own. Maybe instead of brushing your teeth and washing your face at the same time, you separate them. Try out the slow, intentional process of single tasking rather than multitasking.

Day One Hundred and Seventy-Six: Play Is Productive

Play is an invitation to make fun the sole purpose of your moment.

Many times you can't play with your child for good reason. You have things that must be done—like making dinner and paying the bills. Then there are other times where you technically have the time to play with your child, but the call to stay productive is strong—there's a pile of laundry waiting to be folded, a house to be organized, and emails to be answered. But did you know that play is productive too? Play is not only productive in building and strengthening the relationship you have with your child, but it's also productive for your nervous system. Play is one of the very few things you can do that's purely for enjoyment, and when you're fully invested in fun—even if it's only for ten minutes—your body is given the chance to be in the present moment and is released from the constant thinking of the future or the past. So the next time you think playing is a waste of time, know that you're not only going to feel more connected to your child, but you're also going to feel much more connected to yourself.

If playing is difficult for you, start small: Set a timer for five minutes with your child and tell them they get to pick any game they want and you'll play that with them, then after the five minutes are up, you get to pick your fun activity.

Day One Hundred and Seventy-Seven: The You of the Past

The you of the past is who brought you to the present—be kind to her.

If you've heard the phrase "Comparison is the thief of joy," you may have nodded your head in acknowledgment of how unproductive comparison can be. Today you're going to take the phrase and apply it to yourself: comparing the you of the past with the you of the present. The you of yesterday, last week, and last decade deserve to be free from today you's judgment. Why? The only way you're the you that reads this today is by the wins and the losses of the you from the past. Guilt can be tricky; it may creep in to make you feel bad about the past—the time you yelled or the time you forgot a birthday party invitation—but it can only serve you if you use it as a tool to move forward, not backward (where you have no power or control to make changes). So remember, the you of yesterday was doing the best she could and she's who you can thank for getting you here today.

Think about one of the biggest lessons the past version of you has taught the current version of you. Thank her for that; she's done some great work.

Day One Hundred and Seventy-Eight: Remember to Float

You can't control your child's feelings, but you can control how you respond to them.

Learning the best way to approach parenting is a lot like swimming. Sometimes there are the biggest waves imaginable—waves of feelings and behaviors—and as much as you feel like you should fight your way through them, don't. Instead *float your way through them.* Floating isn't the same as giving up or sinking; it's keeping your head above water and conserving precious energy. When your child is having big feelings, you aren't able to control those feelings, but you are able to control how you respond. Imagine yourself floating in a huge body of water: You're calm; you're okay. You're neither swimming nor sinking; you're just making your way through the moment. Floating in a tough parenting moment means less talking and less convincing and more observing and allowing the big feelings to pass. While it may feel passive, it's actually rather productive. Allow yourself to float the next time you feel the urge to fight the waves of your child's emotions. See where the floating takes you, and hopefully it will lead you and your child to calmer waters.

Swimming 101 is all about learning to float, right? Most children are taught to float before they learn to swim, and this is no different in parenting. Today take a moment that feels tough and practice floating through that moment.

Day One Hundred and Seventy-Nine: Time Away

Connection to yourself fosters the connection to your child.

You know that taking time to yourself and away from your child is healthy, but when you finally get that time away, you can't help but feel a little guilty. What if you miss something? What if your child is upset with you for leaving them? These are all valid points, yet there is one other very important point to note: When you take time to reconnect with yourself, you create the opportunity to create a deeper connection with your child. How? When your needs are met, you feel more grounded and able to stay present with your little one. Not that every nonparenting move you make has to somehow benefit your child, but it does in fact support you and your child. When in doubt, take care of the human who takes care of all the humans in your family—and everyone will benefit.

Today make a plan to do something just for you within the upcoming week.

Day One Hundred and Eighty: Replace "Use Your Words"

Replace "Use your words" with "I'm here when you're ready to talk."

Hypothetical situation here: Imagine crying to your friend or spouse and their first response was "Use your words," could you imagine? You'd probably feel even sadder, more misunderstood, and less likely to turn to them again. So why in the world would you use this phrase with your child? Of course it's okay if you've said this before, but if you'd like a more effective way to get your child to communicate their feelings and needs, think about what you would like in those moments. Would you like comfort? Would you like validation? Take what would help you through your sadness and try that out with your child instead. If your child is too upset and emotional to speak, it's okay to sit with your child until they're able to talk. When in doubt, always ask yourself what you would need in a tough moment and use that approach with your child.

Think about an older approach to parenting you weren't too keen on from your childhood that you've replaced with an updated version that works for you and your child. It might seem small or obvious, but it's huge. Take a moment to soak in the shifts you've already made for your family; they are pretty wonderful, aren't they?

Day One Hundred and Eighty-One: Look Beyond Big Behaviors

Behind every big behavior is an even bigger feeling.

Your child comes home from school and slams the door. While you aren't fond of their behavior, something tells you to focus on that later and first tend to the feelings that may have prompted their behavior. You knock on their door and let them know that you'll give them space, but that you're here to talk when they're ready. Eventually they let you in, explain what happened at school, and start to cry. You're able to connect with your child, help them through tough feelings, and solidify that you'll always be their safe place. This was able to happen because you know that *behind every big behavior is an even bigger feeling*—a feeling that longs to be noticed, tended to, and cared for. Sure, you'll address the door slamming, but because you've prioritized open communication, that behavior will no longer serve a purpose and has been replaced with healthier coping mechanisms like talking, writing, and pausing.

Today create a code word for your child to use when they are feeling too upset to talk. Give your child ideas like "porcupine" or "raspberry" or let them come up with the word all by themselves. This will give your child more awareness over their feelings and give you a heads-up to address the feeling before the behavior.

Day One Hundred and Eighty-Two: Quality Time over Screen Time

Children will choose quality time over screen time when you do the same.

Screens play a role in your family's day-to-day life, and while they can enhance, educate, and entertain, they can also be a source of strain, stress, and separation. If what once became a fun pastime or a short-term babysitter now prevents you and your child from quality time, here are three steps to shift from screen time to quality time:

1. Assess what your own relationship with screen time is like: What do you use screen time for? Is it to check out, to avoid tasks, to pass time? Or do you use it in ways that enhance your life like entertainment, education, connection, and so on?
2. Slowly reduce screen time by replacing it with highly enjoyable alternatives.
3. Be kind to yourself; it's not easy to make changes in our own patterns or our families'. Remember, small, doable shifts are what create true, lasting changes.

Make a plan to replace screen time with quality time by taking a sheet of paper and making a "fun menu." On that menu, list three to five fun ideas that your child can choose from instead of screen time. Ideas: ice cream date, dessert-before-dinner night, movie night, board games, tag, family charades, home spa night, or freeze dance.

Day One Hundred and Eighty-Three: Softness and Sturdiness

Motherhood is a balance of being soft and sturdy.

Motherhood has a way of taking two things that seem so incredibly opposite and making them pair perfectly together. A great example is how as a mother, you possess the ability to be both soft and sturdy. Your softness is what allows your child to feel seen and cared for—your ability to tune into your child's feelings and meet them with compassion. Yet at the same time, your sturdiness is what keeps your children feeling safe—you are anchored and you hold boundaries that keep your family safe, healthy, and resilient. Finding this balance in softness and sturdiness is the very art of motherhood you are mastering today. When your softness isn't rooted in sturdiness, it often leads to you and your children feeling lost, frustrated, and chaotic. When your sturdiness lacks softness, your family can feel disconnected and resentful. Take a moment to assess which you lean toward more and how you can add the other into your day-to-day to feel more balanced.

Today take a sticky note or a piece of paper (and tape) and on it write "soft and sturdy." Place it on the mirror above your sink and let it be a reminder to you each day that you have the ability to be both of these at the same time.

Day One Hundred and Eighty-Four: Asking For Help

Knowing what you don't know is actually a sign that you know a lot.

As a mother, is it difficult for you to ask for help? While this is a common motherhood struggle, it's one that exists because at one time it was adaptive, necessary, and helpful. The good news is that because this is a learned behavior, it can also be unlearned. The first step is to gain awareness behind why asking for help is foreign to you. Here are four common scenarios:

- As a child, you learned that other people in your family had needs or wants that took precedence over yours, so you unconsciously learned to quiet your needs.
- You learned that asking for help is a sign of weakness, so you learned to hush that vulnerability.
- You learned the pain of being let down by others, so you learned to do things on your own.
- You've been so busy helping everyone else that you've never learned how to ask for help yourself.

If all or some of these scenarios sound familiar, allow this understanding to turn into compassion. This is a building block for you to create a new pattern for yourself that requests, accepts, and welcomes support.

Today reach out to the safest person in your life to ask for help. Use this prompt to let that person know this isn't easy for you: "I really want to ask you for help, but this is difficult for me because I don't want to inconvenience you, make you think less of me, and so on . . . "

Day One Hundred and Eighty-Five: Teaching Your Child to Feel

Punishment creates fear-based obedience; modeling teaches confidence-based learning.

Think back to when your child was learning to talk. How did you help them utter their first words? It's likely you modeled and encouraged language, cheered them on, and didn't take their language development personally. It's highly unlikely that you used punishment when your child made the wrong sound or didn't say the right word. So why is it so common to use punishment when teaching children, tweens, and teens how to manage their feelings? The answer is twofold: First, we forget that behavior is driven by feelings and solely focus on the behavior. Second, as parents, *we* are still learning how to handle our own feelings. As a mother, because you want to give your child healthy communication skills, modeling, rather than punishment, will be the most effective tool to do so. The next time your child uses an undesirable behavior, don't jump right in to addressing their behavior; instead respond to the feeling: "I heard you slam the door. You're probably pretty upset; that stinks and I'm here for you when you need me."

Open up the Notes app in your phone and type this cheat sheet as a reminder of common childhood behaviors and their corresponding feelings.

BEHAVIOR	FEELING
Yelling, hitting, kicking	*Anger, frustration, embarrassment, hurt*
Hiding, silence, ignoring	*Hurt, shame, fear, embarrassment, overstimulation*

Day One Hundred and Eighty-Six: Connection-Seeking Behavior

Every child is just looking to get the most love and connection possible.

It's time to rebrand your child's need for attention. Mothers are often taught to see a need for attention as a behavioral issue, but this attitude only furthers the distance between you and your child. Today take a new approach and look at your child's attention-seeking behavior as a *connection-seeking* behavior. This will help *you* feel less irritated and more compassionate and create a bridge for connection. Here are three steps to change the narrative:

1. The moment your child ignores chores, skips curfew, or lashes out, label the behavior as a need for something.
2. Ask yourself, "What need could my child be trying to meet?"
3. Address the behavior assuming it is connection-seeking: "Hey, I saw you forgot to do your chores; what's going on? I'm here to help if you need something."

While it will take time to adjust how you see your child's behavior, over time it will strengthen the connection with your child. You are your child's most trusted source of support, and at the end of the day, your child is behaving in ways to meet their need for connection.

Have a quick conversation with your child about a recurring behavior that causes tension between the two of you by saying, "You know how you do XYZ? I've been thinking a lot about that and I want to know how I can help you when this happens. What do you think you I can do to help?"

Day One Hundred and Eighty-Seven: When Your Child Loses

Your children can be winners even when they lose.

It's generally easy for mothers to celebrate their children's wins. However, it's much harder to witness your child lose. The thing is, your child is a winner when they learn how to lose. Here's how you can support your child in the moments of defeat:

- First, honor the disappointment that comes with losing. Yes, it's okay to be sad, upset, disappointed, or even angry—these are valid human emotions to experience.
- Second, give your child the time they need to move through those feelings even if you want them to move on faster. Remember, your child is different than you are; the more your child feels unconditionally loved no matter what feelings they have, the healthier of a relationship they'll have with their own feelings.
- Third, once your child's feelings subside, have a chat about the experience and then guide them into any next steps they may need to take (congratulate others, prepare for the next game, and so on).

Last but not least, monitor your own feelings too. It's likely you may need to take those same steps with yourself.

Tonight have a family conversation at dinnertime about a time when each person felt like they did their best and a time when they felt like they made a mistake. Letting your kids see that everyone has ups and downs, wins and losses, helps normalize those feelings for your children.

Day One Hundred and Eighty-Eight: Make Mornings Fun

It's a great day to add a little more fun into your morning routine.

When you send your child off to school, the last thing you want is for your child to feel tense or stressed. Yet somehow, most mornings are filled with just that: tension, stress, and regret. If starting the day off on the wrong foot isn't a tradition you want to continue, you can make a shift today. First, take inventory of what mornings were like growing up in your childhood home and note what parts of your current mornings are connected to back when you were a child. This awareness will allow you to unsubscribe from unhelpful habits you might be unconsciously carrying over for no reason other than it's all you know. Second, it's time for you to consciously add fun to your morning routine in areas that typically feel stressful. From making a game out of getting dressed to putting on music—you can pick small ways to make tough moments feel more doable and stress-free. Finally, if your morning has already gone awry, take the extra five minutes to reset so you can leave your child on the best note possible. The key part here is for *you* to enjoy the morning more, too, because you set the tone.

Chat with your child about mornings and see what ideas they have to make your mornings together more fun—maybe letting them choose their favorite songs to get ready to or playing a game, like I spy, in the car. Take their idea and make it happen!

Day One Hundred and Eighty-Nine: Handling Impatience

The moment you realize you're impatient with your child's lack of patience is the moment you realize your patience is what needs strengthening.

Most mothers want their children to learn patience, which is certainly a learned skill and not something we're just born with. But here's a funny question: Have you ever become impatient with your child's lack of patience? Often the very thing you want your child to learn is something you also need to learn too! The good news is that motherhood is a constant mirror leading you to see where your own growth is needed, so if patience is something you'd like to work on, here are a few tricks. The next time your child becomes impatient, flip the lens around to monitor your own patience. Remind yourself that enduring *all* feelings is what creates patience, and as you increase your tolerance, your patience will grow. If it helps, you can even call yourself out to another adult, have a little chuckle about your impatience, and remind yourself the journey to patience is a bumpy one. Finally, patience is learning to be in the moment, even when the moment isn't what you want; therefore, remembering that all feelings are impermanent can serve as a great emotional floatation device.

Today use this one-minute "noting" meditation technique to practice strengthening your own patience. Set a one-minute timer on your phone and close your eyes. Each time you have a feeling, thought, or involuntary movement, simply label it "feeling," "thought," "sneeze," or "itch." Once a minute feels easy to endure, move it up to two minutes, and so on.

Day One Hundred and Ninety: Being Present

It's not tough to be present with your children;
it's tough to be present with yourself.

There is no doubt how much you love your children. Yet you may feel stumped as to why you can't sit with them and play longer without drifting off into your mental to-do list. Or why you struggle to listen to your child's story when all you want is to connect with them. Today is the day you stop questioning the love you have for your child and instead question the love you have for yourself. Are there parts of yourself you learned aren't loveable, parts you learned to hide or push down? When your child asks you to slow down, that stillness allows the parts you've pushed down with staying busy to rise to the surface. Feelings of inadequacy, not-enoughness, sadness . . . all the unpleasant ones you try to avoid. Your child has called you to be present with them, but really to be present with yourself. The next time you slow down and start to feel uncomfortable, get curious about the feelings that are present. Practice sitting with them for a few moments and watch how your tolerance for those moments grows; eventually they won't have such a strong hold over your ability to slow down and be present with yourself and your child.

You can strengthen your ability to stay present by getting more connected to your surroundings using this 4-3-2-1 technique. In your current surroundings, name four things you can see, three things you can touch, two things you can hear, and one thing you can smell. Use this to help calm yourself anytime you feel unsettled in the present moment.

Day One Hundred and Ninety-One: Matrescence

When you welcome a new baby, you're also welcoming a new you and this is the process of matrescence.

Becoming a mother shifts your identity to the point where you may feel like a whole new person. The truth is, motherhood does create a new version of you and this transition into motherhood is called matrescence. Matrescence can be understood as the motherhood version of adolescence where your mental, physical, social, and emotional self is transitioning to accommodate your new phase of life. These shifts are often the reason why you feel like some days you're loving your new role as mom, but then other days you feel lost, monotonous, frustrated, or confused about how you feel as a mom. Learning more about matrescence can empower you in your role as mom, understanding that you aren't supposed to walk out of the delivery room as an expert being a mom. Instead it's a gradual process of shedding the layers of yourself that are no longer needed as you become the new you—which is stronger, wiser, and more connected to yourself than ever before.

Today take what you've learned about matrescence and share it with another mother. Have a conversation about what social or emotional shifts you've noticed since entering into motherhood; doing so will help you and also help another mother better understand herself.

Day One Hundred and Ninety-Two: Change "What If" to "What Is"

There are many "what ifs" in motherhood, and there are just as many "what is" moments you can ground yourself in.

As a mother, you are constantly assessing the "what ifs" in your family's life. What if your child doesn't hit their next milestone? What if your child doesn't make the next sports team? What if your child doesn't get on the honor roll this semester? As much as you are programmed to think ahead, assess risk, and mitigate danger, the "what if" mentality may be keeping you in a state of fear that's hurting you more than helping you. A great way to balance the amount of "what ifs" in your life is to match each one with a "what is" statement. This means when you are thinking ahead about the endless possibilities of what motherhood will look like, you also plant your feet firmly on the ground by noticing "what is" true and right in the moment. If you're stuck on "What if my child doesn't pass their test," you can balance it with a "what is" that affirms, "No matter what, my child will have the tools to get them through their school year." Your "what is" statements aren't here to erase your real worries, but instead to remind you that behind the fear there are endless truths to anchor you.

Today take out two sticky notes: On the first, write "what if" and on the second, write "what is" and place them on your bathroom or bedroom mirror for one week as a reminder to match any fear that pops up with a solid, supportive truth.

Day One Hundred and Ninety-Three: Love and Care for Yourself

The love you give to yourself as a mother comes back to your children tenfold.

Thinking back to your childhood, can you remember witnessing your own mother, grandmother, or maternal figure who modeled their own self-care? While each generation has their own way of caring for themselves, it's likely that you saw little to no self-care with your mother. Today as you explore your identity as a mother, it's beneficial to identify what feelings come up for you around self-care. Do you feel wrong for needing time to yourself? If so, ask yourself where those feelings originated. Where did you learn it wasn't okay to need space and time for yourself? Once you discover the roots of those beliefs, it's important you know that the love you give to yourself actually comes back tenfold to your children. How? Well, the more you love yourself and model that for your child, the more you get to show up as your best self. Not only does this make a more authentic, connected you, but it creates a tradition you are passing on to your children—to love and care for themselves just like they learn to love and care for others.

Open up your calendar and schedule a self-care-based appointment. It can be an early alarm to do a face mask or have a quiet cup of coffee, a nail appointment, or even lunch or a drink with a friend you haven't seen. Make the time to love yourself and watch how that love multiplies within your family.

Day One Hundred and Ninety-Four: The Mommy Meltdown

Preventing a meltdown is much easier than cleaning up the mess of a meltdown.

Yes, moms have meltdowns and they look something like this: You've asked your child to do something repeatedly, you're on your last nerve, and then . . . you lose it, you're a mess, you may want to cry, and you may even want to shout at the top of your lungs, "Doesn't anyone care about me and all I do in this house?" The first step in preventing a mommy meltdown is noticing the signs before it happens: You are overly tired or hungry, you feel emotional, you're hormonal, or you feel unreasonably angry. Think of those feelings as an alarm that needs to be tended to. Then take a step back from acting toward your child and instead take action toward yourself. Make a cup of tea, hop in the shower, turn on music—do something simple that brings you the tiniest amount of joy. Second, when you find that tiny joyous moment, *praise* yourself for that awareness and for already taking a huge step from feeling out of control. Finally, call yourself out: "Wow, I feel so off right now, I probably need a little time-out." These tiny shifts will add up to create big changes in your most tough moments!

Create a mommy meltdown jar. On small slips of paper, write down a few ideas that can help you in a tough moment, and maybe even throw in a candy or chocolate. Know that you can come back to that jar anytime you need a moment to regroup.

Day One Hundred and Ninety-Five: Business and Pleasure

Motherhood is the ultimate journey of finding the balance between business and pleasure.

If you've ever asked yourself, "Why is motherhood so hard?" it's likely you've come up with many answers. One of the answers to this question is that motherhood is the creation of the ultimate blend of business and pleasure. Finding the balance of those two not only can feel counterintuitive, but also the balance changes each day. The business side of motherhood is full of keeping your children safe, healthy, and on schedule, and it tends to take up most of your time. The pleasure side of motherhood are the sweet moments of conversation, play, laughter, and simply enjoying each other's company. The reason motherhood is so hard is that you have to constantly find that balance so that the business side doesn't always drain your battery to the point that there's no energy for the pleasure side. Take a moment to reflect what parts of motherhood tend to be business heavy and create an "appetizer" of something from the pleasure side to shift the balance. It's these small shifts in your day-to-day life that will help you create a motherhood that feels truer to you: more connected, more authentic, and of course filled with more joy.

Today you're going to pick one part of your "business" role of motherhood and add in a small "pleasure" moment. Here's an idea to use for bedtime: Before the routine of resistance begins, announce a freeze dance party or use freeze dance while everyone is brushing their teeth!

Day One Hundred and Ninety-Six: Raising Confident Children

What you believe about your children your children will believe about themselves.

If you want your child to be resilient, to be confident in their ability to handle what life throws their way and develop a strong sense of self-trust, you must get comfortable allowing your child to struggle. Yes, it's the worst feeling to see your child experience discomfort; however, this is the process your child must go through to learn that they can do hard things. Now, of course you don't sit back and say, "Good luck to you, kid, life is hard!" Rather you affirm the struggle your child has and comfort, encourage, guide, and empower your child to do their part to solve their problem. For school-age children, don't run to school to drop off their forgotten homework; instead help them build a routine to ensure they bring their work next time. In their teenage years, don't call their mean friend to give them a piece of your mind; instead listen to your teen's sadness and let them talk out how they want to move forward with that friendship. This is hard work as a mother because your innate sense is to protect your child at all costs, but in the end you will have given your child the tools to solve their problems.

Today create a family motto that reminds you and your child that they can do hard things. Make it a fun art project together or simply create one on your own for the fridge.

Day One Hundred and Ninety-Seven: Family Vacations Gone Wrong

Families take vacations; feelings do not.

Have you ever taken your precious time and money to plan a magical, fun-filled family vacation only to have your child pout about not wanting to be there? This is a *tough* experience as a mother, to care so much about creating an enjoyable family experience for it to be the exact opposite. The most important thing for you to remember is that families take vacations, but feelings, expectations, and sickness do not. As a mother, your best preparation for a vacation is to prepare for it to not be perfectly planned. Not that you should expect the worst, but instead remember that all human conditions that exist at home also exist on vacation, only there's a bit more pressure to "enjoy every moment" and to get your money's worth. What a huge weight on your shoulders! Here's how you can let yourself off the hook: First, talk to your family about what the trip will look like. Second, allow your child to have a say in an activity or a preference. Third, allow for transition time for everyone in the family. This three-step checklist will not only prepare your family to enjoy your time away, it will also allow you to lighten the expectation of perfection and welcome the reality (and even laughter) at how life rarely goes as planned.

Have some fun with your family tonight by discussing everyone's dream vacation: From the location, activities, food, and souvenirs, take an imaginary trip to everyone's fantasy destination.

Day One Hundred and Ninety-Eight: Holding Boundaries Is Hard

A mother's job is to hold boundaries; a child's job is to test boundaries.

It's safe to say that any parenting approach that promises you a stress-free, easy path to holding boundaries for your children is pure fiction. This is because your job is to hold boundaries and your child's job is to test those boundaries, a forever struggle that is necessary for your child's development. Each time you hold a boundary for your child, you are showing them that they are safe and cared for. You are showing them that they can trust that you will always have their best interest in mind. Think of yourself like an anchor for a boat: No matter how bad the conditions get, you are secure, deeply rooted, and doing your job. So the next time you are wiped out after holding your boundary, take a moment to pat yourself on the back, take a breath, and know that you're doing an amazing job being the anchor of your child's life. Because of you, your child will learn how to be their *own* anchor later in life, and that is one of the best gifts you can give.

Try this one-minute anchoring meditation. Close your eyes, take three deep breaths: three seconds in, six seconds out. Place your feet on the ground and your hand on your heart. Feel the contact between your feet and the earth supporting you. Take three more deep breaths and after each exhale, repeat, "I am deeply supported in this moment." Repeat as needed.

Day One Hundred and Ninety-Nine: Keep Trying

Behind every motherhood win is a hundred failures.

What do you tend to reflect on? Are you more concerned with your wins or are you laser focused on your misses? The answer may be different depending on the parenting scenario, but today you're going to focus on the fact that no matter what, you've continued to try. You see, the parenting wins are wonderful—soak them up, breathe them in, and enjoy those sweet moments. The parenting fails, they hurt, they burn, and they never feel great. But what both the wins and the fails have in common is that you have continued to try, and without those fails the wins would have never come about. Today take a moment to appreciate your tenacity and your ability to try to get things right, to try to do better, and to love yourself more and more each time you try. This reminder can stay with you forever, because even when things haven't gone right, you'll remember it's the fact that you keep trying that matters most.

Today pay attention to any parenting win you notice, whether you got out the door on time or you got an extra hug from your child. Savor the moment and remember to credit your tenacity—even despite many previous failures—for bringing you that precious moment.

Day Two Hundred:
Ask For Feedback

*Children learn how to respect their parents
by being respected by their parents.*

Rarely are children asked for their feedback about family life. Think about it: Did your parents ever sit you down and say, "We'd love feedback on our parenting; how can we do better?" Probably not! Yet what tends to yield cooperation in a company, team, or group is feeling appreciated and respected and being an integral part of a system. You can use this same principle with your child by checking in with them about their experience as a member of your family. Today start by asking your child, "Hey, sweetie, I was thinking about our family and how we could make it even better, even more fun, even more loving . . . I'd love to hear what your ideas are." Your one and only goal here is to listen: Listen to what your child is saying; listen to the words, the themes, and the deeper feelings that lie beneath. Listen without distraction, and if your child isn't in the mood to chat, try again at another time when your child is intentionally trying to get your attention. Small moments of connection like these show your child that you care about what they have to say and that their opinions matter—a feeling that strengthens your and your child's bond, connection, and mutual respect.

Tonight at dinnertime, ask your child for feedback: "How could we make our family better?" Once you ask the question, be sure to practice active listening and reflect back what you've heard.

Day Two Hundred and One: Lighthouse Mothering

You can't control the waves in your child's life,
but you can teach them how to surf.

If you want to have a positive, trusting, loving, and respectful relationship with your child, a great analogy to use is that of a lighthouse mother. A lighthouse mother acts just like a lighthouse on a coastal hilltop: You're a guiding light in your child's life yet doing so at a distance that still allows your child to make their own choices. You don't try to control your child; you allow them to choose a path that you'll continue to watch over. In times of need, you're there to guide them rather than shame them. In times of joy, you shine a light on their wins, successes, and happiness. As a lighthouse mother, you are trusted because you remain steady, sturdy, and reliable—your boundaries and rules are explained so that your child understands your "why." You respectfully communicate with your child, and because of that, your child knows they are trusted, respected, and allowed to share their thoughts without punishment or shame. The next time you feel lost in motherhood, ask yourself how you can be a lighthouse mother and let those principles guide you.

Today cast your light on your child's goodness. Highlight what you see your child doing right and let them know how proud you are of their choices.

Day Two Hundred and Two: Motherhood Isn't a Competition

Comparison doesn't have to steal your joy; instead it can be used to shine a light on ways to create more joy.

In today's world, everything can feel like a competition, including motherhood. Whose child got into honors classes, whose career has pulled ahead, or who has lost the baby weight the quickest . . . all these comparisons are traps that keep you feeling like you'll never be a first-place mother. That's because motherhood isn't a competition. You're not competing against anyone. Sure, you're aware of what other mothers are doing, but you're not running the same race. You have your own path, your own unique set of advantages, and your own individual hurdles. When you notice that you're looking into someone else's lane, note what you admire and ask yourself, "How do I believe achieving this would make me feel?" It's likely you'll find that it's less about the accomplishment and more about how you *believe* you'd feel if you were to achieve that goal or status. So the next time you're in a motherhood competition state of mind, remember to use comparison as a tool to reflect on what it is you truly want to feel.

Think about something you want to achieve as a mother. Maybe it's a clean kitchen sink at the end of the day or maybe it's no more yelling. Now ask yourself, "How do I expect to feel once I achieve that?" Take that feeling and write down two other ways you can achieve that feeling. This will help you use comparison to expand the joy in your life.

Day Two Hundred and Three: After-School Connections

Giving your child the space to "be" after a whole day of "doing" is a beautiful way to say "I love you."

Have you ever tried to chat with your child after school only to be met with one-word answers, frustration, or silence? It's disappointing for sure, but it's important to remember that your child has been at school for most of the day and at school they are required to be "on," meaning they're in a constant state of giving attention, energy, and focus to others. They have to be alert to answer questions, listen, and learn and be emotionally prepared to handle the social aspects of friendships. So the moment your child enters your space, they know they are safe—they don't have to perform, act, or be on alert. Your child's lack of interest in conversation has way less to do with you and way more to do with their need to decompress and wind down. So the next time you feel the urge to ask your child about their day, try replacing a question with a statement: "I'm so happy you're home" or "I missed you today; it's so good to see you." Allow your child to simply "be" in their safe space, and trust that your presence is what welcomes your child to share about their day. This will truly change the dynamic of your after-school environment.

When your child comes home from school today, switch up your usual inquisition and say, "I'm so glad to see you." Hand them their favorite snack and be nearby, ready to chat if and when they are ready.

Day Two Hundred and Four: Avoid Snowball Guilt

The good you've done is never erased by the mistakes you make.

There are moments in motherhood where one mistake somehow feels like it erases all the good you've done. These moments are best described as snowball guilt. Imagine you're on the top of a snowy mountain; you drop one snowball that's filled with guilt and as it rolls down that mountain, it gets bigger and bigger, collecting more snow and making that one tiny moment into a massive snowball of guilt. This happens because of *recency bias*. Recency bias is when your mind focuses on the most recent event, placing too much emphasis on that moment. In other words, once that guilt sucks you in, you look at your day through the lens of guilt. However, there's good news: Knowledge is power. Now that you know about snowball guilt, you can stop it in its tracks by isolating that one moment of guilt. Rather than letting guilt gain momentum, separate that one moment from the rest of your day, acknowledge it, but then place it aside and call attention to the things you've done right in your day—even if they're as small as "I woke up, I got my kids awake, and I made their breakfast." It's the smallest changes you make that create true, lasting change.

The next time you're having a bad day, remember the idea of recency bias. Has one bad moment in the day made you generalize the whole day as "bad"? This very awareness will help stop your guilt snowball in its tracks.

Day Two Hundred and Five: Your Child's Appearance

The attachment to your child's appearance often has roots to your own childhood.

Do you ever feel tension or a power battle around your child's appearance? You know, those mornings where you want to tell your child their hair is ridiculously messy? Or when you have to bite your tongue about what your teen is wearing? The instinct to protect your child is strong, but when it comes to your child's appearance, it's less likely they need your protection and it's time to check in with your attachments to your child's appearance. Perhaps your child's appearance feels like a representation of your parenting: "What will the teachers think that my child heads into school with unbrushed hair?" Or perhaps there are judgments from your own childhood about your appearance that are now living rent-free in your head, altering how you see your child? Did your mother always demand that your hair be perfect? Did your father comment about your clothes not fitting the right way? Get curious about where the narratives about your child's appearance have come from. Now, of course it's your responsibility to teach your child how to care for their body and dress respectfully, but aside from those basic needs being met, it's important to sort out what parts of that tension are from your past so that you can free yourself and your child from those older patterns of thinking and feeling.

Have a discussion with your child about their favorite way to dress or do their hair. Take a moment to really hear how they like to express themselves.

Day Two Hundred and Six: Cultivating Feeling Awareness

Motherhood is more about dealing with your own feelings than your child's feelings.

Your feelings play one of the biggest roles in how you show up as a mother. Which is why motherhood becomes more about dealing with your own feelings than your child's feelings. Understanding this is like a BOGO. Once you practice becoming more comfortable with your own feelings, it flows over to becoming more comfortable with your child's. Take a moment to think about the last time your child had a *big* feeling; you'll probably notice that you either had your own feelings stewing before your child's experience or felt pretty activated by your child's feelings. This is because *your* feelings are behind the driving wheel, and they are controlling how you parent. You can move away from this reactivity-style parenting by becoming more aware of how you feel. Yes, it sounds simple, but when you begin checking in with yourself regularly to identify your feelings, you gain a greater sense of "control" over yourself, which is really just cultivating self-awareness. As you practice more feeling awareness, you'll find yourself becoming more patient and understanding of your child's big-feeling moments.

Set three alarms on your phone today, each with the title "How am I feeling right now?" Set one for the late morning, the late afternoon, and then bedtime. With each alarm, take a minute to close your eyes and assess how you are feeling. The goal here is to simply create feeling awareness.

Day Two Hundred and Seven: Hand Priority Check-In

When you make yourself a priority,
your other priorities will be taken care of.

When you're a mother, everything can feel like a priority. So when too much gets piled on your plate, it's important to sort out your true priorities. This can be done by using the *hand priority check-in*. Look at your hand. Starting with your thumb, assign each finger a top priority and end at your pinky finger, giving you five priorities. While your priorities are individual to you, a sample would look something like this:

1. Yourself/Your health
2. Your children
3. Your spouse
4. Your work
5. Your home

As long as you can remember to look at your hand, you can remember to check in with your top five priorities.

Take a moment today to trace your hand and write five priorities within the outline of your fingers, or simply write out the five priorities in your life. While this may feel silly or obvious, dedicating time to remind yourself where to focus your energy is a powerful grounding process.

Day Two Hundred and Eight: It's Never Too Late

It's never too late to start over, try again, and change your mind.

Motherhood has a way of really catching you off guard, doesn't it? As much as you try to get it right, it's inevitable (and normal) that you'll have moments when you get it wrong. So when you've made a mistake, the most important thing you can remember is that it's never too late to start over. It's never too late to try again. It's never too late to shift, change, or alter how you handle a parenting situation. Here are three reasons why keeping this in mind will not only help you as a mother, but also help your entire family:

1. Forgiving yourself actually encourages you to do more than shaming yourself.
2. When you give yourself grace to start over, your child will learn to give themselves this same compassion throughout their own lives.
3. The key to successful relationships of any kind is openness to new perspectives, so when you're open to changing what isn't working, you'll be able to navigate the toughest moments in parenting.

Putting your thoughts down on paper increases your chances of creating that change. So today write down one situation in motherhood you'd like a fresh start on and three small steps you can take to make that shift.

Day Two Hundred and Nine: Making Others Happy

There's no better feeling than creating and witnessing moments of joy for your child.

In motherhood, so much joy is found by seeing your children happy, especially when you're a part of creating that happiness. The joy of making your child happy is much different from the *need* to make your child happy. That fine line between wanting to make others happy and needing to make others happy is often blurred for mothers. Most women were raised to prioritize other's feelings and to be kind, caring, and considerate. However, when others' happiness becomes your priority, there's little room for your own feelings, thereby making your happiness dependent on the happiness of others. Often called people-pleasing, this way of living quickly turns into a life of obligation. This becomes tricky in motherhood, because while your intellectual self knows everything your child wants isn't what's best for them, your emotional self feels pulled to eradicate any feelings your child experiences that aren't joyous ones. A question to help ground yourself in these tricky moments is to ask yourself, "Do I want to make my child happy, or do I feel like I have to make my child happy so that I can feel okay?" Be patient and kind with yourself and remember it's the tiny steps you make that add up to create lasting change.

Plan a mini date with your child to do something that truly brings your child joy and be sure to tune into your child's joy—you've created that moment and you deserve to bask in it.

Day Two Hundred and Ten: Releasing Filters

Anytime you use the word "should," make sure your ask yourself, "Where did that 'should' originate?"

If you use social media, you're aware that there are endless filters available to alter your appearance. While the ideas behind these are fun, when they're used regularly, you start to feel like the filtered you is how you *should* look. Similar to those social media filters, you likely grew up with "filters" for your personality, your wants, and your needs. Yet now that you're a mother, those filters aren't working for you anymore and you're starting to take them off. This can be confusing and have you questioning, "Who am I?" and sometimes you may not even notice yourself anymore. So as you grow into motherhood with fewer of these filters, you owe yourself grace and compassion. This is a process; you'll see progression, you'll see regression, and you may even go from one end of the spectrum to the other, but eventually you'll find a balance that feels right. With this new balance you can start to live your life more authentically, more comfortably, and of course more connectedly.

Make time for a conversation with someone you love about what parts of your life would be better without a filter. Filters that might resonate with you: people-pleasing, perfectionism, martyrdom, over-achieving, chronic busyness, type A control, or a victim mentality.

Day Two Hundred and Eleven: Swap Guilt with Gratitude

Gratitude practiced becomes gratitude that's permanent.

When you get time away from your child, a mix of feelings can swirl around inside you. From feeling excited and relieved to feeling worried or guilty, it can be confusing how to handle balancing being a mother and being your own person who needs time to be alone, recharge, and have fun. A great practice is to swap that guilt with gratitude. Rather than pretend your guilt doesn't exist, acknowledge that it's there and then bring gratitude to the front of your mind. Gratitude can come in many forms: You can be grateful for childcare, for the resources to take a vacation, or simply that you have loved ones and friends that you get time to connect with. The goal in using gratitude is to allow yourself to experience the pleasant feelings in your life just as much as you experience the not-so-pleasant emotions. The more you seek out the good, the more it will be accessible to you on a regular basis.

Today make a plan to take time for yourself, whether it's a vacation or a coffee date with a friend. You owe it to yourself to have time on the calendar where you can be grateful to yourself for making that time.

Day Two Hundred and Twelve: What Is Underneath This Anger?

The more you get to know anger, the more you realize it's not so scary after all.

Have you ever been angry at your child for being angry? You don't want your child to be angry, so you use your anger to stop it. The irony! There's a difference between being angry together with your child—feeling indignant or protective when they've been mistreated by others—and being angry at your child's anger. The latter happens not because you lack love for your child, but because you lack the coping mechanisms to handle anger. One of the most helpful tools in dealing with anger is remembering that underneath anger is a vulnerable emotion. Visualize an iceberg: Anger is the part above the water, but underneath that water are feelings of sadness, fear, worry, hurt, powerlessness, injustice, embarrassment, and more. Knowing this is key to understanding what is driving your anger and to helping you disarm it: "I'm angry because I am worried I can't control my child" or "I'm angry because I'm embarrassed my child yelled at me in front of others." The more you can get in touch with what lies beneath your anger, the less likely your anger will have control over your stressful parenting moments.

The bonus to understanding anger is that you'll also be able to help your child with their anger. Today pay attention to any anger you see your child experiencing and get curious about what vulnerable feelings might be driving their anger.

Day Two Hundred and Thirteen: Use the Three Cs Against Rigidity

Curiosity and compassion paired with confidence are the three Cs that will never let you down in parenting.

When your child is stuck in a moment of rigidity—for example, your child isn't willing to change their mind or they are unable to adapt to a new schedule—you may respond with that same level of rigidity: "Sorry, kid, you have no choice; it is what it is." While of course it's your job to hold boundaries, fighting rigidity with rigidity may create an unpleasant experience. Instead try using the three Cs approach: curiosity, compassion, and confidence. Using *curiosity* means you ask yourself what underlying feeling or feelings are holding your child back—perhaps it's fear or discomfort. Using *compassion* means you understand that deeper feelings exist and you meet your child at the emotional level rather than the behavioral. Using *confidence* means you utilize the first two Cs in knowing you are still in control yet you allow wiggle room to assert that control: "Listen, it probably feels unfair to have to do things you don't want to do and I know it's hard to be a kid because of that, but today our plan can't change, so let's talk so we can get you feeling better about this." Using the three Cs will not only help you; it will also show your child how to move through being stuck.

Take a sticky note and write down the three Cs for you to remember this week. Place the note on your fridge, bathroom mirror, or front door to remind you the next time you need them.

Day Two Hundred and Fourteen: Dealing With Unsolicited Parenting Advice

No mother desires unsolicited parenting advice.

If you've ever received unsolicited opinions about your mothering, you've probably felt an array of emotions: angry, hurt, and bothered, to name a few. When this advice comes from someone in your family, it can feel tricky to navigate. You want to kindly make sure your boundaries are known, yet you may also feel under attack and the need to defend yourself. When you feel caught off guard and are not sure how to respond, know that you *don't* have to respond. You can simply nod, take time to process, and respond later. Another option is to respond with "I've never thought of it that way." However, if this is a recurring issue, it can be helpful to talk with this person. Here's a framework for a productive conversation around your boundaries: Assume their good intentions, share how you feel, and ask for a change. For example: "I know you mean well, but when you share that kind of advice it feels like you don't trust my abilities as a mother. I'd love you to support me in other ways, and here's how . . . " Of course you can tweak this to your needs, but the goal is to create a kind yet firm boundary as to how you will be treated so that you don't end up being the "bad guy" by reacting without a plan.

In a notebook or in your Notes app, draft a brief statement you plan to use the next time someone gives you unsolicited parenting advice.

Day Two Hundred and Fifteen: Try Bedtime Chats

Time is love.

The moment you see your child after school, you're dying to know how their day was, but all you get is a one-word answer: "Fine." You wonder: What gives? Is your child mad at you? Did something happen at school? Why won't they talk to you? The truth is, at that moment you aren't going to get the answers or the connection you're seeking. So instead give yourself and your child the permission to revisit their day when they are more open to discussions. For most kids, it's around bedtime. Bedtime is an amazing opportunity for you to connect with your child, mostly because *they* are ready to connect. To do this, you may have to shift around your evening routine, as you'll need to add more time to account for chats. To your child, your time is love. Therefore, making adjustments that work for you *and* your child will continue to deepen your connection; the more you can open yourself to making small shifts, the more likely you'll start to see real, lasting change.

Tonight at bedtime, consciously carve out an extra ten minutes for conversation and let your child know, "Hey, I really wanted more time to hang out with you." It doesn't have to just be questions about their day; it can be fun, like dreaming up vacation ideas or asking them, "If you could invent something, what would it be?"

Day Two Hundred and Sixteen: Let the Mess Become a Memory

Let a mess become a memory instead of a lesson.

Motherhood is messy, figuratively and literally. As much as you need order in your home, sometimes the stress of being on mess patrol can be draining. It not only drains your energy, but it can drain the fun you have with your child. Sometimes it can be helpful to let a mess become a memory. If your toddler dumped their toy bin, your child moved all their stuffed animals to the living room, or your teen has a collection of bath towels strewn along the floor, rather than make it a fight, make it fun. You can use sarcasm or dramatic play or simply laugh at the ridiculousness of the mess. The goal here is to disarm yourself and look at your child as a human who has their own agenda that's likely not keeping everything clean. It's also a chance to join your child in the predicament that they've created: Race your toddler to clean up, start talking to the stuffed animals, or playfully applaud your teen for bathing so frequently. You can absolutely have discussions about order and caring for their things, but you can also have fun while doing so.

Who said cleaning can't be fun? Schedule a relay race of cleaning in your home. Take three tasks and make them a race. Make it a fun family tradition to take towels and scoot your bottoms across the floor to mop. See who can make beds the fastest or who can fold laundry the quickest. Sprinkle in fun wherever you can!

Day Two Hundred and Seventeen: Learning Emotional Language

*Your children might not always hear what you say,
but they certainly "listen" to what you do.*

As a mother, you want to give your child the world, and when it comes to giving your child the emotional tools to thrive, you may struggle in some of these areas. This is because as much as you have the best intentions, you are likely still learning to develop these emotional tools for yourself. Think of it in the same way as wanting your child to learn a foreign language; you could buy your child all the books, courses, and even a tutor, but when you don't speak the language yourself, it's going to take much more time for your child to learn that language. This is why motherhood calls you to become the most conscious version of yourself—the things you want to give your child must also be given to yourself. So the next time you feel upset your child doesn't have patience, look inward to see where you can foster more patience. The next time your child is worried, look inward to see what your relationship with worry is. The more you can look inward, the more you can project what you've learned outward to your child.

Make a plan to invest in yourself. Know that you're already doing that by reading this book, but take it one step further and save a podcast, take a course, or book a session with a therapist or coach. The more you learn about you, the more comfortable in your skin you'll become.

Day Two Hundred and Eighteen: The Reverse Golden Rule

Treat yourself how you treat others.

The golden rule is "to treat others the way you want to be treated," and is one of the most beautiful phrases to encourage kindness, respect, and support. Yet as a mother, it's likely you might need to reverse this golden rule: to treat yourself how you treat others. Yes, you give your children the world; you think about your family, your friends, your kids' teachers, and probably the mail carrier too. But what about you? Do you treat yourself how you treat others? Are you more likely to pick up a brand-new outfit for your child because it was cute rather than do the same for yourself? Are you compassionate when others make a mistake, but when you mess up you drag yourself through the mud? If so, let's make you the focus of the golden rule today and ask yourself, "In what ways can I treat myself more like I treat the ones I love?"

Today's takeaway is to pick one thing you are most proud of that you do for your child, partner, family, or friends. Whatever that thing is, make a plan to do the same for yourself.

Day Two Hundred and Nineteen: Parenting with Compassion

Parenting is hard; compassion helps.

It's not easy being a mom; you're in charge of keeping everyone in your family on schedule even when they don't want to be. And because of that, it's also not easy being a child, having someone else in charge of most of your decisions. Pause for a moment to let that sink in, that both you and your children have tough jobs at times. When you acknowledge that, it brings space for compassion. But what does compassion look like? Here are *four real-life practices* to breathe more compassion into your life during challenging moments:

1. Compassion is acknowledging that the situation you are in *is* hard rather than gaslighting or shaming yourself that somehow it shouldn't be.
2. Compassion is acknowledging that the situation you're in may not have a quick and easy solution.
3. Compassion looks like truly forgiving yourself for not handling your present moment perfectly.
4. Compassion means remembering your child has little autonomy over their life and is still learning how to communicate their feelings and needs.

Finally, remember that compassion is simply allowing yourself to accept that what you are experiencing is tough while still taking the steps you need to move forward.

Take one of the four compassion practices from this entry that feels most relevant in your life right now and set a daily calendar morning reminder for the remainder of the week to remind yourself that you can add compassion in the tiniest moments.

Day Two Hundred and Twenty: Reflect Back

The you from five years ago would be so proud of you today.

Have you ever taken a moment to reflect back on all you've accomplished as a mother? Mothers rarely stop and admire their accomplishments. But from the minute, daily tasks that are completed over and over to the deeper, inner work that's helped you grow into your role as mom—they are all worthy of acknowledgment. Why? Because the more you soak in and savor the good you do, the more you'll be able to enjoy motherhood—not just in the good moments, but the tough ones too. A great way to do this is by asking yourself, "What would the me from five years ago be proud of today?" First, focus on an external accomplishment: creating a family, keeping a home, your career, your volunteering, your caretaking, and more. Second, focus on your inner achievements, your inner-world wins: trusting yourself, choosing yourself, listening to yourself, healing yourself. The you of today has come so far because of the you from five years ago. You're here right now, with this book in your hand, because of her—and she deserves to be acknowledged, thanked, and loved because of that.

Passing on this experience is a great way to support other mothers in your life: Pick one other mother in your life that you can reach out to and share how proud you are of her—not only will it make her day, it will make yours too.

Day Two Hundred and Twenty-One: Three Stages of Motherhood Identity

Every stage of motherhood is best paired with compassion.

There are three stages of your motherhood identity: the mother you dreamed you would become, the mother you are today, and the mother you hope to be. You may have dreamed of becoming a mother who only serves healthy homemade meals, a mother who never raises her voice, or a mother who keeps an immaculate home. And perhaps now you look around and realize what you thought would be isn't. The truth is that before you became a mother, you had no idea the mental, emotional, and physical journey you'd experience. So naturally, your idealistic vision was bound to not manifest exactly as you planned. However, today you are doing so much more than just dreaming for life to be perfect. Today you are doing the work to create a life where you feel comfortable in your own skin by allowing yourself to experience compassion in motherhood. That compassion you're working on is what will guide you into the mother you hope to be. Whatever your goals are as a mother, know that you can absolutely achieve them when you allow compassion to be along for the ride.

What's one area in motherhood you give other mothers compassion for that you could also extend to yourself? Make this a goal for yourself by the end of the week. Tell your spouse, partner, mother, father, or friend about this to hold you accountable!

Day Two Hundred and Twenty-Two: Your Greatest Parenting Struggle

Your greatest parenting struggle points to the exact place that needs the most healing.

Sometimes your greatest parenting struggle as a mother points to the place where you need the most healing. Sure, it's easy to just chalk it up to your kids being difficult—because they certainly can be! Yet when you reflect on your greatest hurdle in motherhood, it can reveal so much about yourself. The following struggles are meant to open your mind and heart as to why certain areas in parenting might feel impossible for you: The struggle to accept parts of your child can often reflect your own self-judgment. The struggle to handle your child's big emotions often reflects your inability to sit with your own big emotions. The struggle to control your child often reveals how you struggle to feel in control of your own life. The struggle to trust your child often reflects your relationship with your own self-trust. The struggle to feel compassion for your child often reflects the lack of compassion you have for yourself. The struggle to hold boundaries reflects your own self-doubt and self-commitment.

Today take out your phone or a journal and write down what you're feeling after reading this entry. Maybe something has clicked for you, maybe a light bulb went off, or maybe you feel curious or doubtful. Whatever you feel, write it out and allow yourself to process your feelings.

Day Two Hundred and Twenty-Three: The Benefits of Chores

Children must know they are needed and wanted and are a crucial part of the family.

Getting your children to do their chores might be a struggle, so here are three little cheats to use the next time you need to boost motivation for your child to get things done:

1. Start small; break the chore into smaller parts that feel doable. For example, if your child has to do laundry, make one part scooping up the clothes and then the second part tossing them into the washing machine, like a basketball game.

2. Model the chore in a fun way for your child; if they clean the windows, take the window cleaner and make a smiley face to show them how they can still have fun.

3. Make sure your child knows how much they are needed and wanted in the home. Talk about how important their job is; let them overhear you telling another family member how helpful they are or how you like how they do their housework.

Chores are about teaching kids responsibility and to help care for the home, but they are also beneficial because children benefit from feeling needed and from being a crucial part of the family.

Write down three doable chores your child can pick from this week. Next week they can alternate with you or a sibling. Keep chores rotating so that everyone can feel the weight of their importance.

Day Two Hundred and Twenty-Four: Change the Story

The stories you tell yourself become the life that you live.

Let's look at a classic motherhood situation where your child isn't listening to your instructions. When this happens you may ask yourself, "What story do I tell myself about why my child isn't listening?" Meaning what reasoning, explanation, or assumptions have created the story about why your child isn't listening? Perhaps the story might be "My child doesn't respect me," or maybe it's "My child never makes it easy on me." These stories are automatic, unconscious, and a huge contributor to keeping you stuck in a negative pattern. The good news is that you can change the story, and here's how:

1. Identify a pattern in motherhood that you're stuck in.
2. Ask yourself, "What story am I telling myself?"
3. Think about where this story came from and what flaws it might have.
4. Think about what a better story might be that gives you and your child the benefit of the doubt.
5. Replace the negative story with a new and improved story like "My child needs me to follow through more so it's clear I mean what I say."

As you start identifying and replacing the stories that keep you stuck, you'll start to see those patterns break.

Today you're going to dissect one motherhood scenario you want to see change. Open up the Notes app on your phone or grab a sheet of paper and write out the numbers 1 through 5, then use the steps in this entry to find out what story you've been telling yourself.

Day Two Hundred and Twenty-Five: Listen and Reflect

*Children gain confidence to solve their problems
by being allowed to solve their problems.*

As your children grow older your role as a mother is less geared toward solving problems and more geared toward being supportive as your child navigates their own problems. This shift happens slowly; one day you're cleaning up scraped knees and the next your solutions aren't the magic bandage they once used to be. As you enter into this era, your new MO will be listening and reflecting: Take in what your child shares and reflect back what you've heard. Sure, you'll still offer your opinions, advice, and corrections—but the key word here is "offer." You can ask, "You are dealing with so much right now, do you want me to share what I hear is going on?" or "This is tough; I have a suggestion that might help whenever you're open to hearing it." Being a mom will always mean you're there to help your child; it's just that "help" looks different as your child gets older. You are absolutely supporting your child by listening, reflecting, and taking into consideration their own ability to solve their problems.

Children gain self-esteem and confidence to solve their problems by being allowed to solve their problems. At dinner tonight, take a moment to highlight a solution your child recently came up with and let them know you admire their self-trust, confidence, or problem-solving skills.

Day Two Hundred and Twenty-Six: Triple Check-In

Connection to your loved ones breeds connection and clarity to the self.

As a mom, connection is essential to enhancing your life. But because you're a mom, life moves fast. So fast that sometimes you miss out on moments to connect with the loved ones in your life who aren't your children. People like your old friends, new friends, mom friends, siblings, cousins, aunts, uncles, or neighbors. A great way to create time for more connection is by using the *triple check-in*, where you schedule a goal to reach out to three people each week. It may sound silly, but creating reminders works like muscle memory: At first you rely on a calendar reminder going off to call your sister, but after three weeks, you automatically pop on the phone on your way to the grocery store. Using the *triple check-in* ensures you're reaching out to the people you want to connect with, knowing that timing won't always be perfect, which is why you text or call three of your friends and hopefully one is available! As each week comes and goes, make it a point to schedule quick check-ins to laugh, cry, and touch base with your favorite people.

Open your phone calendar or agenda and set a recurring calendar reminder that reads "triple check-in." Schedule it at a time that you're driving or doing housework or any moment where you can check in. Remember, the goal is to make attempts to connect, so even if you don't get to speak, you've laid the foundation for connection!

Day Two Hundred and Twenty-Seven: The Many Parts of You

There aren't bad parts of you as a mother, only parts that do their job to protect you in your role as a mother.

Have you ever noticed that there are many parts to your identity as a mother? For example, there are parts of yourself that are confident and other parts that feel unsteady or uncertain. There are parts of you that are playful and other parts that may be wound-up and inflexible. It's helpful to recognize that your identity as a mother is made up of *many* parts. When you acknowledge all the different parts of you as a mother, you can also learn to forgive the parts of you that may let you down. The next time you lose your cool and raise your voice, rather than the all-encompassing statement "I'm a bad mom," you can isolate the part of you that yelled and dissect what that part of you was trying to achieve. Perhaps that part of you yelled because you were worried or felt uncertain of what else to do. There aren't any "bad" parts of you, only parts of you that are doing their job to protect you as a mother. So the next time you feel like labeling yourself as one thing, remember your many parts and get curious about what job that part was trying to do.

Jot down all the different parts of yourself as a mother. Take a look at how many there are! If you want to take it one step further (and deeper), ask yourself what job each part fulfills and what it tries to protect you from (feeling).

Day Two Hundred and Twenty-Eight: Teacher Appreciation

Help your child's teacher help your child.

When your child goes off to school each day, they spend just as much time with their teacher as they do with you! Your child's teacher is a very important person in their life, which is why building as much of a relationship as you can with them is helpful. Depending on the school your child attends, there are different levels of involvement you have access to. From back-to-school nights, conferences, emails, volunteering opportunities, virtual classroom bulletin boards, or even school messaging apps—you likely have some access to your child's teacher. Make your presence known. Introduce yourself. Share about your child. Make connections. Let the teacher know you're committed to your child's education. Thank them in advance for all they do. And know that it's never too late to get more acquainted with your child's teacher. You certainly don't have to become best friends, but being visible, being approachable, and being kind can truly go a long way for you and your child.

A great way to get to know your child's teacher is to send them a quick "about me" form. The form asks for their favorite colors, candies, coffees, stores, and flowers. Search on the Internet for a premade form, print it out, and send it with a note and a pen for your child's teacher to complete.

Day Two Hundred and Twenty-Nine: Familiar Feelings

Motherhood might be new, but your feelings in motherhood are anything but new.

Motherhood may be uncharted waters, but the emotions that come with motherhood are anything but new. Becoming a mother has a way of bringing up feelings you previously were able to avoid, but now you're forced to deal with. Think about having to handle your child's big emotions; that's a whole new experience you never dealt with pre-children. However, *your feelings* about how to handle your child's big emotions—like feeling helpless, uncertain, or doubtful in your ability to make the right decisions—have roots that extend beyond motherhood. So when you're having trouble making sense of your own feelings in motherhood, it can be helpful to ask yourself, "What about this feeling is familiar?" Making connections with your current and past feelings will help in understanding why you feel so activated. You'll be able to say things to yourself like "Ah, this whole 'No one is listening to me' is pretty crummy, but it's that much harder because it's just like my experience when I was younger. But things are different now; I am absolutely in control."

Today ask yourself, "What activates me the most in motherhood?" and then hypothesize what roots that activation has in your earlier years.

Day Two Hundred and Thirty: Coach Mom

Your family is the best little team you could ever have.

Being a mom is a lot like being a coach on a sports team: You're Coach Mom, your children are players, and you're all together on Team Family, which can be hard to do when your players want nothing to do with your rules, requests, or regimen. Just like a coach makes the best choices for their team by making them do challenging warm-ups, drills, and exercises, you enforce chores, grooming, and homework. You are getting your children ready to be the best version of themselves. While you know you're all on the same team, it doesn't always feel like it in those tough moments. It might just be a phrase, but quietly repeating to yourself, "We're on the same team" can help you regroup and recalibrate. The discipline you teach your children becomes their own self-discipline, the boundaries you hold for yourself become the boundaries your children learn to hold for themselves, and the respect you give to your children as active members on the team becomes their own self-respect. Your family is the best little team you could ever imagine, and you deserve a big pat on the back for being the wonderful coach that you are.

Have some fun with your family tonight by creating your own Team Family. Give yourselves a team name, which can easily just be "Team [Your Last Name]," along with a mascot, a team motto, and team colors.

Day Two Hundred and Thirty-One: The Wonderful You

Praise yourself because you keep trying. Effort alone is praiseworthy.

Because you're a mom, you have the incredible ability to balance business with pleasure. You get your children up and ready for school, they're fed and clothed and cared for, while also giving them all the love in the world, laughing, and enjoying the small moments. For that you deserve a pat on the back every minute of every day! You deserve praise for *attempting* that balance, not just for achieving that balance. Why? Because you keep showing up, you keep making efforts to care for yourself more and your children more, and that is praiseworthy. So today it's important that you take these three minutes to praise yourself for three ways that you balance the business and pleasure of motherhood. List one thing you do out of love that keeps your children safe, list one thing you do out of love that allows your children to feel joy, and list one thing you do for yourself that allows you to be the mother that you are.

Don't just mentally list your three statements, write them down too. Writing down your thoughts and beliefs will help you retain all the wonderful things you do as a mother, which you absolutely deserve to have ingrained into your memory.

Day Two Hundred and Thirty-Two: It's Not about You

*You can respond instead of react when
you stop taking your child's behavior personally.*

If your child's ever gotten upset because you said no to more dessert, it's not about you. If your child has ever stormed off to their room because they can't have their way, it's not about you. And if your child has ever asked for your advice but then didn't take it, it's not about you. Sure, it can feel personal; after all, you've created, cared for, and loved them for their whole life! But what usually happens when you take your child's behavior personally? You fall into the trap of a self-sabotaging motherhood: Taking it personally sends you into a defensive, revengeful, or victimized mindset, which is far from the strong, confident, and loving mother you are. Taking your child's behavior personally causes you to react rather than respond. So rather than act on your feelings of defensiveness, use them as an alarm. An alarm signaling "This isn't about me." So, what is it about? Your child's feelings: feelings they are unsure of how to express or handle, so they use any behavior accessible to them. By not taking your child's behavior personally, you're able to help your child with those feelings and to correct and show how to replace their behavior from a calmer, confident state.

Today if something your child does feels personal, ask yourself, "How is this personal to my child?" This will help you replace defensiveness with understanding and allow you to respond instead of react.

Day Two Hundred and Thirty-Three: Return To Yourself

Motherhood is a return to the most authentic version of yourself.

Becoming a mother changes you. Your body changes, your emotions change, and even the way you see the world changes. Yet what if instead of motherhood changing you into a different person, it's actually bringing you back to yourself? As a child, you unapologetically felt your feelings and you sought out joy regardless of what others thought; you were simply you, your true self. But as you grew up, all parts of you weren't necessarily accepted, so layers around your true self formed. Layers like forming coping mechanisms, pushing down vulnerable feelings, or tending to other people's feelings. Cue motherhood, and some of those layers start to shed. It can feel like you don't even know who you are anymore. Maybe the type A personality that once served you is starting to hurt you, or the people-pleasing person you once were feels burdened by trying to make so many people happy. Motherhood is helping you return to your authentic self. This is the beautiful, yet sometimes brutal process of motherhood, so be patient and compassionate as you get to know the most authentic version of yourself.

Try this one-minute meditation: Close your eyes, take three deep breaths, and put your hand on your heart. Travel back to a time in your childhood where you felt happiest. Imagine what the girl you were then was doing that made her so happy and savor that memory. Take three deep breaths before you return to the present and open your eyes.

Day Two Hundred and Thirty-Four: Two-Ingredient Boundaries

Holding boundaries for your child is how your child learns to hold boundaries for themselves.

Setting boundaries in motherhood is one thing; holding boundaries is another. It can be rather difficult to stand strong when your child is doing everything they can to resist your boundary. There are two very important ingredients to holding your boundaries: *self-trust and self-awareness*. First, self-trust means you trust yourself to set boundaries to the best of your ability. When your boundary is rooted in love and what's best for your child, you can trust yourself. On the contrary, doubting yourself mid-boundary-holding creates confusion within you and creates the potential collapse of your boundary. While it's not about you always being right, it is about your child knowing they can rely on you and trust that you mean what you say. Second, self-awareness means you are aware of your own feelings when holding a boundary. If your child pushes back, you might feel an array of emotions: anger, frustration, helplessness, confusion, doubt, or guilt. Believe it or not, these feelings are more about you than your child; awareness and ownership of your feelings leaves you less likely to react and more likely to remain confident in holding your boundaries.

Think about how you would like to feel when you have to hold boundaries with your children. Would you like to feel stronger or more confident? Would you like to feel more compassionate or empathic? Write those words on a sticky note to remind yourself of where you are headed in your boundary-holding!

Day Two Hundred and Thirty-Five: Searching for Perfect

You might not be the perfect mother,
but you're the perfect mother for your child.

You probably would agree that there is no such thing as a perfect mother, right? Yet most mothers still have this deeply ingrained belief that perfection is the goal. This unconscious drive toward perfection often shows up in motherhood by never feeling good enough. If that feeling is familiar to you, unpack where this idea of perfection came from by going all the way back to your younger years. First, what did "perfect" mean in your family as it related to being a perfect child? Did it mean you never raised issues, never shared your true feelings to keep the peace, or was it being the golden child who always got it right, achieving and pleasing like it was your job? In the present day, how are those beliefs showing up for you as a mother? While you don't always have to dive deep into your past, it's incredibly liberating to realize the past is often what's holding you back! Understanding that old beliefs are in charge of your present-day self can help you sort through which beliefs are worth keeping and which are no longer serving you.

Music is a beautiful tool to release energy. The next time you're in your car or around your kitchen cleaning, play a song that makes you feel free. Let this song be your own little reminder to yourself, each time you hear it, that perfection once helped you—but now it no longer serves you.

Day Two Hundred and Thirty-Six: The Friends You'll Meet

*Every mother needs and wants connection
to the sisterhood of motherhood.*

Throughout your life you form friendships. One of the most pleasant surprises in motherhood is the friendships you've made or the friends you will meet. If you've ever felt alone in your motherhood journey, know that different women will come into your life and serve as supportive, loving people in your life. It can be daunting as a new mom with the pressure of "making friends" and finding your child a friend group, so let this serve as a reminder to trust the process of motherhood. Endless opportunities will continue to unfold during motherhood, from friendships with your children's friends' families to sports, activities, volunteering, parenting support groups, and more. Don't be afraid to reach out to mothers who you've enjoyed interacting with; just because your children aren't friends doesn't mean you can't form a friendship that will support you in motherhood. The truth is, every mother needs and wants a connection to the sisterhood of motherhood. And while schedules and timing don't always align, the more you allow yourself to connect, the more you will naturally attract mothers who want the same thing.

Think about any friendships that need tending to. Take a moment to send a text message to check in with the friend or make a quick phone call to let them know you were thinking of them. A little connection goes a long way.

Day Two Hundred and Thirty-Seven: Hidden Messages

Children are tapped into the truth of your family.

Have you ever made plans to attend a social gathering only to find that your child is in complete resistance? Whether your child says they don't like the people there or they're too tired and need rest—your child is loud and clear about what they want and what they don't want. Have you ever looked at your child in those moments and silently agreed? You might even be thinking, "You know, you're right. I don't want to go either." Should you cancel plans every time your child resists? Absolutely not. Could your child be reflecting a deeper truth that you've continued to push through or ignore? It's possible. Children are wired for truth and are tapped into the unspoken feelings of the family: They say things no one else wants to say, they share feelings no one else is used to feeling, and they are truth tellers. While not everything your child utters is the absolute truth, it's incredibly eye-opening to ask yourself, "Is there any truth in what my child is saying?" The more you can listen for your child's inner wisdom, the more it might guide you to your own.

Look at your calendar for the next month, and with each "extra" on your schedule, check in with yourself by asking, "Does this still serve me and my family?" Perhaps there are a few things you can shed to make more room for what's needed.

Day Two Hundred and Thirty-Eight: Trusting Your Gut

How do you know it's your gut?
Because it comes from love rather than fear.

Have you ever made a decision and then *after the fact* you realized you went against your gut? Maybe you weren't 100 percent certain, but you had a "feeling"? It can be disappointing to realize you didn't go with that deeper, gut feeling, but instead of being upset with yourself, there's something incredible to note: You do have a deeper "knowing" about what feels right for you. Right now it's a whisper, a knot in the stomach, or a funny feeling. Hindsight will allow you to tune into what small signals were going off that you maybe didn't notice beforehand. So the next time you feel regretful over not listening to your gut, remember it's a beautiful opportunity to reflect on your "knowing." It *was* there. You're just learning how to tune into the subtle signals, and over time the signs will become more apparent and you'll have moments when you're wildly comfortable in your decision-making abilities. Keep leaning into your innate wisdom to know what's best for you and your family.

Do a body scan: Think about a trait or quality that you're certain of about yourself, something you've always known to be true. Maybe you're confident in your kindness, intelligence, or humor. Close your eyes and think about that certain quality. Now scan your body from the top of your head down to your toes and note where in your body you experience that quality most.

Day Two Hundred and Thirty-Nine: Are You Overstimulated?

*Awareness is one of the most beautiful
tools in reducing overstimulation.*

A million things going on at once? You must be a mom! You know that nothing about being a mom is easy and sometimes it really is too much all at once. So the next time you feel like you're going to snap, when you're frustrated over a relatively innocuous situation, ask yourself, "Am I mad or am I overstimulated?" Overstimulation is when too many of your senses are stimulated at once and your brain is unable to process that information smoothly. And guess what the most common symptom of overstimulation is? It's irritability. So the next time you notice overstimulation is the root of your anger, there are three things that can help you:

1. **Awareness:** Noting when you're overstimulated helps deactivate your anger.
2. **Switching your setting:** A quick walk around the room or a breath of fresh air can help you recalibrate.
3. **Breathing:** You might not be familiar with breathing exercises, but it doesn't mean you can't learn.

A breathing technique of 4-7-8 is great to help you reduce overstimulation. Try it right now: Close your mouth and inhale through your nose for four seconds, hold for seven seconds, and release your breath through your mouth for eight seconds. The goal is to exhale double the amount of time you inhale. Practice this anytime you need to reset your nervous system.

Day Two Hundred and Forty:
Three Tricks for Meltdowns

The first step in helping your child calm down is calming yourself down.

Children of all ages experience big feelings where they are completely unhinged, dysregulated, and irrational. From toddlers to teenagers, "meltdowns" are difficult for your child to get through, and they are difficult for *you* to get through. So how do you stay calm and prevent your own meltdown? Here are three techniques to keep yourself calm the next time your child loses their cool:

1. Find common ground in what your child is feeling. You know what it's like to not get what you want, to be disappointed, or to feel powerless. This helps you connect to your child in the moment rather than judge their feelings.
2. Remember that your child isn't giving you a hard time; they're having a hard time. This is about your child learning how to handle disappointment and how to handle boundaries.
3. Let your child be upset. Don't resist it. The more you try to stop their feelings or change them, the more you create disconnection between you and your child.

Wait it out, and as difficult as it can be to tolerate your child crying or being angry with you, you are allowing your child to ride the wave of their feelings without shutting them down or shaming them.

In the Notes app on your phone, create a folder for "parenting" and type out these three reminders so that you have them readily available the next time you want support in staying calm amid a meltdown.

Day Two Hundred and Forty-One: Disarm with Humor

You have the power to turn frustration into silliness.

There are the delightful sounds of motherhood like your children's laughter and then there are the not-so-delightful sounds like your child calling your name ten times in a row. Sure, you can ask your child to only ask once or to wait until you're available, but your irritability might still get the best of you. A great tool to help you disarm is humor. And while silliness isn't applicable or appropriate in every scenario, it can be used to take your frustrations down a notch. Here are four fun ways to use humor: First, you can playfully say, "Mom, Mom, Mom . . . Ah! I think my head is going to pop hearing my name so much, you must love me so much." Second, you can turn it into a game by asking your child, "How many times do you think you can say my name? Let's count, go!" Third, say the "moms" to the tune of a song you all know like "Old McDonald Had a Farm." Fourth, you can pretend you're a robot, restaurant server, or butler to overexaggerate your response to their every need. The goal in using humor is to help you regroup and have some fun instead of letting frustration and anger take the wheel.

At some point today, try being silly and playful with your children. Try using a funny voice, dancing, or doing what makes you feel most comfortable playing. Let humor be a part of your daily routine.

Day Two Hundred and Forty-Two: Toss Unrealistic Expectations of Yourself

At any given moment you have the power to create new expectations for yourself.

Just like a retail store takes inventory to manage their business in the best way possible, you can do the same in motherhood. Taking inventory of the expectations you've set for yourself can be an eye-opening experience. First, let's take note of the basic needs you meet for your child every day, because these are often overlooked, and come up with five acts you do without hesitation. Now, let's say on that list you have "prepare meals"; what expectations have you placed on yourself for those meals? Are these expectations helping or hurting you in your business of motherhood? How can you adjust your expectations to enjoy your role as mom more? Second, let's take note of all the extra expectations you've set for yourself. Do you have to have your kitchen spotless every night? Do you have to attend every birthday party you're invited to? Do you have to answer every text message or email right when you get it? There are many expectations you live your life by each day that are likely outdated or incompatible with how your life has changed. Take inventory of your expectations so you can liberate yourself from what no longer serves you!

Expectation inventory: List three nonnegotiable expectations you have for each category: "basic needs" and "extras." List two expectations that you might consider changing. List one expectation you're ready to let go of right now.

Day Two Hundred and Forty-Three: Fix Cranky Mornings

The quickest way to disarm is to make a connection with your child's feelings.

Not everyone is a morning person, and if your child isn't, you know how difficult it can be to manage a morning with a cranky child! There are some small shifts you can make that will release pressure off you and your child. The first shift is to make a connection between your child's crankiness and your own, meaning that instead of being frustrated by their mood, relate it to your own past cranky moments. This reconnects you to your child because you're able to be a bit more understanding. The second shift you can make is to not try to change your child's mood. Often when you try to change your child's feelings, it is received as if you're trying to change them. Instead name what you see: "You seem so tired! Ah, I feel the same. I just wanna stay in bed too!" The third shift is to shift your expectations. If you approach the morning expecting your child to be cranky, you are likely approaching your child with defensiveness, dread, or frustration. Instead use the first two shifts to slowly change your outlook. Applying just one of these shifts will change the dynamic of your morning.

Make a little sign that has two sides: one that says "cranky" and the other that says "not cranky." Announce to your family where this sign is, and that they can use it when they don't want to discuss how they feel, but want to let everyone know. This adds lightheartedness to a tense environment.

Day Two Hundred and Forty-Four: Don't Minimize

Just because you can carry it doesn't mean it isn't heavy.

As a mother, you take on a lot for your family. You do so much, you're just used to it. Your full capacity might even be your status quo. If this sounds like you, a coping mechanism you might be using is *minimizing*, or downplaying, the amount of stress in your life. Even though minimizing convinces you that there's nothing to be too stressed about, your body still experiences the effects of stress. You may brush off headaches, exhaustion, stomachaches, and other physical symptoms when in reality they can be directly correlated with your stress levels. You can change your relationship with minimizing by simply acknowledging the load that you carry. This isn't throwing yourself a pity party, feeling sorry for yourself, or being weak; it's being honest and realistic. The simple act of allowing your mind and body to acknowledge what you carry releases the unnecessary stress of suppressing your truth.

Envision getting a call from your best friend where she tells you she's feeling down and doesn't know why, but then she lists everything she's managing in her life right now. What would you say to her? Now list out everything on your plate right now. Can you say the same thing to yourself?

Day Two Hundred and Forty-Five: The Right Way to Say No

It's not what you say; it's how you say it.

While saying no is a very important ingredient in setting boundaries in parenting, it's ineffective when it's said without any other support. Think of cooking a delicious meal for dinner; do you use one ingredient? It's unlikely. The same can be said when you're delivering an effective and productive no; you need more than one ingredient! The first ingredient is the no—that's the base of your boundary—but you can say no without actually using the word "no," for example: "Screen time is over for tonight" or "We're done with TV for tonight." Now let's add the second ingredient: empathy. The truth is, it stinks when your parent has the power to take away something you want, so remember and show empathy, compassion, and understanding. The final ingredient is replacement. Offer your child a path out of their disappointment; you can give them the next task to focus on or let them know when they can resume their desired activity: "Hey, let's go take a walk before bedtime" or "I can't wait to watch you play your video game tomorrow and finally reach that new level."

Have a chat with your school-age children to get their input. Ask your child, "I've been thinking about when screen time is up. What would be an easier way for you to hand over your iPad? Would you like a five-minute timer? Let's figure this out together."

Day Two Hundred and Forty-Six: Strengths and Weaknesses

*Invest in your child's strengths and watch
how much your child will flourish.*

When you look at your child, you probably see their strengths, their talents, and what makes them so uniquely special. But there are also other parts of your child you see, the parts of your child that you worry aren't "good enough." As wild as it sounds, that has become a defense mechanism for *you*. It's the narrative of "Well, if I'm always on high alert, aware of all the areas I might have a defect or a flaw, I'll be less upset if someone else points that out." Except, when you read that out loud, you realize it keeps you in a constant state of fear and worry and really robs you of the joy to appreciate all the great parts of yourself! So now as a mother, you are hardwired to look at your child the same way. If this sounds like you, here's a great way to shift out of that parenting rut: Start doubling down on all the good you see in your child. If your child is great at math but not so great at reading, get them on a math team; build up the muscle they have! While you'll always help your child develop their areas needing improvement, building your child's confidence through their strengths is just as important.

Today talk to your child about something they're great at or have a great interest in: From sports, video games, movies, or music, you can find a topic that they love and watch them light up as you ask about their strengths.

Day Two Hundred and Forty-Seven: Humor Is a Life Raft

Find the humor in motherhood and let yourself have a good laugh.

As you fine-tune your mothering skills like compassion, holding boundaries, and discernment, there's one skill you certainly have—but it might be buried underneath all the adulting you've had to do—and that's humor. Yes, allowing humor to become a regular part of motherhood is not only essential, it's also a life raft. There are so many parts of motherhood that are unexpected and unimaginable, and sometimes humor will let you float through those moments. Not every situation calls for laughs and chuckles, but when you find yourself in the middle of the biggest mess your toddler has ever made or a pile of laundry your teen has kept hidden for way too long, you can let your anger get the best of you or you can let humor help you float along the way. Let yourself laugh at how ridiculous the traffic is on the way to school instead of shout at the cars that refuse to move. It is beneficial for your child to see that laughter can heal moments of pain, but mostly humor is for you. You deserve to sprinkle moments of joy into your day. Find the humor in motherhood and let yourself have a good laugh.

Today look around for the humor in your day and make sure to write one funny thing down to talk about with your family at dinnertime. Ask everyone else to share something fun that happened to them today too!

Day Two Hundred and Forty-Eight: Navigating Disappointment

You can be grateful and disappointed.

Has your child ever opened up a birthday gift only to have a look of disappointment on their face? Perhaps they were expecting a different toy or a different color shirt. Whether your child "makes a face," forgets to say thank you, or lets you know they don't like the gift—often their disappointment is mistaken for ungratefulness. As a mother, you can use those moments to teach your child about disappointment. Validating a normal human emotion for your child will allow them to be comfortable processing that feeling. Rather than shame a child or tell them they shouldn't be disappointed, you can show them *how* to be disappointed. Here is how to help your child the next time they're disappointed:

1. **Name the feeling:** "You seem pretty disappointed that's not the present you had hoped for."
2. **Normalize the feeling:** "Last year Daddy got me perfume instead of the book I wanted. I was pretty disappointed too."
3. **Model manners:** "You can always come to me and let me know how you feel, but whenever someone gives you a gift, it's important to thank them for their kindness—even if you don't like it!"

These three steps will help you and your child navigate the tricky feeling of disappointment.

Today intentionally model being disappointed in front of your child the next time you encounter your own lighthearted disappointment by thinking through the three steps out loud.

Day Two Hundred and Forty-Nine: Motherhood Is an Experiment

Motherhood isn't about how often you get it right, but how you always show up.

Becoming a mother is similar to being a scientist. A scientist makes her prediction, conducts her experiment, and collects results to find her conclusion, and even if her hypothesis may have not been correct, there is still a great deal of evidence to help her move forward. The tricky thing about motherhood is that rather than see the unfavorable result as valuable, you judge yourself and deem it a "failure." But today you're going to rewire that thought: Your missed attempts in motherhood are part of your scientific method; this is your process as a mom. You make the best choices you can, and when they don't turn out as you'd hoped, you make the small shifts needed. When making these shifts, compassion for you and your child will be extremely helpful. Perhaps you've been doing things a certain way for a while and they "used to" work but now they don't, or perhaps this is your second child and what worked for your first isn't working for your second. This is a process that will take time and patience. So the next time something stops working in your motherhood experiment, remind yourself to nonjudgmentally collect that data and use it toward your next experiment.

What's one motherhood hypothesis you predicted that was successful? Today you are being awarded first place in motherhood for that prediction because it sure is difficult to be a scientist in the field of motherhood (hope that gave you a chuckle).

Day Two Hundred and Fifty: Boundary versus Power Struggle

*Boundaries are rooted in love,
coming from a core family value or belief.*

If you've ever found yourself in a power struggle with your child, this entry is for you. There is a big difference between a power struggle and holding an unfavorable boundary for your child. How do you know the difference? A boundary is rooted in love. It's coming from a core family value or belief like safety and health. When it's a power struggle, it's rooted in fear or anger. You'll know it's a power struggle when your point is less about your core beliefs, you've lost sight of the boundary, or you need to be right to show your authority. It's incredibly humbling to notice when you're in a power struggle. And the truth is, if you're in a power struggle with your child, it's a losing game because being the authority isn't about dominance; it's about knowing you're secure and rooted in doing what's best for you and your child. If you have a hunch you're involved in a power struggle, it's time to give yourself compassion because it's not easy to step back and notice you're carrying on parenting methods that aren't true to your motherhood mission. Take this entry and ask yourself, "Where do I see myself in power struggles and how can I turn them into strong boundaries?"

Make a list to differentiate between what is a boundary and what is a power struggle. Reference this the next time you feel like you might be in a power struggle.

Day Two Hundred and Fifty-One: Strong-Willed Children

All feelings are valid, but all behaviors are not.

It's a proud mom moment when you see that your child knows how they deserve to be treated and they advocate for themselves. Do you love your child's tenacity to create their own boundaries? Absolutely! Do you love that same passion when it's used to resist your boundaries? Probably not!

No one tells you about how hard it is to raise children who know what they want, when they want it! If this sounds familiar, remember to separate your child's feelings from their behavior. You don't have a say in what your child feels, but you do have a say in how your child behaves, so separating the two will help you make space to allow the feelings while not allowing the behaviors. It can be helpful to state it out loud: "You can be mad, but you can't be mean" (this phrase can be helpful to say to yourself too!). You're modeling a way to set boundaries with compassion—a practice your child will learn from you and carry on into their adulthood.

Here are a few ways to separate your child's feelings from the boundary that must be applied: (1) Your child says no to you: "I get that you're angry about dinner, but this is the only option we have." (2) Your child hits their sibling: "You can be angry, but you can't hit. I'm separating you for now." (3) Your teen won't do their laundry: "I'd be pretty upset if I had all this piled up too. How can I help you get started?"

Day Two Hundred and Fifty-Two: Three Rules with Extended Family

The only feelings a mother can manage are her own.

When you became a mother, you certainly had an idea you'd be managing your family, but you probably didn't think that you'd also be managing adult family members: your parents, siblings, nephews, nieces, aunts, uncles, cousins, in-laws, half-families, stepfamilies, and so on. If you're overwhelmed with all the different colorful personalities, requests, or even "demands," then today you're going to get your bearings.

- First, prepare with priorities: Have a conversation with a partner, spouse, sibling, or parent to become a united front. Decide your priorities and boundaries around extended family.
- Second, prepare for "boundary backlash": It takes time to adjust to any new changes in life, especially with family dynamics. Knowing this will help you stay grounded when you learn there are hurt feelings or expressions of disappointment.
- Third, manage plans, not feelings: No matter how hard you try to make everyone happy, someone will still be upset. So rather than try to manage feelings, manage plans instead.

Remember these three steps to approach your extended family with confidence.

Tonight sit down with your partner or spouse to go over your priorities and boundaries for extended family to become a united front: What is working? What would work better? How can you move away from managing feelings and instead managing plans?

Day Two Hundred and Fifty-Three: Stop Overcommitting

Just because you can do it all doesn't mean you have to do it all.

As a mother, energy is your most precious resource. You dedicate most of that energy to the mental, emotional, and physical load of caring for your children, and even when those resources are bordering on empty, you somehow gather up reserves to keep going. Here's the thing: *Just because you can do it all doesn't mean you should do it all.* Today ask yourself, "Am I doing it all because I want to, or am I doing it all because I believe there's no other way?" If your answer is the latter, glimpsing back into your younger years can help you understand where this belief originated. First, where did you learn that you should be able to do it all? When you were a child, were you asked to carry more than you should? Did you hear your parent say yes even when they probably should have said no? When you understand how deeply rooted your desire to overcommit is in your past, you gain more clarity as to why it's not so simple to say no. So the next time you feel compelled to overcommit, ask yourself, "Am I doing it all because I want to or because I believe there's no other way?"

Today you're going to practice saying no to something that doesn't serve you. It can be saying no to a phone call you don't have the energy to pick up or an email to answer or making plans because you simply want more rest.

Day Two Hundred and Fifty-Four: What Makes a Good Mom?

A good mom shows up whether she's at 100 percent or 1 percent.

A good mom doesn't always have their child's hair brushed. A good mom loses her temper and forgives herself for it. A good mom doesn't attend every single school event. A good mom apologizes when she knows she's messed up. A good mom sometimes feeds her kids fast food because it's easy. A good mom says no to playdates because she knows she needs rest. A good mom enjoys time away from being a mother and is unashamed that she wants that time away. A good mom has a messy kitchen. A good mom takes time for herself. A good mom doesn't take time for herself, but wants to. A good mom lets a mess become a memory instead of a lecture. A good mom lectures and then laughs when she realizes her kids probably weren't even listening. A good mom sends her kids to school in mismatched socks and wrinkled clothes. A good mom lets her child have more TV time just because. A good mom lets her kids have ice cream before bed (but probably regrets it). A good mom doesn't have to fill her child's schedule with an activity every day. A good mom does fill her child's schedule every day with an activity. A good mom shows up whether she's at 100 percent or 1 percent. And that good mom is you.

A good mom doesn't always have to be working on herself. Today just be you.

Day Two Hundred and Fifty-Five: Think Before Picking Up Your Phone

*Mothers are allowed to protect their
most precious asset, their attention.*

You are in the first generation of mothers to deal with "urgency culture." You have a constant flow of information coming at you from your phone and computer to the point where you can experience "urgency overload." Urgency overload is the incessant bombardment of being contacted, alerted, and notified. While of course there are phone calls, text messages, and emails you must answer in motherhood, most of that noise is not urgent. Here are three strategies to deprogram that "urgency culture":

1. When your phone rings, ask yourself, "Is this a good time for me to speak?" If not, let the call go to voicemail and call back when it works for you.
2. When you receive a text message, you don't have to reply right away. You can take time to think about your response.
3. When you reach for social media, ask, "What am I hoping to achieve by scrolling?" Perhaps you're bored, avoiding, taking a break, wanting connection, or looking for news or entertainment.

Knowing your intention can help you make more productive, relaxing, or supportive choices like a walk, a talk, or picking up this book.

Time to minimize alerts in your phone: Create a custom Focus filter on your phone that only allows designated alerts or calls. Also, visit the Notifications section on your phone to turn off unnecessary notifications like social media, games, or retail apps.

Day Two Hundred and Fifty-Six:
Get Curious about Your Bossy Child

Inside every bossy child is a child who wants to feel safe and secure.

Do you have a bossy child? Are they always telling you exactly what to say when you're playing together? Are they telling you exactly how they want their hair brushed or dinner plated? It's common to feel embarrassed that you've arrived at this destination in motherhood; you never wanted your child to be bossy, inflexible, or rude. You *can* break free from this cycle by getting a better understanding of what is really going on with your bossy child. As much as it may seem, your child doesn't actually want to be the boss; they want to feel safe, secure, and watched over by you. When your child needs to be in control, it's often from a place of fear or worry. Rather than punish or give in to bossy demands, you can investigate what feeling your child is trying to avoid feeling. You can reassure your child that it's hard to not get what you want, but as their mom you will always make the best choices for them. Getting curious about bossy behavior can help you meet your child's deeper needs.

Create specific moments in the day when your child can be the boss or make a choice. A great way is "this or that": Give your child a choice about their clothes, snack, dinner, book, or TV show. You can also add in a choice you need to make and offer them two approved choices to select for you.

Day Two Hundred and Fifty-Seven: Connection for Connection's Sake

You can connect with your child to get something in return or connect with your child simply to connect with your child.

There is no right or wrong way to connect with your children. You love those special moments of connection to simply enjoy their presence, and you also live in the real world where you make deposits of connection in the hopes that you get to withdraw their love, patience, or obedience when it's needed. Your child certainly can feel the difference when you're with them just to be with them, but you will also feel the difference. How? Because your mind is always thinking of ten things at once, yet when you truly take time to set your phone down and just lie next to your child, you let the noise of your mind stop for just a bit. Whether you're watching your child play a game, noticing how excited they are to show you their skills, or just sitting by their side, admiring how they're playing or laughing—you let yourself take a mental snapshot of that moment. Allow yourself to connect for connection's sake, and your child will be way more inclined to give you that same connection back.

No matter how old your child is, ask them to play the staring game with you today. It can be just you and your child, or you can make it a family championship. Connecting can be fun and silly (and sneaky because this gives you an excuse to stare into their beautiful eyes!).

Day Two Hundred and Fifty-Eight: Look with New Eyes at a "Difficult" Child

Change the way you look at your "difficult" child, and your "difficult" child will change.

You love your children equally, of course you do, but most mothers can admit that one child is "easy" and the other child is . . . not so easy. Your child who sleeps through the night or goes with the flow makes you feel like you're the best parent! Your child who challenges you or always seems in conflict with what the rest of the group wants probably makes you feel like not the best parent! Here are three lenses to see your "difficult" child through:

- **Different:** What if your child is just different from you? Perhaps they aren't as concerned with pleasing others and going with the flow as you are.
- **Determined:** What if your child is simply determined to stay aligned to what feels right for them? Perhaps your child doesn't have the words to express it, but they have unmet needs their "difficultness" is protecting.
- **Duplicate:** What if your child is simply a duplicate of you? Is your child reflecting back parts of yourself that could use more flexibility?

By no means does changing the lens of how you view your child sugarcoat the struggle of motherhood, but it does give you a path out of feeling trapped in a pattern that isn't working.

Remind your child of your unconditional love when they have a rough patch today. Say "I love you no matter what" without a "but" attached to it! Note how that feels to give that love freely without needing a response or action.

Day Two Hundred and Fifty-Nine: Boundaries Equal Trust

Boundaries teach your child that you say what you mean and you mean what you say.

If you've ever picked up a book on parenting, chances are you've read about boundaries. There are endless reasons why boundaries in motherhood are imperative, but one aspect that's not addressed often is how boundaries solidify trust in your parent-child relationship. Your child is hardwired to trust you as a mother, and yet, you must continue to build upon that trust each day. When you set a boundary and follow through, your child receives a message: "My mom means what she says; I can trust her." Even if your child despises that boundary, they can rely on that foundation of trust: "My mom keeps her word; I can trust her." Every time you hold a boundary for your child, you're showing them that you can be trusted. Does this make holding boundaries any easier when your child's doing everything they can to make you budge? Probably not! But what it will do is remind you that you have a very important foundation you're building and it's worth every drop of tears or sweat because you're making sure your child can always trust you.

Build that trust! Remember that cheesy trust fall exercise? Yep, today you're going to have some fun and let your child try the trust fall. Place pillows and blankets underneath them and give it a go!

Day Two Hundred and Sixty: Help Your Child by Helping Yourself

A mother's capacity to handle her child's feelings is only as deep as her capacity to handle her own.

How you can love your child more than anything in the world, and yet somehow that love can't translate into having more patience for your child? Well, it really has nothing to do with your child. Your capacity to handle your child's feelings is only as deep as your capacity to handle your own feelings. When you have uncomfortable feelings like sadness, disappointment, or indignance, are you able to sit with the discomfort until it passes or are you more likely to distract yourself, push down the feeling, or cover up the feeling with something comforting? Most people aren't taught how to feel their feelings; they learn how to get rid of them instead. So naturally, when your child is in the thick of their own big feelings, it can feel wildly uncomfortable for you to witness. You certainly want your child to develop healthy coping skills, yet it requires you to develop those skills for yourself too. You can practice this the next time you feel upset: When you're by yourself, name out loud how you are feeling and explain to yourself why you feel that way. It's incredibly effective to allow yourself to process your feelings before you move past them.

"Sit with it" is a term used often in therapy and coaching. The "it" in "sit with it" can be used as a reminder for today's exercise: I—Identify the feeling; T—Talk about why you feel that way. Try this the next time you're alone.

Day Two Hundred and Sixty-One:
Ride the Wave

Just like a wave doesn't last forever,
neither will your child's big feelings.

Riding the wave is a great way to envision how you can handle your child's big feelings. At first when you see the wave coming, you can mentally prepare yourself: "Meltdown, straight ahead." You can relate to your child's feeling of disappointment and pour on the compassion. Yet after an extended period of time, you might run out of patience. You're all for your child "feeling their feelings," but there is a time limit on that because you and your child have to get back to your lives. Unfortunately, children can be in their feelings for a long time, so this is where you ride the wave. Just like a wave won't last forever, neither will your child's feelings. So ride the wave. It might not be easy, but you know there is an end in sight. You might experience all the feelings—frustration, uneasiness, anxiousness, sadness, anger—but you keep riding that wave because you know that all feelings are temporary. Not only is this helpful for you to remember, but it's also helpful to share this with your child when they feel like their big, uncomfortable feelings will never end.

Is there a difficult situation your child is experiencing right now? If so, think about a story you can tell your child about a time they were able to move through their feelings. Retelling a story of their own resilience is a powerful confidence-building tool.

Day Two Hundred and Sixty-Two: Creating a Narrative for Your Child

What you believe about your child will become what your child believes about themselves.

Can you hear the stories your family's told about you over and over again? You know the stories, the ones that say, "She was the easiest baby, she barely ever cried!"; "School was so hard for her!"; "She was such a picky eater!" Regardless of whether those stories had positive spins or negative spins, they stuck with you. Here's the thing: Those stories aren't really you. Those stories are someone else's *perspective* of you. While you might automatically accept those stories as your truth, it's important to ask yourself how that idea of you has shaped you today. Because here you are, decades later, remembering this story about who you are. This is the power you hold in creating your child's narrative. Who you think your child is, what you think your child can or can't do, is exactly who your child believes they are. Today think about creating a narrative for your children. What do you want them to grow up knowing about themselves? Believing about themselves?

Rewrite your narrative today. What were your strengths as a child? How did the challenges of your life affect you and ultimately make you who you are today? This can be a few sentences, but think about what qualities you wish were highlighted and encouraged more and be sure to include those.

Day Two Hundred and Sixty-Three: Preparing for Mondays

*At any given moment, mothers have the
power to change the mood of their home.*

You know how when there's a possible storm coming, you prepare your home accordingly? You stock up on batteries, water, and food, and you also mentally prepare yourself to be stuck in your house with your family! You can use that same preparation strategy for heading into Mondays. After a long weekend of being out and about, going to bed later, and knowing there might be some crankiness on Monday, you can prepare yourself and your home for the possibility of a "storm." Here are some ideas for you to get started "storm prepping" for your next Monday:

- **Make dinner easy:** Order out, pre-prep on the weekends, or use paper plates for an easy cleanup.
- **No-laundry Mondays:** Only tidy up as needed or make it a rule to do no laundry on Mondays.
- **Fun Mondays:** Don't create unrealistic expectations for the first day of the week; maybe even create a fun ritual on Mondays to watch a movie and call it "movie Mondays," or play a board game.

You have a great deal of power in shaping the mood of your home, so do what you can to help your family enjoy (or at least endure) Mondays.

Weekly rituals create a sense of calm, connectedness, and belonging within your family. Today, pick a small "Monday Funday" idea to add to your family.

Day Two Hundred and Sixty-Four: Rest Is Productive

Rest is productive, and for mothers it's a necessity.

Productivity has a stronghold on a mother's worth. When you think of needing rest, what comes to mind? Do you feel guilty? Does it make you feel like something is wrong with you? That you're somehow weak and not productive? Well, today you're going to rewire those beliefs because *rest is productive.* Now if you've already overplanned and are overcommitted, the idea of rest probably makes you even more stressed because time you take away from "doing" will set you back even further. But here's something to think about: When you're constantly on the go, the "stress hormone" cortisol is released. Over time the extended release of that hormone affects focus, memory, and sleep—three things mothers really need. When those three areas are affected, you can't be as productive as you want to be! So what's a great way to lower that stress hormone? Rest! Rest becomes a productive part of being a mother because you're able to reset, recharge, and rejuvenate so that you can be the best version of yourself. So know that taking time to slow down and relax is a great way to keep being the amazing mother you are.

Take out your phone and look at your calendar for next month; pick a thirty-minute block of time and schedule rest for yourself. This might feel silly, but the more you prioritize rest, the more energy and strength you create for yourself in motherhood.

Day Two Hundred and Sixty-Five: Your Parenting Path

It's natural to grow and evolve throughout life,
and evolving as a parent is no different.

As a mother raising your own family, you have the beautiful ability to continue, alter, or retire parenting traditions from your family of origin. You might have already consciously done this by continuing your grandmother's bedtime song, changing the way you discipline your child, or getting rid of parenting phrases like "Children are seen, not heard." However, just because you're the one raising your family doesn't mean relatives, like in-laws or parents, will simply stand back and approve. It's not easy to be critiqued as a parent, so as you grow your own family, it's important to remind yourself of these three things:

1. You know what's best for your family. You are always making the best choices with the best intentions.
2. If a relative challenges your parenting, they're likely taking it personally. Thank them for caring enough to share their thoughts and politely decline engaging in that conversation.
3. You're allowed to change your mind. Just because you've parented one way for a few years doesn't mean you have to stick to it. It's natural to grow and evolve throughout life, and evolving as a parent is no different.

Let's talk about traditions: Tonight ask your child, "What's one of our family's traditions you love?" and "When you have a family, what family tradition will you start?"

Day Two Hundred and Sixty-Six: Your Child's Biggest Fan

You're the biggest fan your child can ever have,
so keep cheering them on.

You are your child's biggest fan. You're one of those die-hard fans, the ones who stick with their team through the best of seasons and the worst of seasons. A fan isn't recognized for their everyday loyalty, but the team still feels it; they know their stands are full because they're loved. The same can be said for motherhood. You show up every day; you cheer your child on; you stand by their side even when you're exhausted, upset, or even disappointed. You're the one your child looks for in the crowd; you are the one they thank for the unconditional support when they receive awards; you are the reason your child believes in themselves. The older your child gets, the more fans they'll gather, yet you'll always be their number one fan, the one who's been there since day one. So as you look at your child today, admiring their successes, know that you had a pretty important role in helping them become the person they are . . . and that is something to celebrate. Forever their number one fan you'll be.

Today make a point to cheer your child on using encouragement that speaks to them most. Maybe it's a high five, a hug, or a compliment as to how hard they've worked.

Day Two Hundred and Sixty-Seven: Tweens, Teens, and In-Betweens

Mothers with teenagers: Keep your mind strong and your heart soft.

As the mom of an older child, those early motherhood responsibilities like bottles and diapers are no longer on your radar, but now you have the complexities of parenting a child who doesn't think they need parenting! You're not just setting boundaries, you're also starting to question yourself more when your child is adamant that your boundaries are ruining their life! As a mother, the last thing you want to see is your child upset, but now more than ever before, your child is upset and you're the cause. These are tough moments, but it's important for you to remember two things: *strong and soft*. You can remain *strong* with your mind. You stay strong with your boundaries, because even though your child feels like their life is over because of those boundaries, you see past their present moment's feelings and into the future as to how these boundaries will help them. You can remain *soft* with your heart; you have compassion for your child's experience. As you create the balance between being strong and soft, you know you're doing a great job navigating this phase of motherhood.

Today look at the tires on your car: Are they strong? Yes! They handle a lot of bumps in the road. Are they soft? Yes! They have to be able to adapt to the surface they're on to accommodate it. Use those tires as a reminder that you can handle these tween and teen years.

Day Two Hundred and Sixty-Eight: Three Paths for Handling Differences

Curiosity will take you further than resistance.

Naturally the way you've lived your life before children is the foundation for how you live your life with children. If you lived that type A life, with ironclad schedules and immaculate organization, you're going to try and implement that as a mother. If you lived that "make everyone happy" life, where you never missed a chance to say yes to a favor, you'll likely apply that same template in motherhood. The thing is, your child is their own person and the ways you've learned to cope with life might not be conducive to your child's unique and individual spirit. There are three paths you might find yourself on:

- The first path is that you are in constant conflict with your child; they won't conform and you're always at odds.
- The second path is that your child is resistant to your ways, but realizes they need to be like you to get the most love possible, so they conform and become just like you.
- The third path, which is available to you right now, is that you realize your old way of living might not be the right way anymore. You slowly let go of the unrealistic expectations of yourself and your child, and you allow yourself to grow into a different version of yourself.

Think about this entry and ask yourself, "Which path am I on?" and if you aren't satisfied with that path, ask yourself, "What small shift can I make to start changing my path?"

Day Two Hundred and Sixty-Nine: Time Away from Your Child

There's nothing wrong with time away from your child to be reminded that it's possible to love them and yourself at the same exact time.

Two things can be true as a mother: You can love your child, and you can love taking time away from your child. Yet taking time away as a mother can be difficult for many reasons. Nevertheless, you need time away from your child, not because you don't love your child or you don't love being a mom. Time away from your child is needed because you love yourself. You're a better mother when you do things for yourself. Get started today by first making the internal shift to validate yourself: "Knowing that I require time away from my kids is what makes me a better mother." Look around at other mothers you admire that are okay with taking time away and ask them for advice. Then start making shifts to carve out some time for yourself. First it might be time where you read a book and your kids get to watch a movie, and then you upgrade to making babysitting arrangements so you can have an evening out—allowing you to return home filled up with some much-needed fun. Make the call and let yourself enjoy time away.

Pick three possible dates in your calendar that would be a great night to grab dinner. Open up your texts and see which nights work best for your spouse or friends. Finally, reach out to your babysitting resources and make those plans happen.

Day Two Hundred and Seventy: Boundaries Are Like Fences

Boundaries are made by you, for you, and enforced by you.

Boundaries are often confused with expectations. Boundaries are made by you, for you, and enforced by you, whereas expectations are made by you, for others, and followed by others. One of the best ways to understand boundaries is imagining a fence. Imagine you had a beautiful field of crops you wanted to protect from unwanted animal visitors. You would build a fence for yourself. You would make sure that the fence is firmly rooted in the ground and made with sturdy materials. Sure, the animals might try to cross over, but once they realize your fence is secure, they stop trying and realize your fence means business. Now, if your fence was more like expectations, you'd build the fence, but once the animals knocked it down, you'd be upset at them for not honoring your rickety fence (even though it wasn't secure!). The same can be said for boundaries; when you firmly root your boundaries in your core beliefs and you're committed to enforcing them, your boundaries will be successful. Sure, you might have other family members try and push back on those boundaries, but because you remain firm, eventually they'll realize your boundaries aren't budging.

Boundary tune-up: What boundary of yours needs tuning up? Use this three-point checklist to make sure you have a boundary rather than an expectation: Is the boundary made by me? Is the boundary for me? And how am I enforcing the boundary?

Day Two Hundred and Seventy-One: Bad Words Happen

There are no bad children, just bad moments, bad moods, and bad influences—all of which you can guide your child through.

Ah, the moment when you hear your little one say a "bad word" . . . it's certainly something you never forget! Depending on the context, your family values, and your sense of humor, you might find it shocking, horrifying, or maybe even humorous! Here's the thing: Regardless of how you feel about "bad words" or cursing, you can handle these moments without shaming your child.

- First, you might need a moment to process how you feel, and depending how old your child is, you might realize they have no idea what this word means!
- Second, in an age-appropriate manner, have a discussion about how there are many different words and some words are hurtful or harmful.
- Third, open up the conversation to where they've heard that word (and whoops, if it was you, explain that it's okay to make mistakes).
- Fourth, offer your child a new world to use in place: You can even make up a funny word together.

In these moments, it's important to give your child the benefit of the doubt, explain to them the consequences of using these words (at home and out in the world), and then choose more effective, appropriate words for them to use.

Get creative with your children tonight to come up with some funny words to use when you're feeling frustrated or angry. You can brainstorm together or tear up tiny pieces of paper, write the words on them, and then throw them in a hat to read out loud and laugh.

Day Two Hundred and Seventy-Two: Don't Let Yourself Down

Sometimes choosing yourself means letting others down.

As much as motherhood is about raising your children, you're also raising yourself. You're realizing that you haven't always chosen yourself before others, and you want to create a life where you trust and care for yourself more. But there's a problem: Sometimes choosing yourself means you'll have to let others down. This probably doesn't feel great to you. If you've built a life around making others happy and now as mom all you want to do is make your children happy, the last thing you can handle is letting others down. But here's the thing: You want your children to be kind, generous, and helpful, right? But would you tell your child to be kind, generous, and helpful at the expense of their own selves? Probably not! This is where your own parenting journey comes in—the one where you start raising yourself because you notice the way you treat yourself becomes the way your child treats themselves. So the next time you have to choose between yourself and letting someone down, ask yourself, "What would I encourage my child to do?" and let that simmer for a bit to help you find your answer.

The next time you are faced with the choice to let someone down or let yourself down, put your hand on your heart, close your eyes, and use this question to sort through your decision: "I care about myself and I care about others; who needs that caring most right now?"

Day Two Hundred and Seventy-Three: It's Okay to Be Angry

The simple act of accepting what is creates a path to move forward.

Did you know that allowing your child to be angry will help them let go of their anger easily? You may not like that they're angry. You may not agree with why they're angry. You might be annoyed with the inconvenient timing of their anger. But it's okay for your child to feel angry because anger is a natural, human emotion. When we accept feelings, it allows them to pass. When we deny our feelings, they linger, create resentment, and pop back up at unexpected times. So when your child gets angry and you can feel your resistance rising, pause and remember "It's okay for my child to get angry." Repeating this to yourself and eventually believing it is like a weight lifting off your shoulders. You can work with your child's anger instead of against it. You can allow your child to be upset while you stand firm about what behaviors are acceptable to express. And most importantly, when you allow your child to be angry, you allow that anger to be felt in the present so that it doesn't carry into the future.

Practice this with yourself today. If you get angry about something, remind yourself that your feeling is allowed and valid. The simple act of accepting what is creates a path to move forward.

Day Two Hundred and Seventy-Four: Introducing New Behaviors

Double the amount of time it took to learn a behavior to unlearn it.

Is there a new behavior you've been trying to teach your child, but it won't stick? Here's a trick that you can use to build up any new desired behavior: *Start small, start slow, and start silly.* When something is new and not so desirable, you can help your children by breaking it down to make it feel easier and doable. Let's use an example of getting your child to sit at the dinner table:

- *Starting small* means you start practicing this behavior in small increments. You say to your child, "I'm curious if you can sit at the table for twenty seconds, okay, go" and start a timer. Chances are your child will be able to accomplish this task. After they've accomplished the task, let them choose a desired behavior like running around or jumping.
- *Starting slow* means you pace the increments, maybe one or two a day. This requires patience on your part!
- *Starting silly* means you make practicing the behavior fun, turn it into a game, or create a fun paper certificate for each new achievement.

As you gradually make this a fun, achievable behavior, your child will gain confidence in themselves and so will you!

Patience is hard . . . for everyone! Pick a board game at home to help everyone practice patience in a fun way. Game ideas include matching games, hide-and-go-seek, Go Fish, Jenga, or keeping a timer that only you can see and asking everyone to guess when a minute is up!

Day Two Hundred and Seventy-Five: Yes Day

In a motherhood full of no it can feel pretty good to say yes and have some fun.

If just reading the title of this entry got you worried, you most certainly are a mother thinking about the absolute absurdity of creating a whole day of yes for your children. But before you close the book, listen to this: Your children live most of their lives being told what to do, when to do it, and how to do it. So creating a day where your child has way more control can truly bring your family together for some much-needed fun. What is a Yes Day? It's a day where you let your child pick two to three of the weekend activities. Maybe you let them pick the meals or a fun destination. Maybe they finally get you to put on a swimsuit, wet your hair, and go swimming. Or you finally go to the pet shop to see them play with kittens and puppies. There are ground rules of course and those can be for you to decide: things like budget, timing, and of course not making any decisions that can't be reversed. The goal of this day isn't to let chaos ensue, but to show your child that life can be fun; it doesn't always have to be the same thing every day.

Another alternative is to download a "spin the wheel" app on your phone and enter up to ten fun ideas, then surprise your child after school with the app and have them spin for a fun surprise.

Day Two Hundred and Seventy-Six: Unconditional Love

Imagine how your life would shift if you loved yourself as unconditionally as you loved your child.

As a mother, you love your child no matter what. Have you ever thought about where that deep, unconditional love came from? Did your child have to earn your love? Nope, it was naturally there, present since the day they came into your life. Now pause for a moment and ask, "Do I have that same love for myself?" Do you love yourself that same way, unconditionally? Or is your love contingent on how much you do as a mother, how you look, or how much you possess? Not being able to give yourself unconditional love as freely as you give it to your child is a product of years of *unintentional* reinforcement from your childhood, where you learned your love (in the form of attention and approval) was based on your actions. Those same conditions were applied to your own self-love. Here's the good news: All of this was learned, so it can be unlearned and replaced with what you know to be true about your child. This is a form of re-parenting yourself. The moment you notice you're conditionally loving yourself, apply how you'd handle the same conversation with your child. Why? Because you're no different from your child in deserving unconditional love.

Open your phone and set a calendar reminder for the next three days that says "Love yourself like you love your child" as a reminder to be extra compassionate, understanding, and forgiving to yourself this week.

Day Two Hundred and Seventy-Seven: Parenting Differently from Your Mother

You can love your mother and still parent differently from her.

Your motherhood journey is different from your own mother's journey. Whether you borrow from the most beloved parts of your childhood or you're raising your children in a completely different way, it's helpful to remember that you can love your mother *and* parent differently from her. You can also have a strained relationship with your mother *and* still use what worked for you from your own childhood. This is because many things can be true at the same time. The key is using the word "and." "And" releases you from feeling trapped by absolute thinking, to be free of an all-or-nothing mentality. "And" gives you permission to have an array of beliefs, feelings, and practices as you continue along your motherhood journey. As you make your way through motherhood today, make it a point to use "and" instead of "but"; you'll witness a shift in how you feel: less conflicted and more comfortable with your choices.

Using "and" can be helpful in your motherhood journey in many ways, specifically when you're separating your child's feelings and behavior, for example, "You can be mad and you can still be kind."

Day Two Hundred and Seventy-Eight: Perfect Is Boring

The beauty in motherhood lies between your imperfections and the journey of learning from them.

Perfection is overrated. You might strive to be the perfect mother, but in reality, it would be pretty boring. Think about the funniest moments in motherhood: All that laughter came from imperfection. Think of the most heartfelt moments: Those were filled with love between two imperfect beings. Think about the closeness in your mother-child relationship: That relationship has nothing to do with perfection; in fact, it's the acceptance and love of each other's imperfections that make it so special. So before you look down on a mistake, remember that the beauty in motherhood lies between your imperfections and the journey of learning from them.

Today share a story with your child about a time a mistake turned into something that ended up being something great. This reflection will help both you and your child see the beauty of imperfection.

Day Two Hundred and Seventy-Nine: Practice Makes Progress

Practice doesn't make perfect; it makes progress.

One area in motherhood that might bring you a great deal of strife is getting your child to stop an unwanted behavior and replace it with a new behavior. While it would be lovely for this to happen after the first time you asked, that probably isn't the case. Next time, try practicing the new behavior with your child. This might sound odd to "practice" a behavior, but repetition is the key to learning any new behavior, and when children are involved, creating a low-stress, low-stakes practice environment is key. Let's say you want your child to patiently wait for you while you're on the phone. Start with a pretend phone call that's only thirty seconds long. Once that's mastered, bump it up to one minute, two minutes, and so on. Next make a real phone call that isn't too important. The replacement behavior you give your child can just be the "waiting" behavior, or you can also introduce another behavior, like your child tapping your arm once when they need you and you tapping them back to let them know you'll be with them soon. Practicing *before* you encounter an important situation is how to make real progress; you'll find it will be way less stressful for you and way more successful for your child.

In the Notes app on your phone, type out one new behavior you'd like to work on this week and create a stress-free simulation for you and your child to practice.

Day Two Hundred and Eighty: Let Them Figure It Out

The greatest way to build your child's resilience is by letting them figure things out on their own.

As a mother, you give your children everything you can to succeed in life. Yet there are some things you can't give your children, like resilience, where the gift is letting them figure things out on their own. Say you're in the car on the way to school and your child realizes they've forgotten their homework. Or you arrive at the park and your child's upset they didn't bring the right toy. Or your child has $5 to spend at a toy store, but there are two items they want. Let them figure it out. Don't rush to bring the homework, go back home to get the toy, or give them the extra money; let them figure it out and show them that they can make it through tough moments. If your child gets overly emotional about having to figure things out on their own, work on staying calm and confident in your child. Your sturdiness and confidence in them will take them much further than you scrambling in fear to do it for them. The greatest way to build your child's resilience is by letting them figure things out on their own.

The antidote to learned helplessness is productive struggling, and this can be practiced with your child as early as toddlerhood by letting them crawl farther for a toy. How can you help build resilience by creating a productive struggle for your child?

Day Two Hundred and Eighty-One:
Choose Your Focus

The bittersweet moments of motherhood are
"Two things can be true" moments.

You hear the phrase "Two things can be true" a lot in motherhood. You may have used this phrase with your children, teaching them that they can experience different feelings all at the same time. Have you ever used this phrase for yourself? For example, when you hear your name called over ten times before 10 a.m. and in that same moment you know it's only a matter of time before your children won't need you the way they need you now. The bittersweet moments of motherhood are "Two things can be true" moments. Where this can help you is where you choose to focus your energy. This is by no means an attempt at toxic positivity or forced gratitude, but rather acknowledging your ability to experience two truths and choose to direct your focus on the truth that feels best. Remember this the next time you find yourself in a motherhood predicament and ask yourself, "What two truths are present right now, and which truth deserves my primary focus?"

Today's takeaway is optional. It's helpful only if it feels right for you: Take a task in motherhood that you're less than excited about and find another truth that makes it more enjoyable. Now focus on the second truth and see how you feel at the end of the day.

Day Two Hundred and Eighty-Two: Saying "Calm Down" Never Helps

If you want to calm your child, find your own calm first.

Imagine you've had plans with your girlfriends for weeks to get dinner. You're dressed and ready to go and then you get a call from your babysitter saying they can no longer watch the kids. You're so disappointed. You call a family member to vent about how upset you are and they say, "Calm down." What are the chances that phrase helps you calm down? What are the chances that phrase makes you even more upset, misunderstood, and frustrated? As a mother, using this phrase is always well-intentioned; of course you don't want your child upset. But who are you really needing to calm down the most? The answer is you. The phrase "Calm down" is probably best used on yourself rather than your child. Meaning find your own calm when your child isn't calm, otherwise you're both spiraling in your emotions. So rather than try to calm down your child, calm yourself down by remembering that *feelings are temporary*. Your child will move past these feelings, not because you told them to "calm down," but because of your confidence in knowing that feelings are temporary.

Practice telling your child a story about a time you had a feeling that you thought would never go away. Children love to hear stories about their mothers as children, so get creative with your details and share away.

Day Two Hundred and Eighty-Three: Add Play Confetti

*Sprinkle play into your day like it's confetti,
a little here and a little there to brighten up your routine.*

Play is not just important in childhood, it's important in motherhood too. The thing is, play isn't just imaginary play; it can be incorporated in small, normal moments throughout the day. Think of it like confetti, "play confetti," and you need to sprinkle a little bit here and there. The best part about this approach is that you can keep your family on their usual routine, but sprinkle the fun in without deterring from your plan. Here are some ideas to get you started: In the morning, turn breakfast into a pretend restaurant meal by draping a towel over your hand and using a pad of paper to take your children's orders. Play red light, green light as you make your way to the car. If someone isn't listening, instead of yelling, use a singsongy, opera voice to get their attention. Write a silly little note attached to your child's folder or place a joke in their lunch box. On the car ride home, play I spy, car freeze dance, or a humming version of a favorite tune. The goal isn't to add more to your plate and make fun feel like a burden, but instead to allow the moments of stress, tension, or silence to be filled with something that will not only make your child's day better, but your day a little bit brighter too.

Today chat with your child and ask what would make their morning a little more fun.

Day Two Hundred and Eighty-Four: Overreacting

Children don't want to behave badly; they simply feel bad.

Has your child ever experienced big emotions and you couldn't help but think, "They're overreacting"? Sure, they might be laying it on thick, but labeling your child's reaction as an overreaction just ends up creating a bigger separation between the two of you, and that doesn't help anyone. Instead make the goal connection. Connection allows you to help your child (and yourself) through the tough moments. Here are some steps you can take to increase connection:

1. Reframe "They're overreacting" as "This is really impacting my child."
2. Remember, all feelings are allowed, but all behaviors are not. Meaning it's important for you to be able to separate what your child feels from how they are expressing their feelings. Children never want to behave badly; they feel bad.
3. Remind yourself you are on your child's team. Even if your child doesn't want help, it's important that *you* remember that so you can stay focused on connection.

These three steps help you disarm rather than unintentionally and judgmentally react in a way that further distances you and your child. Using even just one of those three steps will bring you closer to where you want to be.

Has anyone ever told you you're overreacting? Did you agree or did you really feel those emotions in the moment? Reflecting on your own experiences can help you understand your child a little bit better.

Day Two Hundred and Eighty-Five: Good Vibes Mostly

If you want to experience your positive emotions more fully, allow your negative emotions to be experienced more fully.

Who doesn't love an uplifting, positive message to brighten their day? Well, sometimes you might not! Why? Because those messages aren't always realistic, especially when you've had a rather rough day in motherhood. The phrase "good vibes only" is one of those messages that is lovely in theory, but impractical in reality. The idea of "good vibes only" creates the unrealistic idea that it is somehow possible to only experience positive emotions. Sure, we want to maximize the good feelings, but rejecting the not-so-good feelings doesn't achieve that. What will work is accepting all your emotions, even when they aren't what you'd like to be feeling. Rather than "good vibes only," why not make your motherhood motto *"good vibes mostly."* You'll always try to feel your best and do your best, but when that doesn't happen, you won't banish or shame your experience; rather you'll remember that it's "good vibes mostly."

Head to Google Images search and type in "good vibes mostly." Save an image that you like best and use it as your phone wallpaper for the week.

Day Two Hundred and Eighty-Six: Feelings Are Like Laundry

A little feeling each day keeps the emotional clutter away.

Feelings are a lot like laundry. You're never excited to deal with them, but the longer you wait to tackle them, the more they pile up and become unmanageable. As a mother, you're busy doing a hundred other things; why would you make time to unpack your feelings? Well, just like when laundry sits there for a while, your feelings start to stink. Your feelings need and deserve to be tended to and cared for. You don't have to handle every feeling at once; rather you handle each feeling little by little, as needed. First, identify what that feeling even is. Sure, you can feel sad, but when you sit with that sadness, what other feelings are attached to it? Sometimes it can be loneliness, grief, abandonment, or fear. Then, ask yourself what associations and judgments you have with those feelings. Does it feel vulnerable to sit with those feelings? Finally, write out how you feel. Just let it flow as to what you feel, why you feel that way, and anything else that comes out. Allow yourself to experiment with actually feeling that feeling. Toss or delete what you've written when you're done. Just like laundry, if you handle a few feelings each day, they start to become much more manageable.

You get a pass on your feelings laundry today. No, seriously, even though this was about doing a little each day, the heavy lifting of talking about your feelings is more than enough work. Go enjoy the day!

Day Two Hundred and Eighty-Seven: Get in the Photos

Grab your children, get in the photos,
and let yourself be part of the memory too.

If you open up the photos on your phone, chances are there are way more photos of your children, spouse, and family members than you. That's because you're usually the one behind the camera! Sure, you're a mom, but you're the family photographer too. Whether or not you enjoy being in photos, you deserve to be in those photos too. Not only for you, but also for your family. Get in the photos. When you snap a photo of your husband walking in the distance with your children, make sure you pass the camera and ask him to do the same. Attempt to take selfies with your teenagers (they're even more of a memory when you surprise them). Take photos of your friends with their children and have them do the same for you. Just get in the photos, because no matter how you look or feel, your children will treasure those photos of you one day. You'll have those photos that let you dive back into memories you'd otherwise forget. The next time the cameras are out, grab your children, get in the photos, and let yourself be part of the memory too.

Try a family photo night. Make plans with your kids to host a home-made family photo shoot. It can be a 1980s awkward theme, a "kids get to pick the outfits" theme, or anything you can think of, and of course make sure you get in those photos too!

Day Two Hundred and Eighty-Eight: Motherhood Is Tough Because You Care

Children aren't a problem, but parents are the solution.

It would be much easier to continue on an unconscious path where you see your children as the "problem" and refuse to look within yourself, but you care, so it's tough. You're here reading this book, continuing to expand your heart and your mind in ways that help you show up more authentic, connected, and conscious. You might overlook the small wins, but they're there. Each time you look at your child with compassion, that's a win. Each time you have a setback, like when you lose your cool and shout, it hurts, it's hard. Not because you're doing it wrong, but because you're doing it right enough to know you'll grow a little bit more next time. Just like building a muscle, it's hard, it hurts, but you heal and become stronger. Motherhood is tough because you care, but the more you continue to give yourself the gifts of forgiveness, compassion, and gentleness, the more those same things will flow over to your children.

Today look for the small wins you've achieved in motherhood. Acknowledge how far you've come and allow yourself to feel good when you notice the wins.

Day Two Hundred and Eighty-Nine: Sharing Isn't Always Caring

A child forced to share learns very little about sharing and a great deal about who is deserving of that caring.

The phrase "Sharing is caring" has been a popular phrase for decades. You've probably said it yourself, and rightfully so because sharing is a rather caring thing to do. But sharing isn't always caring, especially when the caring is one-sided. Rather than force your child to share, you can teach them how to share. Let's use a common scenario at the playground: Imagine your child sits down on a swing and another child runs up to ask for a turn. You could certainly force your child to share the swing, but that wouldn't take into account your child's feelings or teach them about sharing (other than what other people want is more important than what they want!). Instead try narrating the scenario and offer solutions if needed: "Looks like this little guy wants a turn; what are you thinking about that?" or "You just got on the swing. Do you want to let the other child know they can have a turn when you're done?" Not only are children more likely to act on a decision that's their own, but it's incredibly empowering to make choices that feel true to them and that positively impact another.

A great way to teach about sharing is by thinking out loud about how hard it is for you to share something in your home. Let your child weigh in on how you should handle the situation.

Day Two Hundred and Ninety: Empathy and Vulnerability

Where there is no empathy, there is no vulnerability.

Sitting with your child or spouse while they're in pain, sadness, or fear is hard because you don't want to see your loved ones suffer. It's also difficult for another reason: Sitting with another's raw feelings exposes you and makes you vulnerable to your own feelings. Maybe they're feelings you've unconsciously avoided, feelings you aren't comfortable with, or feelings that scare you. So while you so badly want to comfort and console your loved one, you might cringe, want to shut a feeling down, or even hide until it's all over! This is nothing to be ashamed of, but it is something you understand more deeply by learning about your relationship with vulnerability. Empathy has a hard time existing without vulnerability. To feel empathy for another, you have to open up your heart, which means you are vulnerable. Empathy is vulnerability; it's saying, "I see you, I feel you, and I'm not scared of your feelings because I feel those same things too." Rather than judge yourself, know that empathy for others has nothing to do with loving them, but has everything to do with you learning to love the parts of that person that you see in yourself.

Today try and think of someone who shows you empathy, compassion, and understanding. Is that person closed off, shallow, or vague? Or are they openhearted, unguarded, and deeply feeling?

Day Two Hundred and Ninety-One: The Beauty of the Emotional Thermometer

Rather than get frustrated with your child, get curious.

Do you have an emotional thermometer in your family? In most families, there's someone who doesn't hide their emotions, someone who isn't afraid to cry or stand up for what they want, and they usually come in the form of children. These are the children who don't go with the flow; they go with what they know to be true for themselves. When you think of your child as the emotional thermometer of the family, the idea that they are "difficult," "sensitive," or "overly emotional" switches to the idea that they are actually the most honest with themselves and are the most honest members of the family. What if we saw these children as more aligned with their needs? More attuned to their feelings? Less likely to self-abandon? After all, isn't that what you're learning to do in your motherhood journey? Leaning into authenticity and getting more in your own skin? Rather than get frustrated with your child, get curious. Ask yourself what truths in their feelings you can identify within yourself. What about their behaviors do you understand and secretly appreciate? These children are a sign to slow down, a sign to tune in, and a sign to drop deeper into your most authentic self.

Think back to your childhood. Did you, a sibling, or a cousin go against the grain of the family often? Looking back, are you able to notice them or you as an emotional thermometer?

Day Two Hundred and Ninety-Two: Use the Three Cs to Foster Resilience

Connection, confidence, and compassion help build your child's resilience.

Let's set the record straight: Resilient children don't bypass their feelings. Resilient children experience their feelings, and because of that, they adapt, bounce back, and carry on. How can you raise your children with emotional confidence? Because resilience is a learned skill, here's how you can foster your children's resilience using the three Cs: connection, confidence, and compassion.

- **Connection:** Your child has a strong sense of belonging in their family, school, and various communities. They are supported by others and know they're important members in those relationships.
- **Confidence:** When you let your child do hard things, they learn that they can do hard things; they discover where they are competent and gain confidence in themselves.
- **Compassion:** Your child experiences compassion from you regularly; therefore, they develop self-compassion and share compassion with others.

The more you foster connection, confidence, and compassion, the more those skills will build your child's resilience.

Which of the three Cs can you lean into more? Connection: Get your child to connect with their friends this weekend. Confidence: Let your child get extra practice at something they're already great at. Compassion: Make it clear you understand and support your child (rather than try to fix them) when they're having a hard time.

Day Two Hundred and Ninety-Three: Don't Fight the Current

Just like the currents in the ocean shift and subside, so do your feelings.

When you live near the ocean, you know that if you get caught in a strong current, in order to survive you have to let the current take you on its path. As long as you relax and float, you'll make it out just fine. This is easier said than done, because the moment you're pulled against your will, your instinct is to panic and fight, draining your energy and putting you in jeopardy. But if you can let yourself float, eventually the current will subside and you'll be able to swim back ashore. The same rules apply in motherhood. Motherhood certainly pulls you into its own rough waters, especially when you get wrapped up in your own feelings. You might want to fight your way out—to do anything but feel. But sometimes the fight hurts you more than the feelings. So rather than fight, float. When you float with your feelings, you're accepting your feelings, which isn't giving up or pretending you like them, but instead just allowing them to be present so that they can run their course. Just like the currents in the ocean eventually subside, so will your feelings.

When was the last time you floated in water? Make a point to float the next time you're in a pool, lake, or ocean (maybe even the bath?) to experience the feeling of letting go of control and allowing yourself to float.

Day Two Hundred and Ninety-Four: Be Curious with Questions

When your child asks you a question, you can answer, "Yes," "No," or "I want to hear more about why you're asking."

Does your child ever ask you to do things for them that they absolutely can do on their own? "Mom, can you please help me get dressed for school?" or "Mom, please cut me up some apples!" If it's happening more than usual, rather than shut them down with a "You can do this on your own," you can use this opportunity to understand your child more by asking questions: "Do you wish Mommy could help you more because you see me helping your brother a lot?" or "Are you wanting more time together?" or "I wonder if you're nervous about using the knife. Do we need more cutting lessons together?" Asking questions helps your child learn two things: how to connect their feelings and their behavior and how to problem solve on their own. Rather than giving your child a yes or no answer, asking questions will open up a whole new path to understanding what your child needs more of, whether it's more attention, quality time, or confidence—asking questions is the key to understanding your child more.

Asking questions is a great way to change up a routine that has lots of whining in it. Try asking, "What about this is tough for you right now?" or "You really don't like this part of the day; if you could change it up, what would you do differently?"

Day Two Hundred and Ninety-Five: Children Are the Greatest Teachers

Your children can be your greatest teachers.

Have you ever thought about what your children have taught you? Of course they've taught you random facts about monster trucks, the solar system, or Taylor Swift, but there are also deeper life lessons they've shared with you that they aren't even aware of. Your children can be your greatest teachers when it comes to presence. Has your child ever called you out when you said you were listening, but you really weren't? They are *so* good at that! Children are masters of being in the present moment, and they call us to join them. When your child says, "Hey, Mom, come sit with me!" you have the choice to see your child's requests for presence as a reminder, an invitation, or a nudge to join them and savor a moment or two. But this doesn't mean you can always do it! These are simply *reminders* that you can choose small moments of presence, that they're always right there in front of you, and your child is simply an adorable invitation to enjoy where you are.

Today if your child wants your presence and you are unable to give it to them, take a second to stop, look at them directly, acknowledge what they've asked, and let them know you can't wait to join them when you are done with your task. That one second of acknowledging their presence will set the tone for you and your child when you are able to join them.

Day Two Hundred and Ninety-Six:
Not a Victim

Your child believes the stories you tell about them, so when you tell your child the story of how they've overcome hard times, they'll remember and believe they are able to conquer what comes their way.

There are times in motherhood when you have to help your child handle being hurt or made fun of. Maybe someone pushed them at recess or called them names at lunch. These are hard moments, hard days where you will be the rock to help your child process the situation. One important distinction to be made is that your child may be a victim in that moment—but do not victimize them. You acknowledge what happened to your child was not okay; however, you also want them to know that they are strong and have power over their life. This is the difference between being a victim for a moment and having a victim mentality in life. We want our children to know that even when bad things happen to them, they have the support from their family and strength within themselves to move forward. A great way to help your child is to allow them to retell the story with a narrative that is empowering. Retelling this story over and over again lets your child process what happened and feel confident that they can handle situations like this with confidence.

Tonight tell your child a story of a time they conquered their fears or made it through a rough moment and came out on top.

Day Two Hundred and Ninety-Seven: Choose Your Battles

A mother who chooses her battles isn't weak;
she knows when to use her strength.

You are likely choosing your battles in motherhood. You want your child to eat nutritiously, but when they refuse to eat anything but peanut butter and jelly sandwiches, you choose your battles, because you'd rather they eat that than nothing at all. You want your child to go to bed at 7 p.m., but you realize they have extra energy, so you let them run a few laps around the kitchen because you choose your battles; you'd rather have a pleasant bedtime than a battle of epic proportions. This is a reminder that it's okay to choose your battles in motherhood. You aren't a weak mother for not always following through; you're actually being a finely attuned mother. Rather than use an authoritative approach, where you demand what you demand no matter what, you assess what's going on in the present moment. You take things into consideration like what time it is, who has eaten, what moods everyone is in, what has happened so far in the day, who has energy that needs to be burned off, and most important, what your energy level is. Choosing your battles is a wise motherhood move, not a weak one. Its strength is knowing that life is situational, and you teach your family how to adapt.

Remember this mantra the next time you choose your battles: "I choose my battles because this is what's best for me in this moment."

Day Two Hundred and Ninety-Eight: They Can Handle It

Sometimes all they need to hear is "I hear you and I'm here for you."

If your child comes to you with a problem that you aren't sure how to handle, you probably feel worried, anxious, and unsettled. It's not easy as your children get older; bigger kids have bigger problems, which requires you to think "bigger" than just giving them a ready-made solution. There are two words—you can call them your homophone helper—that will get you and your child through these moments: "hear" and "here." For example: "I hear you and I'm here for you." To be heard and held through a predicament is often all our children need. While you might want to solve their problems and have all the answers, your attention and presence are what give your child a supportive foundation to make the best choices for themselves. Make no mistake, this is a learning curve as you move through motherhood. You'll want to bite your tongue many times, but in the end you're showing your child you trust that they can handle what life throws their way.

Write a note and remind your child that you love them, you're here for them, or any other sentiment that reiterates what they very much know, that you're their biggest supporter.

Day Two Hundred and Ninety-Nine: Keep It Present and Factual

Natural consequences are the best untapped parenting hack.

You want your child to be accountable for their actions without feeling overly responsible for others' emotions. Let's use an example of your child hitting you with a toy after getting a little too passionate. Help your child understand accountability by letting them experience the natural consequences of their actions. Say things like "Ouch, that really hurt," "I'm upset I got hit by that toy," and "I'm going to keep this toy away while we talk about how to play safely." This is much different from making your child feel overly responsible for your feelings by saying, "I'm in a bad mood because of you" or "Since you hit Mommy in the face, now you have to be a good boy all day." The key to this balance is for you, as the mother, to keep the situation *in the present and factual* rather than bring it into the future or add anecdotal accounts. You keep it present by focusing on what's happening right now and you keep it factual by sticking to what happened, how it made you feel, and how your child can change in the future: "You threw that toy and it really hurt me. Next time let's play with that toy outside."

The next time your child does something wrong, try to let natural consequences take the reins.

Day Three Hundred:
Let Them Vent

Just like a kettle lets off steam to reach the right temperature,
so do your children when it comes to settling into their feelings.

Motherhood is a lot like being the Chief Human Resources (HR) Officer of the family; everyone comes to you with their complaints. HR professionals are trained to handle tricky situations like when company rules have been broken, but most of the time employees just need to vent. The same can be said for you, Chief HR Officer and Mom. You'll always be there to enforce the family rules, but most of the time your kids just need to vent. So let them vent. You can even think of it as being off the hook because you don't actually have to solve the problem; instead you're there to listen. They might complain about their siblings, a friend, a teacher, or maybe even the other adults in the family. Everyone needs a moment to let out their thoughts and their feelings, and your children are no different. So next time your child comes to you with their complaints, listen and make sure you let them know how happy you are to be there for them.

If you're on HR Mom duty today and receive a complaint, be sure to tell your child, "I'm so glad you came to me with this" so that your child knows that your door is always open.

Day Three Hundred and One: ABCs of Active Listening

Children want their parents' full attention.

Okay, you're probably wondering why any mother would need a lesson in active listening when it's their children who need to learn how to listen! Well, in reality, mothers need to actively listen, too, because the opposite of active listening is passive listening. Passive listening leads children to assume that your lack of attention means their topic isn't important or that they aren't important, which couldn't be further from the truth! Your children, tweens, and teens know when you're *really* listening, so try using the ABCs of active listening the next time your child wants to discuss something important:

- *Attention:* Give your full attention. Put down the phone, shut off the TV, stop what you're doing, and with your full attention, sit close to your child.
- *Be Quiet:* Don't interrupt your child while they're talking; instead show them that you're listening by your normal nonverbal cues.
- *Clarity:* Once your child is done speaking, clarify and summarize in a nonjudgmental manner; use their words instead of infusing your own ideas into the summary.

Great news, active listening is a wonderful tool to use in your marriage and friendships and at work. Try it out and see how your connection in those relationships grows!

Day Three Hundred and Two: Pushing Buttons

*Children might push buttons, but they're
not responsible for uninstalling them.*

Your children likely have a special way of pushing your buttons. Your first thought is probably "My child shouldn't push that button," and yes, this can be true. However, the most effective change comes from deactivating your buttons so there are no buttons to push. The first step is to understand how this button was installed. There are two questions to help find the culprit for your button. The first: "Were you able to act the way your child acts to push your buttons?" If the answer is no, there may be feelings of resentment toward your child for being able to act this way when you couldn't. Perhaps you weren't able to share how you felt or you weren't able to be extra silly. The second: "Is there a part of you that feels upset that your child doesn't act how you acted as a child?" Perhaps you never shared when you disagreed or you had to act like you were always happy. While you don't want your child to hide their feelings, there's misguided anger toward your child for not suppressing their emotions like you did. The best gift you can give yourself is compassion while you slowly deactivate your button, knowing it's less about your child's behavior and more about the old, unprocessed feelings you have.

Use a simple one-minute meditation to reset your mind. Close your eyes; take six deep breaths in through your nose (four seconds each) and out through your mouth (six seconds each).

Day Three Hundred and Three: When Parenting Scripts Don't Work

The best script to use is that of authenticity.

Have you heard a wonderful parenting script, but when you try and use it with your own children it crashes and burns? Maybe you loved how someone else used it, but when it came out of your mouth, it felt awkward and inauthentic. This is a common situation because scripts are a starting point. Think of scripts as a foundation for what boundaries you want to set, what points you want to make, and what words or sayings you want to avoid. Start with the foundation and then make it your own. First, use your usual tone. Your children will sniff out the inauthenticity when you try a new voice that's so far from your normal one. Second, use your usual words. Sure, a new word or two is fine, but getting fancy will bring confusion. Third, if you try a script that doesn't work, it can't hurt to be honest with your child about it (especially with your tweens and teens). They'll appreciate your honesty, and that authenticity will go a long way in your mother-child relationship.

"You're feeling really angry right now" . . . This is a script that's often shared to validate your child's feelings, yet for older children this can be overkill when it's clear they're angry. A great swap is using natural empathy, concern, or basic active listening.

Day Three Hundred and Four:
Unintentional Shame

*Recognizing your child's effort is just as important
as recognizing your child's accomplishments.*

"Don't you want to be a big kid?" Mothers know that their kids are excited to grow up and be like the older children they admire. So naturally you've used the terms "big girl" and "big boy" to let them know when they're being mature, responsible, or really doing anything you deem a "big kid" would do. You can use the term to motivate and encourage your child, and you can also use the term to unintentionally shame them. The key word here is "unintentionally," because of course you don't intend to use shame as a motivator. So how does that happen? When it's used as a punishment or penalty: "I guess you're not a big girl because big girls know how to tie their shoes." A great replacement is to honor your child's attempts, efforts, and tenacity: "Wow, you're learning how to tie your shoes and you keep trying no matter what!" If you're ever unsure about using rewards, punishment, or penalties, the best way to assess is to make sure it's motivating your child by love or encouragement rather than by shame or fear.

Recognizing your child's efforts starts with recognizing your own. Take a moment to recall a time you tried something new and it didn't lead to success right away or at all. Sit for the next minute and see if you can find small amounts of pride.

Day Three Hundred and Five: Respect Redefined

Respect is a two-way street: A child has to experience what it's like to be respected in order to show true respect.

Have you ever noticed how the word "respect" means two different things for adults and children? When you use the word in regard to a child respecting their mother, it's associated with the child following rules, listening, and doing what they're told. When it's used in regard to an adult respecting another adult, it's associated with holding them in high regard and admiring their achievements, how they treat others, or the good that they've done. It makes you think about how we twist the meaning of the word "respect": Children bear the responsibility to carry out respect, regardless of the parent's behavior receiving it, whereas with adults we place the responsibility on the other adult to earn our respect. What if we redefined respect in parenting to include all of the above? Take a moment to shift your thinking about respect and view it as a two-way street: Teach your child what respect looks like by showing them how it feels to be respected by being considerate, polite, attentive, and caring.

Who would have thought respect would bring so much up for mothers? What is your definition of respect? Write it out and get curious about how you've come to define respect that way.

Day Three Hundred and Six:
Exceptionally Average

Raise your child to be the best at something, to be their best selves.

Have you noticed how motherhood has shifted from raising a child to raising the most exceptionally gifted child that ever lived? It's almost like the goal is to raise a professional athlete, superstar, or a genius. That's a lot of pressure on mothers, but most of that pressure falls on our children. Here's a thought: What if your kids were allowed to be exceptionally average? Imagine how loved and accepted you would have felt if your parents had said to you, *"Doing more, achieving more, that's amazing, but all of that doesn't mean you're worth more, because you've been worth all the love in the world since the day you were born."* Today take inventory of the areas you strive for your child to be better and ask yourself, "Is this coming from a place of love for my child or fear that if they don't succeed, they'll somehow not be enough?" Remember, you aren't raising your child to be the best at anything other than raising them to be their best selves.

Is there any correlation with your expectations for your child and the expectations you had (or your parents had) for you as a child? If so, ask yourself where the source of that expectation is coming from: love or fear? If it's fear, read the italicized quote in this entry and see how it feels to receive the message that you've always been enough.

Day Three Hundred and Seven: Zooming Out

When you feel lost in motherhood,
zoom out to remember the bigger picture.

Do you ever feel so consumed with getting your child to do something (or not do something) that you lose sight of the bigger picture? This often happens because you're so zoomed in to the struggle at hand that you totally forget your "why" in motherhood. So rather than freak out, zoom out. Zooming out means you're looking at the bigger picture. Think of it in terms of looking at the Maps app on your phone: When you're zoomed in on every little detail, you get distracted with traffic, detours, and pit stops. But when you zoom out to see the destination, where you want to go, you're able to refocus on what matters most (things like love, connection, joy, and trust). The same goes for motherhood, because in the stressful moments, you're so zoomed in that you forget this is just a drop in the bucket on your journey. Today remember to zoom out—not because the zoomed-in tasks aren't hard (they really are)—but because the bigger picture reminds you of the beauty of the journey you want for your family.

Three questions to ask yourself when you're zoomed in: One, how does this rule/routine serve my child at this moment? Two, is this rule coming from a place of caring or control? Three, how will my handling of this moment affect me and my child five minutes, five hours, five months, or five years down the road? This will help you assess what needs to happen in the grand scheme of things.

Day Three Hundred and Eight: Bedtime Challenge

Sometimes the best moments of connection come during the moments of routine.

You're probably tired at the end of a day. You've mothered all day long and getting your child to sleep is the last thing on your list, so naturally if you can get bedtime done quickly, you're a happy camper. But what if you notice that your child isn't so tired? What if your child really wants to talk to you about something? Today invite yourself into a bedtime challenge to not hurry your child to sleep when you notice they might need more time with you. Now, this can be a stall tactic on your child's part (they're so darn good at that, aren't they?), but even if it is, it's really just your child wanting more alone time with you, right? Bedtime gives you an incredible opportunity to learn more about your child, their day, and their thoughts and feelings. Bedtime has this magical effect on kids to open up and share what's in their heart. Yes, routine and structure are essential for our children's well-being and health, but these moments of connection are important too. So the next time you have a slight inclination your child is needing more of you, challenge yourself to lean in and enjoy soaking up that time together.

Set a calendar reminder for the next seven days right before bedtime that says "bedtime challenge" to remind yourself to lean into connection if the opportunity presents itself.

Day Three Hundred and Nine: "Would You Still Love Me?"

Reminding your child that they're loved no matter what is always a good idea.

You love your child unconditionally. You know this for sure, and you show them this through your actions by hugging them after they've disobeyed you or telling them you love them after a disagreement. Another fun way to remind your child of your unconditional love is to play the Would You Still Love Me? game. You tell your child to come up with the craziest ideas about what they could do and then they ask you, "Would you still love me?" Here are examples: "Mommy, would you still love me if I ate a popsicle without asking you?" and you reply, "I would tell you we can't have popsicles for a while, and yes, I'd still love you." "Mom, if I hit my brother, would you still love me?" and you reply, "I would make sure he's okay, ask you why that happened, and yes, I'd still love you." The game can be fun and silly, but the goal is to make sure your child knows the love you have for them is truly unconditional (even when the love you have for their behavior is not!). Take this game and make it your own to remind your child they can always tell you the truth and always let you know how they feel because no matter what, they are unconditionally loved.

The next time you have spare time with your child (in the car, in a waiting room, or at bedtime) bring up this game to add a little extra love (and fun) to your day.

Day Three Hundred and Ten: Supply and Demand

You have an unlimited supply of love for your child.

Motherhood supply and demand goes like this: Kids have an unlimited demand for love and connection, and mothers have a limited supply of . . . themselves (there's likely only one of you). Your children have a cup for love and connection that can never be overfilled. There is no such thing as too much love, which is why your child is always asking for more of it (in many different ways of course). But that endless demand can make you feel that somehow you're not doing it right or that you're not a good-enough mother no matter how much you do. It's important to remember: *Just because your child is always asking for more love and attention doesn't mean they're deprived of it.* Children are programmed to take it all in and rarely turn it down (until the tween and teen years come). So for now, know this: When you've done your best for the day, believe that you've done your best. Just because the demand is high doesn't mean something is wrong with your supply, because you will forever have an unlimited supply of love for your child.

Take a moment to ask your child three ways they know you love them. This is a fun way to get them thinking about how you show love and a great way for you to recognize what's top of mind when they think of what it feels like to be loved!

Day Three Hundred and Eleven:
Three Ways You're Conscious Parenting

You are the true conscious parenting expert because you're the only one who knows what feels right, true, and best for you.

Conscious parenting may seem like another parenting-advice-from-experts trend when really it's about connecting to your inner expert. Here are three ways you might be already consciously parenting because you're connected to the expert inside you:

1. You know it's okay for your child to have big feelings (but that still doesn't mean it's not hard for you to watch and handle those big feelings).
2. You're parenting differently from your parents (not as a diss to them, but because it feels natural and good to grow, evolve, and change).
3. You recognize that your child's behaviors are a form of communication. (You're able to see behaviors as a signal of what your child needs rather than take the behavior at face value or take it personally.)

You are the expert of what feels right for you in motherhood. As you get more comfortable in your skin, you know the connection to yourself and your child is all you really need to be a conscious parent.

Bonus: Another way you're consciously parenting is by holding this very book. You've invested minutes of your day to learn more about yourself (the good, the bad, and the ugly!), so take a second to pat yourself on the back. You're doing it!

Day Three Hundred and Twelve: You Are the Mom You Were Meant to Be

*Someone else's definition of being a good mom
has no business in your personal motherhood library.*

There sure are a lot of opinions out there about how a mother should mother! If you asked five different mothers in your life what the definition of a "good mother" is, you'd likely get different answers. So if someone else's definition of being a good mom makes you feel like you're doing it wrong, remember that their motherhood dictionary has no business in your personal motherhood library. This applies to everyone: your mother, your mother-in-law, your grandmother, your sister, your therapist, your doctor, your neighbor, your best friend, and even your favorite parenting expert. This isn't about being confident; it's about being connected to yourself and therefore connected to your child. It's these two connections that make you the true expert on how to mother your child and how to be a "good mother." So rather than focus on other people's definitions of how to be a good mother, focus on what you know it means to be a good mother to your child.

Think about the mothers in your life and what makes you believe they're doing a great job. Now do the same for yourself and don't cheap out on this! Actually take out a pen and paper (or the Notes app on your phone) and write it out!

Day Three Hundred and Thirteen: Parenting Without Parents

Nothing makes you realize the importance of your role as a mother than mothering without your parent(s).

If you're parenting without a mother (or father), today's message is for you. Whether your parents left this earth too soon or your parents weren't able to be the parents you needed, there's one thing for sure: Parents are some of the most impactful people in our lives. Despite what you've had to endure with your own parents, you are showing up like never before. You're processing your feelings about your own childhood experiences with your mom and/or dad not because you have to, but because you want to . . . to be the mother your child needs. You are seeking out authentic connection to yourself and your child, and because of that you deserve to be proud of yourself. You are the breaker of patterns, the healer of your own wounds; you are everything your family needs. And even though not many people can see it, you are doing big things . . . quite possibly the biggest and most impactful thing: to parent without the parents you so badly need.

Type a letter to your parents (not to send), telling them about the wonderful things you've done so far being a mother, how proud you are of yourself, and how proud you are of your children. This is for you, not them. Sit with it and feel the pride you deserve.

Day Three Hundred and Fourteen: Healing, Not Fixing

Children don't need to be fixed; it's the parent that needs to be healed.

Gone are the days where parenting is solely child focused, geared toward "fixing" the child to be how the parent believes they should be. Today you're being challenged to look at parenting much differently and ask yourself, "Does my child need to be fixed, or does something inside me need tending to?" Yes, the focus has shifted to you, not because something is broken or wrong with you, but rather because something needs to be healed in you. Healed from what? From the unprocessed feelings and buried wounds you've been carrying around that are getting in the way of you being your best self as a mother. For example, you're unbelievably triggered when your child doesn't listen to you and you realize this is a deeper wound being poked from when you weren't heard as a child. Turning the lens on yourself allows you to be free from unnecessary strain between you and your child and helps heal what causes that strain. While this is no easy feat, taking small moments to recognize what might need to be healed within you is one of the most beautiful gifts you can give to your child.

Today practice a self-compassion mini meditation while closing your eyes. Breathe in: "This moment is hard." Breathe out: "It's okay, because this is what hard feels like." Pause: "May I give myself what I need to move through this." Repeat three times or as many times as you need.

Day Three Hundred and Fifteen: Get Comfortable in the Gray Area

Your motherhood is defined by you—
it's not black or white; it's your own shade of gray.

Motherhood seems like it should be clearly defined; after all, there are so many definitions out there as to what motherhood should be. However, motherhood is very much a gray area. You had a whole life before you became a mother; you had other responsibilities that occupied your mind, heart, and time. Becoming a mother changes all of that, even when you keep the same job, home, friends, and lifestyle . . . or try to cling to them the best you can. Rather than try to fit your motherhood into a box, say as a "stay-at-home mom" or a "working mom," why not allow motherhood to be many different shades of gray, your gray, the shade that works best for you where you're at today? Sure, there might be other mothers out there you watch "do it all" in the way you imagined, but the truth is, you really have no idea what their lives really look like. Your motherhood is defined by you. And it certainly doesn't belong in a box that was designed for someone else other than yourself. Get comfortable in your gray area and make it your own.

If you want to define your motherhood status, take a moment to find a phrase that works best for you, maybe "I'm a home parent." If you don't feel the need to define your status, get comfortable saying that too: "I don't like slapping a title on my role; it's too hard to define!"

Day Three Hundred and Sixteen: Compassion Legacy

The way you speak to yourself affects the way you speak to your child.

"What were you thinking?" "How could you do that?" "Why can't you just do what you're supposed to do?" Unfortunately, all mothers have moments when they think or say these things to their children. But how often do you say these things to yourself? The way you speak to yourself often affects the way you speak to your child. The frustration and disappointment with our children often resembles the feelings we have about ourselves. When you speak in a less than loving way to yourself, the same dialogue pops in your head with your child. The good news is, recognizing this connection is a gigantic first step. Once you recognize this connection, give yourself a big dose of compassion because this type of talk was most likely involuntarily passed down to you. Second piece of good news: You can be the breaker of patterns for your family. Again, this requires unlimited self-compassion, so here's what your compassion legacy is going to look like: You speak to yourself with compassion. You speak to your child with compassion. Your child learns to speak to themselves with compassion. This is the new legacy you're creating for your family.

If your friend came to you and shared the unkind words she said to herself, what would you say to her? Now take that and say it to yourself today, because it's important you hear it from a trusted source: yourself.

Day Three Hundred and Seventeen: You Are Not Your Feelings

Noticing and naming how you're feeling is the practice of mindfulness.

In motherhood you have a lot of feelings. Your feelings don't define you. They describe what you're going through in a moment of time. It's easy to get caught up feeling like you are your feelings; for example, it's common to say, "I'm so sad" or "I'm anxious" when really what you mean is "In this moment, I feel sadness" or "Right now I'm feeling anxious." Making that small distinction that your feelings come from you—but they aren't you—allows you to watch your feelings come and go like visitors rather than permanent residents. So the next time you feel stuck in a feeling, practice acknowledging the feeling by saying, "In this moment, I feel frustrated." PS: This practice of acknowledging your feelings in the present moment is the practice of mindfulness!

Experiment time: Note how you're feeling right now. Are you feeling calm, anxious, happy, apathetic? Whatever you are feeling in this moment, open up a calendar reminder in your phone, title it "I'm feeling XYZ" and set it for two hours from now. When you get the alert, note how you're feeling: Do you feel the same feeling at the same intensity? Did it lessen, intensify, or subside?

Day Three Hundred and Eighteen: Boundaries Workout

Holding boundaries is like building muscles;
the resistance lets you know you're making progress.

Creating boundaries in motherhood is a lot like going to the gym to work out. At first, it's hard and painful. You question "Is this even worth it?" and maybe even contemplate giving up. But as you stick to your plan, the pain starts to subside. You get stronger and more confident in your ability. So how do you remain confident when things get hard? You return to your "why." Remember why you've created these boundaries: to create a healthier family life for you and your children. And just like some people will tell you, "Skip the gym, who cares," you'll have people tell you that your boundaries are too stringent, too strict, but you stick to what you know works best for you. Boundaries are just like any other muscle; you have to put in the hard work and effort, but the results are a healthier, happier family.

Be patient with yourself as you build your boundary muscle; start small with a small no today when something doesn't work for you. Let the no come from a place of love for yourself rather than a yes that ignores that knowing.

Day Three Hundred and Nineteen:
Let Go of the Mornings

Never doubt your child's ability to have a good day.

Mornings can be tense. As much as you do your best to get everyone out the door feeling good, loved, and ready for the day, there are times when that's not the case. Having the last moment with your child be one where they are sad, angry, or annoyed can be unsettling. While your child may move on and enjoy their day at school, you're left behind brooding, lamenting, and worrying about your child all day. This does you no good, nor does it help your child. What will help you is to remember that you've laid an incredible foundation for your child, and one tough morning (or even a week of tough mornings) is still supported by the love and connection you've created. Rather than question your child about whether they're okay when they return home, greet them by saying you're happy they're home and stay close by if they want to chat. You'll be there to discuss, repair, or support them if needed, but most importantly, trust in the connection you've built.

A great way to remind your child you love them during those tough moments is to write a few small notes with an "I love you" or other sweet phrase that will make your child smile and keep the notes in a place where you can easily get them. Then when you think your child needs one, tuck a note into their hand or pocket before they leave for the day. Write a few of these today.

Day Three Hundred and Twenty: Mind and Body Connection

Your mind, body, and emotions are always talking to one another.

In your quest for change in motherhood, whether it be more quality time with your child, less yelling, or healthier eating habits, it's important to understand how deeply connected your mind and body are to the emotions driving change. Your body can be in two states: (1) fight or flight or (2) calm and connected. While the fight-or-flight state will motivate you to change, the change is less sustainable because survival mode keeps your mind in a feedback loop of fear and negativity, so even when you make a change, you'll feel like it's never enough. The calm and connected state won't give you the same sense of urgency, but it will allow you to stay motivated because the change you make is rooted in compassion, understanding, and love. This state allows your mind to be in a positive feedback loop, focusing on the good rather than just eliminating the bad. Not only is this helpful for you in motherhood, it's also great for helping your children make changes by using motivation that's rooted in compassion, love, and encouragement.

Do a body scan: Close your eyes and take three deep breaths. Staring at the top of your head, imagine a warm beam of light slowly scanning your body as it makes its way down to your toes. Notice how your body feels. If you feel calm, use this scan when you want to drop into a calm and connected state.

Day Three Hundred and Twenty-One: The "Why" Behind Resentment

Listen to the messages your feelings are sending you.

Your spouse goes off to play a round of golf, and even though you gave your blessing, you're irritated. Sure, you know how important it is to have "me time," but you're resentful that your spouse gets this time and you don't. Is what your feeling anger? Envy? Resentment? It can be all three! But let's help you get to the bottom of this. Ask yourself, "Am I upset because I want that time for myself?" If the answer is yes, great! Now you know you want that same enjoyment. Take a moment to process why you aren't making the same arrangements to have your "me time." Perhaps you feel guilty for taking time away from your family. Perhaps you don't make plans in advance, so when the opportunity presents itself you can't make it happen. Understanding the "why" behind your resentment is essential in making a change for yourself rather than creating an unearned argument with your spouse. Your feelings are always sending you messages; take the time to listen deeply to what they're telling you so you can continue to feel more connected to yourself.

Envy is a great emotion to play with because it shows you what you really want. Keep envy on your radar today to see what it picks up.

Day Three Hundred and Twenty-Two: Being Comfortable with Not Being Confident

It's 100 percent normal to feel 0 percent confident in motherhood.

It's a funny concept, but you can actually work on being comfortable with not being confident in motherhood. Getting comfortable with the unknown, the unresolved, and the undecided is a useful tool. Why? Well, it's pretty normal to not feel confident with every decision you make in motherhood. It's okay to not know for sure, because you quite possibly won't ever know something for sure. What you do know is you use all the resources you have to make the best decisions possible. Here's a practice to try when you're uncomfortable with your uncertainty:

1. Remind yourself that it's okay to not have all the answers right away; time and experience will bring you closer to them.
2. Remind yourself that when a choice is made, you can always choose differently later down the road.
3. Remind yourself that no one else has 100 percent confidence, but you do have 100 percent confidence that you'll make the best choice you can.

Name one area of motherhood you feel most confident in and allow yourself to soak in that feeling for a moment.

Day Three Hundred and Twenty-Three: Mom Bod

Love your body for what it does, which is a whole heck of a lot.

This wouldn't be a book for mothers if it didn't address the unfair pressure placed on mothers' bodies. Hopefully you're reading this feeling all the love in the world for your body that does so much for you and your family. But if you don't, that's okay, too, because there's a way to love your body that isn't forced. The concept of body neutrality takes away a forced positivity and also moves you away from a negative association. Body neutrality says, "Let's remove the pressure from having to love your body and instead appreciate it for what it does rather than how it looks." This is a more genuine approach to loving your body—for how it functions, which does so much for you and your family.

Replace any body negativity you experience today with a body neutrality statement. Here are a couple to get your started: "I appreciate everything my body does for me" and "My body works hard and deserves compassion and respect."

Day Three Hundred and Twenty-Four: Get That Rest

Rest your body before your body rests you.

Every mother's body needs rest, yet every mother's body demands that rest in different ways. In a perfect world, the moment your body gave you cues it needed rest, you'd lie down, close your eyes, and drift off to sleep. The more likely scenario is that you've learned to push your body to its limits and no longer even notice the subtle signs that it needs rest. Your body then learns to communicate in more overt ways like headaches, migraines, muscle tightness, lowered immunity (getting sick often), lack of motivation, flare-ups, and more. As you get more connected to your emotions, you'll get more connected to your body because the two are inextricably linked. You can start tracking how your body is demanding you to rest by noting what parts of your body are trying to slow you down. Then ask yourself, "Have I been missing signs that I need to rest, slow down, or stop (today or this week) that have now exacerbated these physical symptoms I'm experiencing?" Getting curious about how your body speaks to you can help you rest your body before your body rests you.

Take a moment to make an appointment with any healthcare providers you need a checkup with: primary physician, specialty physician, therapist, chiropractor, acupuncturist, physical therapist, and so on.

Day Three Hundred and Twenty-Five: Don't Change; Heal

You don't have to change who you are; you have to heal what's preventing who you are from shining through.

With all the messages you receive as a mother, the common theme is that you need to change some part of yourself in order to be whole. And while there's nothing wrong with wanting to make changes to feel better, when you're shifting from a place of not being "enough," it can feel like you're on a never-ending treadmill. Not only is this exhausting, it's also untrue, because who you are at your core is your authentic self and doesn't need to change—rather you need to heal. Heal the parts that aren't serving you anymore so you can get back to your authentic self. Healing is the act of making something right again, to make it better and restore it to its original healthy function. So rather than "changing" into some new version of yourself that feels daunting and unknown, you're just healing so you can return to your true self. So the next time you feel like you have to be someone completely new, remember that you don't need to change; you need to heal.

Think back to being a child: You knew who you were, what you liked, and what you didn't—there was no question. This is the essence of your true self. Close your eyes and imagine that feeling right now—to know what you like and don't like with no fear to be honest. Embrace that moment and let it take over your body for sixty seconds.

Day Three Hundred and Twenty-Six: Hold Boundaries, Not Grudges

Holding grudges keeps you stuck; holding boundaries sets you free.

Have you ever held a grudge? If so, you know it feels like a form of protection. Especially as a mother, you'll have even more mama bear energy to protect not just yourself, but your children too. You're not going to let down your guard; you don't want to get hurt. However, a grudge can also have the essence of anger, vengeance, or resentment, which over time can end up hurting you because you're the one carrying it around. This message offers you an option to swap: Hold a boundary, not a grudge. A boundary provides the same protection without the inner turmoil. A boundary has the essence of self-love, confidence, and trust. You hold a boundary because you have love for yourself; you know what's best for yourself, and you trust yourself enough to carry it through. So the next time you feel the toxicity of a grudge impeding your life, swap it out with a boundary. Let the love you have for yourself take the reins to do what's best for you and your family.

There's a saying: "Resentment is like taking poison and waiting for the other person to die." While this is a bit extreme, it shows the impact of holding grudges; they end up hurting you more than protecting you. Ask yourself today, "What grudge can I swap out for a boundary?"

Day Three Hundred and Twenty-Seven: Handling Negative Comments

What others say about you says much more about them than you.

You've received many compliments in your life. So why does the one negative comment stand out among the ninety-nine positive comments? The answer is simple: survival. Yes, even though you're living in the most advanced time ever for humans, your brain is still hardwired for survival in the most primal way: to look for threats and activate the body to protect itself. Your brain might not be looking out for animal predators, but it is looking out for psychological and emotional ones, which show up in the form of constructive feedback, negative comments, and insults. This is why you think about that one snide comment at a birthday party rather than all the comments about how lovely it is. Chalk this up to nature and then nurture yourself back to the truth that you're not in danger and that a comment can be discarded (even though it is hurtful!).

Today practice labeling anything that makes you feel less than happy as a threat and then ask yourself, "Am I really in danger here? Will this really affect my life?" If there's no truth to it, discard it and allow yourself to be free of that unnecessary weight.

Day Three Hundred and Twenty-Eight: You Are Not Your Pattern

To know your ego is to know the biggest bandage ever created.

Ever wonder why you end up in the same situations in motherhood? Maybe it's feelings of frustration for not being appreciated at home or feelings of being misunderstood by your family. These are patterns of feeling—but you are not your pattern. Patterns are a function of your ego—not the self-important ego, but rather the ego that is there to protect you from hurt, keep you safe, and get you the most love as possible. Think of the ego like the biggest bandage for your emotional pain. The ego can take many forms like of a perfectionist, people pleaser, martyr, or type A overachiever. All those identities are not you; they are temporary parts of you. The ego is what has created patterns that once helped you, but no longer help you now in motherhood. The next time you find yourself in a pattern, don't ask, "Why do I keep doing this?" Instead ask, "How did this way of being or feeling once help me?" Understanding the function of your ego's pattern lessens its power and invites you to let go of what no longer serves you.

The ego isn't a bad part of you; it's incredibly resourceful. Take a moment to thank your ego today for all its done for you because it deserves gratitude for working overtime for so long. You can also invite it to take a break, and let it know, "I got this today, don't worry; I know you'll be there if I need you."

Day Three Hundred and Twenty-Nine: Use the Unkind Rewind

"Monkey see, monkey do" can be used to model how to handle old behaviors and replace them with new, desirable behaviors.

No mother is perfect. We all lose our cool, say the wrong things, and wish we had a "redo." But what if you had a way to help you disarm, model apologizing, and start over? Introducing the *unkind rewind*. The unkind rewind only requires two things: acknowledging when you've made a mistake and a dose of lightheartedness. Step one is acknowledging you messed up, were unkind, or did something you're not proud of with your child. Step two is saying out loud, "I need an unkind rewind." Step three is signaling to your children a visual of you "rewinding" what you just did and replacing it with a new, healthier, and more desirable approach. You can actually pretend to rewind yourself in slow motion, or simply say, "I need to try that again" or "Whoa, I didn't like how I said that to you, I'm sorry. What I really meant to say was . . . " Using this redo to right your wrongs will give your child a model to do the same. You can even prompt your child when you catch them being unkind and say, "Hmm, I think you meant to say this . . . Do you need an unkind rewind?" Modeling is one of the best ways for your children to learn how to cope with life situations.

Start using the unkind rewind today. Any small redo will do! The goal is for you to use it around your children so they can learn a shame-free way to handle apologies, self-forgiveness, and starting over.

Day Three Hundred and Thirty: Two Things Can Be True

*Two things can be true. You can love your
kids and need time away from them too.*

When your child learns the "two things can be true" principle, it allows them to accept the complexity that is human emotion. For example, you are a mother who loves her child and yet you can also need time away from them too. While intellectually you agree with this, emotionally you might feel otherwise. A great way to explain the need for your own time away (with or without your spouse or friends) to yourself and your children is to compare it to your children hanging out with their friends or going on playdates or to birthday parties or camp. "You know how you love being with your friends? You love our time together and you love time to have fun with someone else besides me. The same is true for me; I love you and I love having time alone to read, go to dinner, and . . . " The more you can make connections between your and your child's common human needs, the more you normalize what you're both going through in the journey of motherhood, childhood, and just life in general.

You and your child come up with two things that can be true, but make it fun: "Mom loves ice cream, and too much of it can make her stomach hurt!" Or: "You love your birthday as your favorite holiday to see your friends, and you love Thanksgiving because you get to see your cousins!"

Day Three Hundred and Thirty-One: Motherhood Serenity Prayer

May you have the serenity to accept the things you cannot change, the courage to change the things you can, and the wisdom to know the difference.

The serenity prayer gives guidance to practice acceptance, courage, and wisdom. It's certainly a great mantra to utilize in motherhood: *"Grant me the serenity to accept the things I cannot change, the courage to change the things I can, and the wisdom to know the difference."* This is a truly powerful guide in your motherhood journey, as there are so many things you cannot change (your children, spouse, and members of your family of origin), there are many things within yourself that you can change (learning new coping skills), and knowing the difference between the two is key (for example, knowing you can't change how your child feels, but you can help them learn new coping skills to handle those emotions). Perhaps you already know this prayer well or you're just vaguely aware of it—either way, let it be at the front of your mind today as you notice how often you're faced with using the wisdom of knowing what you can and cannot change.

In the Notes app in your phone, type this mantra and commit it to memory this weekend. Let it be a reminder to help you sort through unnecessary added stress by practicing more acceptance.

Day Three Hundred and Thirty-Two: Motherhood Bloopers

Motherhood is a series of bloopers and outtakes.

What you see about motherhood on social media is usually the finished product in parenting. You see the smiling family photos, the winners of competitions, and mostly the good stuff. What you're seeing is the fully edited and executed moments. And there's nothing wrong with sharing the good stuff, as long as you know it takes so much to get there and it's just a moment in time. Think of these social media posts like the final cut of a movie. Motherhood, however, is really more about the bloopers and the outtakes. Without the bloopers, you wouldn't have room to grow. Without the outtakes, life would be pretty boring. So today remember you're allowed to have those moments. You are allowed to wish you had an understudy to take over when you aren't feeling your best. You're allowed to improvise when you have no earthly idea what to do. If you lose your temper, you're allowed to apologize, call it a blooper, and then try it again. Now get out there and break a leg; you got this!

Ask your kids to make a short movie using your phone about being a mom, being a kid, or being any family member and watch the silliness that ensues.

Day Three Hundred and Thirty-Three: Outer Order, Inner Peace

Inner order is what truly creates peace.

To feel like your space is cared for and clear of clutter promotes clarity, calm, and relaxation. But for some, external order isn't just a preference, it's also a requirement. Without it, you might feel anxious, uneasy, less than, or unable to function at your best—your need for order is much deeper than a deep spring cleaning. If this sounds like you, it's likely that cleanliness and order have become a security blanket for you. You feel soothed to see everything in place, and it's almost as if external order is what allows for internal order. But when you can't achieve that external order, it's hard for you to function as your best motherly self. That's when it's helpful to explore where your need for that order and control originated. Think back to your younger years when you didn't feel safe or felt worried, powerless, or unsure of what was to come. It's likely you learned to use control of your environment to cope. Yet now that you are an adult who has much more say in her life, you can tend to those wounds of worry and soothe them by cleaning out the old angst that no longer belongs in your present. Then you will discover it is inner order that really creates peace.

Your need for order isn't negative in any way. So thank yourself for the respectful ways to handle your inner struggles and allow that part of yourself to be appreciated, thanked, and loved. As you make peace with this, growth will follow.

Day Three Hundred and Thirty-Four: Resist the People-Pleasing Mindset

If you don't want to raise a people pleaser, learn how to handle your own discomfort when your child isn't happy with you.

People-pleasing is often about not having to handle your own feelings because you're so focused on others. And having people-pleasing tendencies might have worked for you in the past. But now that you're a mom, the control that people-pleasing gives you goes out the window because you can't always please kids, and that in turn exposes your inability to handle your own uncomfortable feelings. Motherhood is the perfect environment for you to slowly let go of the belief that you must make others happy to be okay. Practice grounding yourself in what boundaries you know are necessary and prepare your heart and mind for your child's reaction that might be less than happy. In the end your job is to keep your children safe, healthy, and loved—happy is just a bonus that comes along the way.

Today use this motherhood mantra: "I'm responsible for my kids' safety, health, and love even when it doesn't make them happy; I know my choices are rooted in that love."

Day Three Hundred and Thirty-Five: How to Not Raise a Perfectionist

Self-esteem is gained by doing "esteem-able" things.

No mother sets out and says, "I want to raise a perfectionist child!" Yet there are sneaky little ways your own coping mechanisms of perfectionism can make their way into motherhood. Here are three ways to ensure you're not raising a perfectionist:

1. Let your child see you fail and cope with that failure. It can be as small as burning dinner and saying, "Gosh, I really messed this one up! That stinks, but hey, I guess it's a pizza night for us instead."

2. Let your child lose. Boosting a child's self-esteem doesn't come from letting them win; it comes from allowing them to see their effort pays off. So when your child doesn't win a game, let them know it's normal to be upset and trying again is what makes you better.

3. Break new tasks and activities into small, achievable goals. This shows your child they can do hard things especially when you take one step at a time.

Today teach your child something new and break down the steps into small, achievable goals. Let your child see their progression and allow them to have whatever feelings come their way without trying to do anything for them. Ideas: Draw a new object, memorize a poem, learn a new dance move, or commit to memory a family's phone number.

Day Three Hundred and Thirty-Six: It's Okay to Not Be Okay

It's okay to not be okay, but don't let that convince you not being okay is here to stay.

There are so many lovely efforts to normalize the human experience of emotions. One you may have heard is "It's okay to not be okay," which is absolutely true because in motherhood there are many moments where you don't feel okay! However, there's a very important addition that needs to be made: "It's okay to not be okay, but don't let that convince you not being okay is here to stay." Why? Because it's important to remember that feelings are not permanent. In the moments when you're not okay, you can accept that it is okay to feel this way, but also that it won't last; it will pass, fade, and lessen. This phrase is a life raft to help you not take the bait of that bad mood, hard moment, or uncomfortable feeling that it's here to stay. Feel what you feel, but also remember you're able to heal.

Visualization technique: Imagine a time in your past that was tough to get through and how it's no longer in your present. A great one to remember is a time you were delayed at the airport: You were probably miserable, tired, and annoyed, yet you did get home, slept in your bed, and were able to carry on with your life. Use a similar memory to help anchor you when you have tough moments to remind you that nothing is here to stay.

Day Three Hundred and Thirty-Seven: Why You Yell

A mother never yells because she feels in control.

If you could remain calm, collected, and confident when you speak to your child, would you choose to yell? Probably not. That's because yelling doesn't feel like a choice; it feels like a last resort. There are three main factors contributing to raising your voice:

1. You feel out of control because you feel worried, frustrated, or helpless.
2. You're taking your child's behavior personally, so you feel under attack, reactive, and defensive.
3. It's all you know. Perhaps your parents yelled at you, so it's the only tool in your toolbox.

For most mothers, it's a combination of all three! It's no wonder yelling happens even when you're not intending it to; there are too many paths leading to that outcome! Rather than be upset with yourself, choose compassion today. Choose compassion because you've learned that you aren't yelling to be a mean mom; you're yelling because you are in need of new coping mechanisms, outlooks, and tools. As you continue reading this book, you'll develop the understanding and tools to let go of those outdated parenting approaches.

Believe it or not, you cannot control your feelings—but you can control your behavior. Today, notice how quickly your feelings prompt your behavior. The moment you notice a feeling, try and delay your reaction just a few seconds. This will build over time, and you'll feel so much more in control of your behaviors.

Day Three Hundred and Thirty-Eight: More Than the Title of Mom

Have you ever stopped to ask yourself,
"Who am I?" outside your role as mom?

A mom is certainly one of the most important parts of your identity, but it is not all that you are. It sure might feel like a mom is your only identity, but you are more than your role, title, or job. You're more than a mom, wife, coparent, coworker, daughter, sister, and so on, because all these roles define who you are based on other people. And while these titles are some of the greatest honors, when your identity and worth are solely based on the people outside you, you're bound to feel like you're lacking. So today, rather than define yourself by your titles or roles, take a moment to define yourself by who you are in your soul. Are you soft, patient, calm, and steady? Are you passionate, energetic, open-minded, and creative? Find the adjectives that describe who you are at your core and write them down on a sheet of paper to see what you've discovered about yourself in just a few moments of pausing to detach yourself from those other identities. When you know who you are aside from your role as mom, you create an anchor tethered to your core self. Remembering this will carry you through the many seasons of motherhood.

It's a bit odd to stop and think, "Who am I?" yet it's important to know, isn't it? Today be sure to do the adjective exercise mentioned in this entry and be sure to write out what you discover.

Day Three Hundred and Thirty-Nine: Thank-You Note

*Your child may not say it today, so thank you
for being a wonderful mother.*

Just in case your child hasn't written you a thank-you note for all you do, here it is:

Dear Mom,

From the moment you knew I would be your child, you wondered who I would be. Yet one thing you never wondered was what you knew for certain: that you could love me just for being me. You let me cry without being scared it will make me weak. You show me my worth is independent of my achievements. You see through my anger and frustration when I can't express my feelings, and you love me harder. You set boundaries for me that I don't like, but are teaching me how to set them for myself. You don't rescue me from my mistakes, but instead you show me how to have compassion for myself while I learn from them. You make me feel safe to be me. You do so much that no one sees, so it's time you get a thank-you from me.

Love,
Your Child

Write a letter to your child today just because you love them. It can be short, silly, long, or heartfelt—taking a moment to write a letter is an act of love we can all use a little more of.

Day Three Hundred and Forty: Deconstructing Behavior

Behind every behavior lies a feeling and need trying to be met.

Behind a child's yelling, tantrums, or meltdowns lies a feeling. Behind that feeling lies a need. The same goes for you too. Your behavior is motivated by your feelings and needs. Let's deconstruct one of the most common motherhood behaviors:

- **Behavior:** You raised your voice when your child wasn't listening.
- **Feeling:** You feel angry, frustrated, or worried.
- **Need:** You want to feel in control, respected, competent, and loved.

After breaking this down, rather than think you're a "bad mom" or "mean mom," you see that you aren't raising your voice to be mean, but because you have needs that haven't been met. As you break down the behavior, feeling, and need, you'll be able to approach the situation much differently: You'll feel more understanding and less judgment. The more you can do this with yourself, the easier it will be to do with your child. Rather than see your child's behavior through a lens of judgment, you can see it as a need that is trying to be met.

The next time your child is behaving in a not-so-wonderful way, ask yourself, "Why would I act this way?" to uncover which need your child is seeking to be met.

Day Three Hundred and Forty-One: Eight Things You Deserve to Hear

You are loved not for what you do, but just for being you.

In case your mom never told you, here are eight things you absolutely deserve to hear. One, you are not responsible for what happened to you in your childhood. Your only responsibility was to be a child, to be watched over, loved, and cared for unconditionally by your caregivers. Two, you are whole and a masterpiece in progress all at the same time. Three, don't be afraid of your feelings; they are key to your healing. Feel them and they will pass; resist them and they will persist. Four, you are not responsible for anyone else's happiness, especially your own parents'. Five, don't take anything personally; everyone's behaviors reflect their own feelings and needs. Six, you are allowed to say no to whoever and whenever because only you know what's best for you. Seven, there's a solution to every problem; it's okay to sit in the unknown until you discover what's best for you. Eight, you are loved not for what you do, but just for being you.

Choose one of these eight reminders to share with a friend that you think could really use the reminder.

Day Three Hundred and Forty-Two: Rejection and Redirection

Rejection hurts; redirection takes the sting away.

Rejection is one of the most difficult human emotions to cope with at any age. Now that you're a mother, you'll also have to walk with your children through their experiences of rejection, so here are a few reminders to help you help them:

- First, your child doesn't have to "get over it" as quickly as you might get over feeling rejected. Everyone processes their own emotions differently, and it's okay if it takes them a bit longer than it would take you.
- Second, you don't have to make your child the good guy and someone else the bad guy. You can teach your child that sometimes things just don't fall in their favor.
- Third, stick to the facts. It's easy to get carried away with assumptions, but this is like sticking your finger in an open wound. Instead help your child stick to the facts: "You tried out for that team and you didn't make it; you have every right to be disappointed."

Finally, rejection hurts, but redirection can help take that sting away. Show your child what can come from this experience—not to take away from what hurts, but to practice looking for the good wherever you are.

Has rejection ever led you to a better outcome? If so, share this story with your child this evening. If they're younger, you can even turn it into the form of a fairy tale.

Day Three Hundred and Forty-Three:
Bad Day Self-Care

*If you cared for yourself like you care for your child,
you'd feel a lot more self-love.*

When your child has an off day or is feeling down or not themselves, how do you treat them? Do you get mad at them for their bad mood, or do you approach them with comfort and concern? It's probably the latter because oftentimes mothers have more compassion for their children than for themselves. You'd probably sit next to your child and say, "I understand, sweetie, you probably need a good meal, a bath, and a great night's sleep." What are the chances you'd care for yourself that same way? Hopefully the chances are high, but if not, perhaps you're less compassionate and more judgmental regarding yourself. If so, you have to work on being more self-compassionate. First and foremost, because you deserve to love yourself like you love your children. And second, your child watches how you treat yourself, and as lovely as you are to them, they'll learn from you what self-love, self-compassion, and self-care look like. As you make your way through motherhood, you can learn to love and accept all the parts of yourself not by pretending to love having a bad day, but by practicing loving yourself even when you have a bad day.

You probably already have specific ways you care for yourself on a bad day, so today pick three actions to identify as your "bad day care plan." An example: Take a hot shower, drink tea, and wear your favorite cozy pajamas.

Day Three Hundred and Forty-Four: Internal Narratives

*Understanding breeds clarity and
sometimes even a little compassion too.*

The internal narrative inside your mind is strong. You might notice it often or rarely at all. The narrative plays like an album on a loop, changing songs depending on what you're doing and how you're feeling. While you likely have positive or comforting narratives, the one that may deserve tweaking is the narrative that plays when you've made a mistake in motherhood: "What's wrong with me?" or "How come I can never do this right?" If narratives like these pop up, they probably keep you feeling trapped or like a victim to your own behaviors. A trick to take yourself out of this loop is to replace the narrative with a question: "What happened to me that makes me respond this way?" or "What about this feeling is familiar from my younger years?" This prompt stops you in your tracks on an unconscious, outdated narrative and switches your brain into conscious curiosity to find real clarity and change. Replacing your own unkind narratives will also help you parent your children through their mistakes.

Using a question that drives true curiosity to understand yourself rather than punish yourself is the path to changing those unhelpful internal narratives. Instead of using rhetorical questions today, replace them with truly helpful questions: "Why does it feel so personal when my child doesn't eat their meal?" or "What is it about someone not hearing me the first time that makes me so hurt?"

Day Three Hundred and Forty-Five: The Silver Lining of Sickness

Sickness lets your guard down just enough to get a glimmer of who you are without all your armor.

If you've ever been sick and still had to take care of your children, you'd probably laugh in someone's face if they told you there's a silver lining there. How could that be, when you're sick and exhausted? Well, as hard as it is to imagine, there are some small glimmers to look out for:

1. **Pumping the breaks.** Sickness has a special way of bringing your life to a halt. It's never planned, yet it tends to show you how much excess is crammed into your life. You're forced to see what matters most.
2. **Receiving.** Sickness has a way of letting your guard down by allowing you to receive help that you normally wouldn't.
3. **Inner child healing.** Sickness strips down your ego self. This lets you face your inner childhood wounds and heal them by experiencing feelings the ego normally covers up.

Whatever your motherhood journey looks like, know there are always silver linings along the way . . . even when they come in the form of coughing and sneezing.

Hopefully you're not sick reading this entry. However, if anyone you know isn't feeling well (especially a mother), text them, pick up the phone, or send a small token of love today to show your support.

Day Three Hundred and Forty-Six: You Don't Complete Me

Children are born complete, not born to make you feel complete.

"You complete me." It sounds so lovely, doesn't it? That thought that someone is the missing puzzle piece to your life. But when you say it to your kids, talk about putting pressure on them! Okay, we know the sentiment behind this statement is filled with love, that life makes more sense with your children in it. However, it's important to note that we're all born complete. Children don't exist to make their parents whole and complete; rather children exist because they *are* whole and complete. Children simply remind us that we all are complete, something we forget along our way in life. As a child you eat, sleep, and play, and it's more than enough. But as you spend more time in the world, you receive messages that your worth becomes contingent on other things like success, education, beauty, and so on. So rather than teach your children that your wholeness is tied to them or anything else on the outside, practice reminding yourself of your own wholeness. This will help you slowly remove conditions from your own self-love. And of course this feeling of true self-acceptance will also flow over to your children as well.

Three times today, close your eyes, place your hand on your chest, and say silently, to yourself, "I am whole as I am, without anything or anyone; I am whole."

Day Three Hundred and Forty-Seven: Honest Greetings

Humans are wired for connection, and mothers have the most powerful ways to create it.

It's interesting how you can spend a whole day interacting with others yet still feel so isolated or alone as a mother. Think about how many times someone says, "Hi, how are you?" yet there's no true interaction about how you're doing. Why? Because it has become a polite and standard greeting met with a polite and standard reply. It can feel like no one cares about your experience as a mother, yet people do care. You see, we are all wired for connection; it's just that our modern society has streamlined communication in a way that feels less personal and more automatic. But you get to change that starting today. Wherever you go today, when someone asks how you're doing, pause and then don't reply with a one-word answer. You don't have to go crazy, but you can widen the scope of connection with some authenticity: "Oh man, I've been stuck home all day with this little guy; it makes me miss being out there in the world like you are, but I'm sure you'd like to be home, too. . . . Funny how that works, right?" Who knows where that conversation will lead, but what it does is restore connection and removes the automatic reply that can make life feel stagnant and isolating.

In the next interaction you have on the phone or in the checkout line, share something more than "I'm well; how are you?" Not only will this spark more connection in your life, it might make someone else's day that much better too.

Day Three Hundred and Forty-Eight: Parentified Mothers

*To give your child a mother they don't have
to worry about is the greatest gift of all.*

If you grew up "fast" because you had life situations that required you to be more mature, take on adult responsibilities, or feel responsible for family members' emotions, you experienced a form of parentification. Parentification is when a child is asked to fulfill a parent's physical, emotional, or mental responsibilities. While now you're a strong woman, you were once a child who carried more than you should have. The effects of parentification tend to show up in mothers in different ways: You struggle to play or be silly, have a hard time connecting to your child's feelings, aren't able to trust others to care for your children responsibly, or feel guilty needing support. These struggles come about because you weren't able to have a true childlike childhood. So now as an adult, things like being playful or asking for help can feel wrong because you never experienced the safety of being able to do so as a child. The good news is that becoming a mother is healing; as you create a safe, loving, and secure environment for your own children, you'll be able to experience through them what you once missed out on.

Find a photo of yourself as a young child and write a short letter to her—perhaps about how much you admire her resilience or that when she becomes a mother she'll be sure to pass on a true childhood to her children and give them all the love and safety she could ever dream of.

Day Three Hundred and Forty-Nine: "Do I Matter?"

*Every child wants to know they're loved; they just
ask you in the most disguised forms of behavior.*

Any mother will tell you she loves her children and in the same breath tell you her children do annoying, bothersome, and frustrating things. But what if you start looking at your child's "annoying" behavior like they're saying, "Look at me, Mommy" for the hundredth time as a way of really saying, "Do I matter, Mommy?" While this reframe may tug at your heartstrings, it's not to make you feel guilty or make excuses for unhealthy behaviors; it's to help you remember that your child always wants to be seen, acknowledged, accepted, and approved of by you. When you factor that into the equation, it helps you move a notch down the "annoyed" meter and meet your child with a bit more understanding. Rather than ask, "Why is my child doing that?" ask, "What is my child seeking right now?"

If you're annoyed with your spouse, do you always tell them right away? Or do you behave in subtle or not-so-subtle ways to let them know? Maybe you huff and puff and say something with an attitude. . . . But what if instead of taking the bait, they said, "Hey, you don't seem like yourself. Can we talk? I want to make sure you know I love you and am here for you." You'd probably feel less activated and more loved, right? Try this with your child and watch how quickly that situation changes.

Day Three Hundred and Fifty: Projection or Protection?

Are you protecting or are you projecting? That is the question.

When you want to give your children the best childhood possible, part of that comes with protecting your children from the unpleasant experiences you faced as a child. This is a beautiful way to heal yourself and give your children a great childhood. The most important part of this process is being aware of where your own childhood wounds lie. Why? Because protection can unintentionally turn into projection, meaning you can unconsciously assume that your feelings or experiences are your child's too. An example of this is knowing you struggled in math, so when your child doesn't perform well on a math test, rather than assume they'll struggle for life, you pause to reflect on what feelings are coming up for you versus what your child is experiencing. So when you find yourself overcorrecting something in your child, pause and ask yourself, "How much of this is mine and how much is my child's?" By knowing what parts of your child's life remind you of your own life, you can prevent yourself from projecting unnecessary problems onto your child and allow them to live this beautiful love you've given them.

Today name one thing you want to intentionally pass on to your child. Maybe it's self-love, confidence, humor, or kindness. Make that your focus for today when you interact with your child.

Day Three Hundred and Fifty-One: When You Don't Want to Parent

Rest is best when you don't feel your best.

Have you ever had a day where you look at the clock and it's only 2 p.m., yet you're exhausted, wiped out, and finishing the day feels harder than climbing Mount Everest? You must be a mom. There might be a battle going on inside you, with one side telling you to get up, be more productive, organize the house, and be on top of the world and another side telling you that you're exhausted, you're over it, and you need a break. It's important that you remember how much you do: Every day you take care of yourself, your children, and your whole family, but you don't just care for them physically, you care for them around the clock mentally and are always attuned to them emotionally. This is a job that never ends, and therefore you'll have moments when you simply don't want to do it all. These moments have nothing to do with how much you love your child or your worth as a mother, but rather it's about being a human being who needs a break. So the next time you feel that "I don't want to parent" feeling, don't shame yourself; accept how normal that is and give yourself as much compassion as you can.

On the days you don't feel like parenting, give yourself permission to do what it takes to have an easy day. Have pizza for dinner, skip bath time, and let yourself off the hook for a day.

Day Three Hundred and Fifty-Two: Big Feeling Moments

The easiest thing you'll ever do is love your child;
the hardest thing you'll ever do is parent them.

Children of all ages experience big feeling moments—heck, humans of all ages do. When your child is having a big feeling moment, things tend to get heated and escalate quickly, so it's important to avoid exacerbating an already tense time. The biggest trap mothers fall into is to make *assumptions* and *judgments* about their child's feelings. You might assume your child's intentions (they're doing this on purpose) or the validity of their feelings (there's no way they're really mad at this) or you might judge their intensity (this is such an overreaction). All of these tend to separate you from your child rather than connect you. So the next time you feel yourself making one of those judgments or assumptions, pause. Even though you might not understand your child's feelings, they're what's present in this moment. You cannot change that, but you can allow it. Rather than resist, deny, or judge your child, accept that this is where they're at for now. Doing so will soften the tension you feel and allow your child to move past their feelings naturally. It's not easy, but it's *easier* when you aren't fighting feelings and instead flowing with them.

Get curious today when you watch your child. How often do you make assumptions and judgments about their behavior: their intentions, the validity, and the intensity? What does it feel like to drop those and instead say, "This is how they are right now; I can't change it, but I can be here when they've moved past it"?

Day Three Hundred and Fifty-Three: Why You Second-Guess Yourself

When you learn to trust yourself, life feels a little less daunting.

It's common to waver when making a big decision. After all, it's healthy to carefully assess your options, especially when you're a mother in charge of decisions for a whole family. But if you find yourself in a constant state of second-guessing yourself, you might be getting lost in what you need to do versus what you think you "should" do. You also might be fearful of making the wrong decision, so you stay stuck instead. Or you make a decision but then torture yourself with guilt and anxiety over your choice. No matter what the second-guessing is about, what lies beneath is a lack of trust in yourself. Lack of trust in yourself is learned, and it's usually unintentionally learned from a young age by your caregivers repetitively invalidating your feelings—being told you're too sensitive or your feelings are wrong, being blamed for others' feelings, or being harshly judged. It's no wonder you hem and haw over decisions; you learned you weren't capable of trusting your own feelings! So rather than beat yourself up for second-guessing yourself, honor that second-guessing for trying to protect you from feeling that pain you once felt as a child. Give yourself compassion and grace as you reconnect to trusting your feelings.

What do you trust yourself the most with? Where are you most confident? Sit with that feeling for a minute, close your eyes, and affirm, "I trust myself to [fill in the blank]." Repeat this three times.

Day Three Hundred and Fifty-Four: When You've Had a Bad Day

Your feelings are fluid and forever changing; the only thing that keeps them stagnant is not letting them be felt.

You made it. You had a choice to make it through a bad day and you did. It's easy to take for granted how often you make it through hard moments, hard days, hard weeks, and even hard months. Always remember that your feelings are fluid, forever changing. The bad won't always be so bad. Your secret weapon to getting through these bad days is really in your ability to acknowledge and accept your feelings. This doesn't mean you like them. This doesn't mean you wallow in them. It's simply being present with them. When you are present with your feelings, they won't stay trapped in your body. You experience them and they eventually subside. You're going to have bad days. Watch them come and go. Do what you can to help them be present so they can leave as fast as they came.

Today you're going to create your own bad day insurance policy, so you know what works for you: Call your favorite people, journal your feelings, do whatever it takes to let your feelings come up and out.

Day Three Hundred and Fifty-Five: The Superhero Myth

The only superhuman thing about mothers is their love for their child; that kind of love has superpowers.

The whole "Moms are superheroes" compliment has great intentions, right? Like you appreciate that others see how much you do all at once with limited resources. That does feel very superhuman, but you're not a superhero. You're human. You need sleep, support, and self-care. The fact that you keep running without those basic necessities isn't being superhuman; it's actually survival. So rather than continue to buy into that unsustainable way of mothering, remember, you are a normal human that needs normal human things. This means saying no to a sleepover your child wants because you need a weekend off to rest. This means calling a family member or friend to come help you for an hour because you just need space and time alone. No one else is going to change the narrative of your motherhood—only you. This is your motherhood, and you get to regain control over it—not to be a superhero, but to be super attuned to yourself so that you can show up to be the mom you want to be.

Have some fun with this and talk with your children tonight about what superpowers they would have if they could be a superhero. You can share what yours would be too!

Day Three Hundred and Fifty-Six: Protection Mode

You can't hate away the parts of yourself that are trying to protect you, so thank them for their service and they'll eventually be on their way.

Imagine you're happily camping in the woods, then all of a sudden a bear comes out of the bushes and immediately your body goes into survival mode and you run to safety. Next week you go camping again; there's no bear, but your body is acting like it did before—the sheer sight of the camping grounds gets you nervous! Why does this happen? To protect you of course. This story helps you understand your emotional reactions in motherhood. If your child is difficult at bedtime in a particular week, the next week you're going to anticipate that same struggle. You're going to be tense, defensive, and ready for the battle. This is where you get to talk to your body about keeping you safe, because being in a defensive state at bedtime only exacerbates the issue. Rather than be annoyed with your child, thank your body for doing its job and then let it off the hook: "I'm actually safe here tonight. I got this, but thanks for looking out." When you befriend and thank your body for doing its job to "protect" you, that part of you can release and allow the more evolved conscious parenting parts to step forward and take the reins.

Think about which parts of motherhood you approach with a preconceived idea of what's going to happen. Try thanking that thought for its protection and invite a new approach to your meeting your child in that moment. Replace "This is always difficult" with "Let's make this fun."

Day Three Hundred and Fifty-Seven: Reframing

When your reframe game is strong,
it strengthens your ability to handle anything.

Let's dive into what reframing is, what it isn't, and how it can really change your motherhood game. Reframing is a cognitive technique where you intentionally shift your view of a situation by looking at it from a different perspective. Essentially, you're looking at the situation differently to help you *handle* the outcome differently. What reframing isn't is a way to pretend your feelings don't matter or cover up a situation that is truly hurtful or harmful. The way reframing can really change how you parent is by allowing yourself new ways to approach the same old situations. If your child comes home from school and doesn't talk to you and you frame that as "My child has no respect or appreciation for me," your approach to connect with your child is limited. If you reframe it with "I wonder what's going on with my child after school; maybe they're overtired, overstimulated, or overwhelmed," you're going to approach your child differently. This reframe doesn't sugarcoat, pretend, or ignore any facts; it simply shifts how you see your child and approach them. Reframes are helpful in any relationship and will truly shape your mother-child relationship for the better.

The next time you feel irritated at someone in your family, try using one of these reframes: "What do I need more of right now to feel calm?" or "What need is my child not having met that they're acting this way?"

Day Three Hundred and Fifty-Eight: Children Aren't Carbon Copies

*Your child has their own unique spirit and soul,
separate from you; honor that as much as you can.*

Your daughter might have your eyes, or your son might have your witty humor, but your children have their own unique, individual spirits. You love to see yourself in your child; it lights you up to watch your genes expressed in the form of the cutest little humans you've ever seen. But one important thing to remember is that just because your child came from you doesn't mean they are exactly like you. As innocuous as "Oh, you're just like your mother: a little mini me!" can sound, it places an unconscious expectation on your child to be someone else. Our children aren't our carbon copies: They aren't here to live out our dreams; they're here to create their own. So while you might be excited to see your child take up the same sport or hobby as you, remember in the back of your mind they're a unique soul, and their journey will be different from yours—not because they don't love you or want to honor you, but because you're raising them to love and honor themselves first.

Honor your child's individual spirit today by drawing attention to their unique efforts and approach to life.

Day Three Hundred and Fifty-Nine: When Someone You Love Is In Pain

There's no wrong way to check in and say, "I'm thinking of you."

You love your children more than anything in the world, and when they're in pain you know how to comfort them. But what happens when someone who's not your child, someone you love, is in pain? You don't have the same abilities to care for them as you do your child, so you might feel at a loss how to approach them. Here are some tips to help someone you love who is in pain:

- First, take a moment to see what their pain is bringing up for you. Acknowledge how it's making you feel and know it's okay to have your own secondary pain.
- Second, remember that as much as you would love to, you don't have the ability to save or take away this person's pain.
- Third, what you can do for them is just be there for them. Make your presence and love known. Text often, call regularly, show up in person when you can, and tell them you love them all the time.

Lastly, the simplest form of checking in is more than enough: "I'm thinking about you; how are you feeling today?" Holding space for others in pain isn't easy; it makes you uncomfortable to not be able to get rid of their pain, so be compassionate and remember that every human being just wants to know they're loved and they're not alone.

Take a moment to send a text to someone you know that could really use a check-in, a hello, or an "I love you."

Day Three Hundred and Sixty: When a No Can Be a Yes

Saying no doesn't make you mean; it makes you stay true to yourself.

There isn't a parent in the world that loves hearing their child tell them "No!" Yet it is so ironic that the word your child says that makes you the most angry is the word *you* truly need to say more often: "No, unfortunately those plans don't work for me" or "No, I can't make it to that birthday party; have fun!" or "No, I'm not available to volunteer that day, maybe next time!" It's hard to say no when you base your worth off of how much you do for others, so try this next time you feel bad about saying no: Reframe it as what you're also saying yes to, yourself.

There's a fine line between being playful with your child's no and mocking them. So try a role-play where you and your child switch roles. Start out gently and see what kind of fun you can have being the child!

Day Three Hundred and Sixty-One:
What Strength Is

*Strength means you aren't afraid to feel, heal,
and deal with what comes your way.*

Did you ever hear these phrases as a child: "Big girls don't cry," "Suck it up," or "Don't feel sorry for yourself"? Society tends to signal that feelings are a sign of weakness because there's a bit of confusion about what strength really is: Strength doesn't mean you're impervious to pain; strength means you aren't afraid to feel, heal, and deal with what comes your way. Think about the trees that withstand the strongest winds in a hurricane: It's the palm trees that sway and move with the winds rather than try to resist them. Even nature knows that strength isn't resistance; it's allowing and trusting that nature will take its course. You get to redefine strength for your children as the strength of being able to feel their feelings rather than fear their feelings, because the more familiar you are with all your feelings, the more comfortable you become with them: less fear, more feeling. Pass it on.

Acknowledging your feelings doesn't make you weak; it lets you heal and get stronger. Today close your eyes to acknowledge a feeling that you normally push away. Welcome it and let it know you're in control, but it's welcome to visit so that you can get comfortable in its presence. Slowly but surely, as you do this each day that feeling won't be as daunting.

Day Three Hundred and Sixty-Two: Being In Charge of Change

The only way children develop confidence is by allowing them to do things that build their confidence.

When your child has a big change in their life coming up, chances are you both have a mix of excitement and anxiety around it! Your child is always looking to you, their mom, to assess what the world is like: Is it scary? Is it hard? Is it safe? Is it fun? Here's a way to create comfort in change:

- Step one: Find your peace first. Before you can help your child find comfort in change, you have to make your own peace with it first! Take inventory to make sure you aren't pouring your own worries into your child's experience.
- Step two: Create the narrative. Create a story for your child that helps them make sense of the change, which creates safety.
- Step three: Simulate the change. The more you expose your child to what the change will look like, feel like, and be like, the more comfortable they'll be in their ability to change.

The more you give your child the tools to handle new experiences, the more they learn they're capable of it on their own. The older your child gets, the less you'll have to create this comfort because they will have learned it always resides within them.

If you're frustrated by your child's inability to adapt to change, try asking yourself, "What does my child need to feel more confident and comfortable with this change?"

Day Three Hundred and Sixty-Three: Self-Compassion

Self-compassion each day keeps the resentments away.

When you find compassion in your heart for *yourself*, the resentments you have *for others* will fade away. How? Because as a mother, all you want is to feel important, worthy, and loved. You look for it on the outside . . . and sure, it's so nice to receive that, but it's never going to be enough unless you find that love for yourself. How? By allowing yourself to *feel* and then have compassion for those cobwebbed feelings that have been cooped up for decades and are now coming out since you've become a mother. So today just focus on one thing: Instead of beating yourself up about what you didn't do, don't have, or don't look like, stop and have compassion for all you've been through in your life. You've made it this far. Have that compassion for yourself; it will slowly allow you to gain power over your own emotions and release that power from it feeling like others control your emotions.

Pick someone you have resentment toward and let go of one tiny bit of that today, not because you aren't hurt, but because you don't have to continue carrying that hurt around to protect yourself. Maybe you can let go of believing their intention was to harm you, or maybe you can let go of needing to be angry and downshift it to annoyance. Any tiny shift you make is progress toward a more connected and contented version of you.

Day Three Hundred and Sixty-Four: Uber for Your Feelings

You are not your feelings; you are simply the feeler of those feelings.

Think of yourself as an Uber driver for your feelings. Imagine you are driving along and you get a ride request from sadness. You aren't the sadness, but that feeling of sadness needs a ride and you're the lucky driver. It's not your ideal passenger because you've been taught to avoid unpleasant feelings, but that sadness really needs to go somewhere. Sure, you can ignore that ride request and only pick up pleasant emotions, but what will happen? Sadness will keep requesting you; it will pop up in places you never thought it could pop up. When you constantly ignore sadness, it turns into other things like anger, irritability, or a deeper sadness that finds its way into ruining your rides with happiness, joy, and fun. That sadness needs to be out in the open; it needs you to sit with it long enough to understand where it came from and what it needs in order to heal.

The funny thing is, once you listen to your sadness, it starts to heal. It's less scary to feel and instead becomes informative and empowering. You just pick it up, take it for a ride, and eventually it will reach its destination and no longer be your passenger.

Turn this into a fun game with your children. Your child can be a driver, and you can be a different "emotion passenger" each time: You can be silly, dramatic, and even informative! You'll be surprised what you might learn about feelings from your children.

Day Three Hundred and Sixty-Five: Un-Becoming

Motherhood is an un-becoming of what no longer serves you and a relearning of your truest self.

A lot in motherhood makes you feel like you need to do more to be a better mother. The world is always suggesting how just this one more thing will finally make your life better, easier, and so on. But what if your motherhood journey wasn't about doing more, accumulating more, or being more than you already are? What if instead of becoming someone better, you're really un-becoming someone you no longer are? Motherhood is more like an artist who is chiseling away at the rough stone. As you chisel away at all the unnecessary parts of yourself—the ego, defense mechanisms, coping skills, and false selves—you reveal the beautifully preserved parts of you that have been waiting to be brushed up, felt, and seen. Motherhood is an un-becoming of what no longer serves you and a relearning of your truest self. Keep doing what you're doing. Lean into the soft parts of yourself, get curious instead of frustrated, and remember you've already come so far, it's only up from here.

Stretch your arms way out in front of you. Now wrap them around your body and give yourself a really good hug. You're truly an incredible mother for dedicating this time to connect more deeply to yourself and your family. They're lucky to have you, you're lucky to have you, and this world is lucky to have you.

ADDITIONAL RESOURCES

Books: Parenting Support

Building a Non-Anxious Life
Dr. John Delony
How to live a more peaceful life as a parent.

Parent Yourself First
Bryana Kappadakunnel
Become the parent you wish you'd had.

Peaceful Parent, Happy Siblings
Dr. Laura Markham
Stop fighting and raise friends for life.

Raising Mentally Strong Kids
Dr. Daniel G. Amen and Dr. Charles Fay
Raise confident, kind, responsible, and resilient children.

The 5 Principles of Parenting
Dr. Aliza Pressman
Five effective strategies for parenting.

The Whole-Brain Child
Dr. Daniel J. Siegel and Tina Payne Bryson
How to nurture your child's developing mind.

Very Intentional Parenting
Destini Ann Davis
Realistic, positive parenting.

Books: Motherhood Support

Atlas of the Heart
Brené Brown
Meaningful connection to yourself and others.

How to Do the Work
Dr. Nicole LaPera
Healing yourself for a better life.

I Didn't Sign Up for This
Dr. Tracy Dalgleish
Finding joy in your relationship.

Mindfulness for Beginners
Jon Kabat-Zinn
Mindfulness made simple and doable.

Moms Moving On
Michelle Dempsey-Multack
Conscious coparenting support.

Set Boundaries, Find Peace
Nedra Glover Tawwab
Reclaiming yourself through boundaries.

Stop Missing Your Life
Cory Muscara
How to be deeply present in an un-present world.

The High 5 Habit
Mel Robbins
Taking control of your life.

The Power Pause
Neha Ruch
How to plan a career break after kids.

Toxic Positivity
Whitney Goodman
An honest, realistic guide to happiness.

Podcasts

Calling Home
Improving family of origin relationships.

Good Inside with Dr. Becky
Effective parenting guidance.

Help Them Bloom
Parent-child expert.

Raising Good Humans
Realistic parenting approaches.

The Rich Roll Podcast
Thought-provoking, impactful self-development.

Websites

www.drsiggie.com
Practical, proven parenting courses.

www.drtanyacotler.com
Parent-child attachment support.

www.erinlevincounseling.com
Postpartum support focused on matrescence.

www.simplyonpurpose.org
Positive parenting courses.

www.theconsciousmom.com
Conscious parenting made realistic.

www.thefamilybehaviorist.com
Parent coaching for behavior change.

INDEX

ABOUT THE AUTHOR

Erin Morrison, MA, EdM, is the creator of The Conscious Mom, an approach to real parenting for real parents. With two master's degrees in psychological counseling from Columbia University, Erin is the down-to-earth, nonjudgmental parenting guide all parents need. As a busy mom of two, she understands the dynamics of parenting—and lives them herself!—so she can help parents everywhere dramatically and positively improve their relationships with their children. Learn more at TheConsciousMom.com.